ADULT CHILDREN
AS HUSBANDS,
WIVES, AND LOVERS

Also by Steven Farmer:

Adult Children of Abusive Parents

A SOLUTIONS BOOK

ADULT CHILDREN
AS
HUSBANDS
WIVES AND
LOVERS

STEVEN FARMER, M.A., M.F.C.C.
Author of ADULT CHILDREN OF ABUSIVE PARENTS

Lowell House
Los Angeles

Contemporary Books
Chicago

Library of Congress Cataloging-in-Publication Data

Farmer, Steven.
    Adult children as husbands, wives, and lovers / Steven Farmer.
      p. cm.
    Includes bibliographical references and index.
    ISBN: 0-929923-21-9
    1. Marriage—Psychological aspects.   2. Adult children of
dysfunctional families—Psychology.   3. Interpersonal relations.
I. Title.
HQ734.F248   1990
158'.2—dc20   90-49819
                                                            CIP

Requests for such permissions should be addressed to:

Lowell House
1875 Century Park East, Suite 220
Los Angeles, CA 90067

Publisher: Jack Artenstein
Vice-President/Editor-in-Chief: Janice Gallagher
Marketing Manager: Elizabeth Wood
Design: Gary Hespenheide

Manufactured in the United States of America
10   9   8   7   6   5   4   3   2   1

Dedicated with love and appreciation to

Richard and Helen Farmer,
who stayed with each other through strife and celebration
and truly did the best they could

and

Michael and Nancy Exeter
who so beautifully and steadily convey
the spirit of the New Heaven and New Earth

CONTENTS

Acknowledgements ix

CHAPTER 1 Love, Sweat, and Tears 1

CHAPTER 2 Emotions 5

Your Family's Rules: Don't Feel and Don't Talk 7
Shutting Down to Stay Alive 9
Childhood Trauma = Shell-shocked Adult 10
Laugh and Play and Cry: Awakening Your Inner Child 14
How Do Men and Women Really Feel? 20
Solutions: How to Feel Better 20

CHAPTER 3 Control 33

Your Family: Lessons in Control 35
"Now That I'm Grown Up . . ." 38
Solutions: Letting Go of Control 48

CHAPTER 4 Boundaries   **63**

You, Your Limits, and Your Family   *65*
Now That We're Adults   *69*
Solutions: Setting and Maintaining Boundaries   *77*

CHAPTER 5 Intimacy   **91**

The Five Ingredients for Intimacy   *93*
Your Family: Training Ground for Avoiding Intimacy   *98*
Past Decisions, Present Barriers   *99*
The Truth About Intimacy   *107*
Solutions: How to Do This Thing Called Intimacy   *112*

CHAPTER 6 Conflict   **129**

Back to the Family   *131*
Adult Child Strategies for Dealing with Conflict   *132*
Why Does It Have to Be This Way? The Cause of Conflict   *135*
Solutions: We Can Work It Out   *138*

CHAPTER 7 Commitment   **157**

'Til Death Do Us Part: Family Ties   *160*
Growing Up Uncertain: Commitment as an Adult   *162*
Solutions: Making Commitments That Work   *168*

Suggested Readings   **183**

Index   **185**

ACKNOWLEDGEMENTS

I want to thank all my clients and workshop participants who by their dedication to their personal growth and recovery have taught me so much about myself and about intimate relationships. Without them this book would not have been possible.

Thanks to those who have educated, enlightened, and inspired me, including John Bradshaw, Alice Miller, Ann Wilson Schaef, Timmen Cermak, Charles Whitfield, Janet Woititz, Robert Bly, Robert Lawlor, John Lee, and John and Linda Friehl.

To my daughters Nicole and Catherine, thanks for your patience and your love notes while I was writing this book. I love you with all my heart.

I also want to thank all my other teachers and friends, starting with some couples whose relationships I appreciate and admire, including John and Pat Allen, Bruce and Vicki Belman, Ron and Susan Clark, Alan and Cindy Francis, Derek and Janice Gallagher, Rupert and Tessa Maskell, Rick and Jane McElvaine, Keahi Pelayo and Linda Palagyi, John and Kelly Steenhoven, and Steve and Patricia Tashiro.

For some wonderful memories and life lessons in relationships, thanks to some people who will always hold a special place in my heart: Linda Barker, Beth Mullane, Susan Coates, Mina Sylvestro, Jan Marie Henry, and Mary Denisenko.

Finally, for their faith and support of my work and their relentless belief in me, a special thanks to Jack Artenstein, Diane Medeiros, Donna Sanford, Walt Murray, Mary Daniels, Paul Fairweather, Rick Potter, Pat Peret, and Ellen Anderson.

Although stories in the book are based on actual incidents, the names, circumstances, and other identifying characteristics have been changed to protect privacy.

CHAPTER 1

LOVE, SWEAT, AND TEARS

*H*ow would you like to have a truly fulfilling relationship, one in which you can really be yourself, one that is supportive and energizing, where love and tenderness are expressed easily and occasional conflict is accepted as part of the deal? How would you like to be in a relationship where you and your partner truly are friends, welcoming personal changes in each other and integrating those changes into your continually evolving, growing relationship?

Sound like a fantasy? It's not. It is possible. I'm not talking about an ideal or perfect relationship; there is no such thing. Every relationship has problems—you can count on it. Instead, I'm talking about a healthy, real relationship, one that is satisfying for both partners. One that has vitality and meaning, one that grows and expands right along with you and your partner.

Everyone yearns for such a relationship. However, if you grew up in a home where there was abuse, alcoholism, or dysfunction of any kind, then as an Adult Child you face some special problems in your relationships. You had a poor start in learning about what it takes to create healthy relationships. When you come from a childhood lacking in healthy models, and the "Father Knows Best" images you saw on television contrasted sharply with the reality you saw at home, it may seem impossible that you could ever have a healthy relationship. But given your willingness to let go of the past and your commitment to learn new ways of relating, you can.

Out of necessity you constructed some defenses that worked to help you survive your childhood but now serve you poorly in creating and sustaining a loving, intimate, committed relationship as an adult. Your early training in co-dependency taught you to shut down your internal sensations and rely heavily on external cues to define how you should feel and act. Without an ongoing awareness of your internal sensations, it's hard to know what your feelings are at any given moment—let alone how to express them. When you rely on some-thing or someone outside yourself, such as your partner, to define your feelings and actions, it's hard to be honest and direct with your feelings—you're still feeling and acting the way you think someone else wants you to. As long as this pattern of denying yourself continues, it will be hard to have the kind of rela-tionship you want. And that's exactly what this book is about: breaking these old habits and replacing them with relationship skills you didn't have a chance to develop while you were growing up.

In my previous book, *Adult Children of Abusive Parents,* I defined and de-scribed in some detail the basic issues and attitudes Adult Children experience as the result of childhood trauma and outlined a program for recovery and change. In this book, I focus on what it takes to make a workable, healthy relationship when you are an Adult Child. In each chapter I'll first pinpoint how the problems you had in childhood have affected your adult relation-ships, then I'll offer specific solutions to your current relationship problems.

The book will cover in detail six of the primary issues that are present in any relationship but are apt to be more challenging for Adult Children: emotions, control, boundaries, intimacy, conflict, and commitment. Each chapter starts with an example of how this issue is played out in an unhealthy relationship, followed by an example from a healthy relationship. The chapter then goes on to identify the source of that particular issue and why it's such a "sore spot" for most Adult Children, and establishes how your present-day problems are rooted in your childhood history. Throughout you'll find other individuals' and couples' stories that illustrate particular points. Although names have been changed, these anecdotes are drawn from clients' and friends' actual experi-ences. I've also included observations based on my work as a marriage and family counselor specializing in Adult Children issues, as well as vignettes from my personal life and my own recovery as an Adult Child.

Once we've established the source of your present relationship difficul-ties, we'll look at precisely how your relationship today is affected. Most im-portant, each chapter will offer some retraining exercises you can work with to develop new relationship skills that will fill in the gaps in your earlier co-dependency training. Once you start consciously using these skills and ideas as an integral part of your recovery program, you can't help but develop a healthy, workable relationship.

If you are in a committed relationship now, I'd encourage you and your partner to read this book and do the exercises together as much as possible. If you're not presently in a committed relationship, this material will still be helpful in understanding what went wrong in your past relationships and preparing the way for your next one. Many of the exercises are designed so that you can do them with a close friend, and many of the skills will be useful in any close relationship. Whatever your particular circumstance, the number one requirement for growth and learning is that you will be willing to risk, and to risk in safety. Risking in safety means not to risk blindly or foolishly, but to risk in ways where you stretch your comfort zone without being hurt.

As you're working with your relationship and your recovery, please remember that you do not have to have it "all together" to start developing new and creative ways to be involved with your partner. A healthy relationship is a process. It is not something that just happens, but something that requires continual attention. While you cannot deny the effects of the past, you no longer have to be ruled by them. You *can* have a healthy relationship. To do so requires risk, commitment, humor, patience, and lots of forgiveness. This may seem like a tall order, but as someone once said to me, that's what a relationship consists of—love, sweat, and tears.

My warmest regards in your journey.

CHAPTER 2

EMOTIONS

*A*ll you do is nag, nag, nag!" shouted Tom to his wife, Tracy, as he slammed his fist down on the kitchen table. "Damn it! Get off my back!"

Tracy jumped at the sudden explosion. Tears welled up in her eyes as she looked at Tom with astonishment. "All I was saying was that Matthew needs help with his homework. He's been having a hard time with his math and I thought you could help him out. I don't think that's asking too much. After all, he *is* your son!"

Tom narrowed his eyes and gritted his teeth. "Knock it off!" he growled. "I'm tired of you telling me I don't do enough with the kids. I do plenty for them. I work my tail off so they can buy their Nintendo games, and what thanks do I get? I don't need to hear about how I'm supposed to be doing more and more. I'm sick and tired of how you constantly complain!"

"All I'm asking is for you to spend a little more time with them, Tom," Tracy retorted, "especially Matthew. The least you could do is spend a few minutes each day with him on his homework. You've never even opened a book with him!"

"That's it! I've had it! You can take your accusations and shove 'em!" Tom lurched out of his chair toward the door. As he grabbed the doorknob he turned and said spitefully, "I'm sorry I ever married you. I don't even know why I'm still in this marriage."

As he stormed out of the house, Tracy yelled out, "Well, you can get out any time you want! The children and I will do just fine without you!"

Mary sat down on the sofa and heaved a big sigh. Roy put down the newspaper he was reading and asked, "What's wrong, honey?"

"Oh, Jillian's teacher called today and said that she wasn't keeping up with her reading and spelling. She's been doing fine until this last quarter."

"I'm sure it's no big deal. It'll pass."

"I'm sure it *will* pass," Mary declared, "but I get irritated when you say it's no big deal, like it doesn't matter at all."

"So it seems like I'm just tossing it off?" Roy inquired.

"Yes, it does, Roy. I really think something's bothering her. Could you talk with her tomorrow and see what you can find out? I've got a feeling that it has something to do with your travels this past few weeks—I think she really misses you."

"Oh, I see. It's my fault, eh?" Roy began to get defensive.

"No, no, no," Mary stated emphatically. "She told me a couple of times lately that she really misses you and wishes you weren't gone so much. I'm not blaming you. I don't like the fact that you've been working so much, either, but I know it's only temporary. I just think Jillian needs some of your attention and a word from you. Maybe some special time together on a weekend when you are here. What do you think?"

"Well, I don't like that I've had to be working so much," Roy said. "This project's just about finished, and I'm ready for it to be done. I get mad that I have to be gone all the time. I really miss you both. And I will talk to Jillian in the morning."

Emotions are the heart of any relationship. They are your life's energy. The pulse of the relationship depends in large part on how you and your partner manage and communicate your feelings. This requires honesty, openness, and lots of tender, loving, attentive care—care for your feelings and for your partner's.

In Tracy and Tom's relationship this kind of care is lacking. Both are Adult Children, and both have brought into their marriage all the attitudes and behaviors from their childhood that cause them to mismanage and miscommunicate their feelings, often at the cost of hurting themselves and each other. Because of their childhood training, it's difficult or even impossible for them to see any other way to work with their feelings. The only resolution they can see when emotions get intense is to break up.

Mary and Roy are dealing with a similar situation regarding their daughter

Jillian. While they are certainly not June and Ward Cleaver, it's obvious that they are dealing with their emotions more clearly and directly than are Tracy and Tom. They state their feelings and acknowledge them without a lot of blaming. They have a healthy dialogue about their daughter's need for extra attention, and in the process they come to understand each other's feelings and arrive at some resolution of the problem.

Emotions are at the core of all the other issues—control, boundaries, intimacy, conflict, and commitment—that you have to contend with in a relationship. These other issues have one thing in common: They require you to pay attention to and communicate your feelings *and* to listen and respond to your partner's feelings. To build a healthy relationship in all other areas, you must develop healthy ways to deal with your feelings.

The emotional exchange between Roy and Mary is one example of the kind of dialogue that can take place in a healthy relationship. When there is emotional honesty in the relationship and in turn in the family, the children benefit. They see their parents expressing feelings without using them to coerce, manipulate, or abuse. In a healthy family, parents acknowledge their children's emotions and encourage them to express their feelings in healthy ways.

However, this was not the case for you. You grew up in a family where you had to follow certain unspoken rules that encouraged you to deny and repress your emotions. These family rules prevented you from learning how to deal with your feelings in a healthy way and in turn have made it more difficult for you to have an adult relationship that works. To understand how you were affected by these rules, let's look at how your family handled emotions.

YOUR FAMILY'S RULES: DON'T FEEL AND DON'T TALK

In your family, denial was the order of the day. Your parents were masters at it. They taught you well how to deny your feelings through their example and by the way they treated you. You concluded that there were two main rules in your family: don't feel and don't talk. You were not supposed to feel anything that was unacceptable to your parents, and you were definitely not to talk about your feelings. If you did break the rules and express an unacceptable feeling, Mom or Dad came down on you hard.

Janet recounts the consequences of having talked back to her mother: "I was always put in charge of my little brother Michael, who was five years younger than me, and I had to watch him all the time, to take him with me if I went and played. One day when I was about eight or nine a friend of mine was supposed to come over to play with our new dolls. My mom told me that I had to be with Michael that day because she was going shopping or something. I freaked. I was so upset, I cried and told her that I was tired of always having to watch Michael and I didn't think it was fair. I'll never forget that look in my mother's eyes. It was so hateful. She started yelling and spewing out all this venom, telling me I was selfish, no good, a crybaby, and how could I hate my brother so much. I was so humiliated that I never once questioned her again about having to take care of my little brother."

When Janet stopped pretending and spoke her true feelings about having to watch her brother so much, she paid a heavy price in the form of her mother's emotional abuse. She learned that an honest expression of emotion was not acceptable. Today in her relationship with her boyfriend she has to force herself to speak her feelings, and she still gets sweaty palms and a rapid heartbeat when she has to express some uncomfortable feelings to him.

In a typical dysfunctional family no one deals with his or her feelings in a direct, honest, and nonabusive way. In some cases the only feelings expressed are extreme anger or hysteria, often followed by periods of silence, denial, and emotional distance. A child who witnesses this kind of emotional mismanagement is bound to be confused about how to deal with feelings and may himself learn to alternate between suppression and overreaction.

"My Dad would come home from work," Lawrence says, "and it was obvious that he had been drinking because he would be singing. He never sang except when he had been drinking. It was a signal to stay clear, because my sister and I knew that the fights would start soon. The night of my thirteenth birthday, when all of us were supposed to go out and celebrate it together, marked one of their biggest fights ever. The next day, nobody said anything about my birthday! For years I told myself that it didn't bother me, but now I realize how much it did." Lawrence is 34 years old and has never been in a relationship longer than six months, and no wonder. To have parents who dealt with emotions in such a chaotic, destructive, and unpredictable way would make any child suppress feelings and avoid close relationships.

You may have come from a family where no one expressed any emotions because they were never allowed. If you did express yourself, these expressions were met with disapproval or outright abandonment—no one was there to receive them.

"Nobody ever came out and told me that I wasn't supposed to feel things," says 52-year-old Cassie. "They didn't have to. My mom had a certain look of disapproval, a sort of scowl, that she would use whenever she was unhappy with me. And she was unhappy a lot, so I got the 'look' a lot. I don't know why this stands out, but one time I was in the living room coloring her a picture. She walked in and had been crying, and when she saw me she just gave me her look and walked away. I figured I was doing something wrong by coloring a picture for her. Being the good little girl that I was and not wanting to upset her, I never gave her my picture. In fact, I threw it away. It was only later as I was dealing with my own depression that I realized that my mother was depressed most of her life and just wasn't there much. And it wasn't my fault."

One of the most difficult situations for a child to deal with is when there is no one there to "mirror" the child's feelings, to reflect back to the child what she is feeling and to help her give that feeling a name. Whatever trauma you suffered in childhood, if you had no significant adult to help you sort out your feelings, to validate them, and to heal the hurt, then, like Cassie, you are at a disadvantage when it comes to an adult relationship.

The very people who would ordinarily mirror your feelings and help you heal from any trauma—your parents—were the ones who traumatized you. They traumatized you through their abuse and neglect. You had to put up with it, but in order to do so you had to shut down your feelings just to stay alive.

SHUTTING DOWN TO STAY ALIVE

I have a lot of respect for the wisdom of our creator. He not only gave us life but also gave us some handy means to survive conditions of hardship and trauma. When you are in any kind of danger, a set of bodily responses takes place that prepares you to deal with that danger. Your adrenaline starts pumping, your heart beats faster, and your rate of breathing increases. Your eyes dilate so you can see more clearly. Your muscles tense to prepare you for any needed action. All your senses become sharper, and you become extremely sensitive to what's going on around you. Your whole system is put on a state of alert, a readiness for fight or flight, thus enabling you to survive.

When you are a child, you rely completely on your parents to provide for you and keep you alive. If your parents provide a reasonably safe environment in which you can learn and grow, you don't have to worry about your survival. You have several years to develop more sophisticated ways to deal with natural and man-made dangers in your environment. If you grow up in a healthy family, you don't have to use your innate survival skills on a daily basis just to get through childhood. This leaves you more available to deal with the normal developmental tasks that all children face. Then when you become an adult your instinctive survival responses, while not operational all the time, are available to meet any real dangers.

Growing up in your family, however, was a course in survival. Your childhood was fraught with dangers, ones you were not physically or psychologically prepared to meet. You could not possibly endure physical, sexual, or emotional abuse and come away unscathed. You could not possibly face the constant abandonment by your caretakers and be unaffected. You had to do whatever it took in order to survive.

You shut down your feelings, and in doing so you developed some qualities that helped you get through your childhood. You learned to be tough, durable, sensitive, and adaptive. Although these can be useful traits, when rigidly applied to a relationship they have their shortcomings. A relationship is not meant to be "toughed out" or endured—it is meant to be enjoyed. As long as your feelings remain shut down and you're operating in a survival mode, you may be surviving, but your relationship won't be thriving.

I spent a good deal of my adult life surviving my relationships, doing what I had to do to "hang in there" but not knowing how to come out from behind the mask of co-dependency. When I think of my second marriage, to Susan, it's sad to think how shut down, how emotionally distant I was. The only time I could feel something strongly was during sex or when we were fighting. I remember how little eye contact we had, even when we were making love. It's only in retrospect that I can see how buried my feelings were. In some ways it seems as if I was a different person then.

To awaken your emotions and learn to communicate your feelings, you must overcome your childhood training and conditioning that have kept you shut down as an adult. This requires an active recovery on your part—it doesn't just get better all by itself. The instinctive methods you used to cope with trauma tend to remain with you as dysfunctional symptoms long past their original usefulness. Keeping your emotions bottled up leads you to live artificially, controlled by your past, and relationships exist in the here and now. To set the stage for successfully dealing with your emotions in your relationships, it's helpful to understand the phenomenon called Post-Traumatic Stress Disorder.

CHILDHOOD TRAUMA = SHELL-SHOCKED ADULT

When you are raised in constant fear or are subject to any type of abuse as a child, you automatically develop ways to shut off the physical or psychological pain. These ways of coping with the trauma are similar to ways in which a soldier copes with the trauma of being on the battlefield. However, when the war is over and all the shooting has died down, the soldier is left with shell shock, otherwise known as Post-Traumatic Stress Disorder (PTSD). Trauma is defined as a "painful emotional experience producing a lasting psychic effect." It's this lasting psychic effect that shows up later in adulthood as PTSD and seriously affects how you deal with your emotions in your relationships.

Timmen Cermak, M.D., who has made tremendous contributions to our understanding of the relationship of PTSD and childhood trauma, states in *Diagnosing and Treating Co-dependence,* "Experience with children from chemically dependent homes reveals that many suffer to some degree from symptoms associated with Post-Traumatic Stress Disorder (PTSD)—a disease seen in combat soldiers, most often today in Vietnam veterans." I would amend this to include children from *any* type of abusive home.

Cermak continues, "PTSD is believed to occur among people with normal defenses who have been subjected to levels of trauma which clearly lie outside the range of what is considered to be normal human experience (especially if the trauma is chronic, of human origin, and sustained within a closed social system)." The abuse you suffered certainly fits this criterion.

I've observed that most Adult Children are "shell-shocked" to some degree. The symptoms serve a useful purpose for the soldier on the battlefield or for the six-year-old who is continually threatened with abandonment or beaten up with words or fists. The problem is that these symptoms persist long after they have served their original purpose and can make it difficult for you to deal with your emotions in a relationship.

There are three major symptoms of PTSD:

1. *Re-experiencing the trauma*
2. *Hypervigilance*
3. *Psychic numbing*

The first of these, *reexperiencing the trauma,* shows up as flashbacks, dreams, and sudden memories of the feelings, thoughts, and behaviors that happened during the trauma. Memories are often triggered by objects and events that resemble the initial abusive situation. As Erica began working in her therapy on some suspected sexual abuse in early childhood, she found that certain images and sensations would uncontrollably appear in her consciousness. "I would turn a certain way while I was lying in bed," she reported, "and I would get these weird sensations deep inside my stomach. It would get all knotted up and I'd flash on this dark stranger sneaking up on my bed. I'm not even sure who it was or exactly what happened, but I think it must have been my stepdad." As Erica later discovered through her recovery work, she had been molested on several occasions by her stepfather, who would sneak into her room at night and fondle her genitals while Erica pretended to be asleep because she was afraid to challenge him.

Erica was having difficulties in her sexual relationship with her live-in boyfriend. She would "turn off" as she became sexually aroused and close to orgasm and was bothered by vague, unspecified fears. Not known to her at the time she began therapy, she was suffering from "shell shock," in particular the symptoms of reexperiencing the trauma. As we worked in therapy, the connection between her present-day feelings and the earlier sexual abuse became obvious. With slow, steady work and the support and cooperation of her boyfriend, Erica has made considerable progress in resolving her issues.

A second major symptom is *hypervigilance*. This is the result of having to continually be on the alert for the next catastrophe at home. Hypervigilance was extremely useful while you were living with your abusive family. As Cermak says: "Individuals under the threat of disaster tend to put their vigilance on automatic pilot so they can continually scan the environment for the smallest sign of impending danger. Many Vietnam veterans found, upon returning home, that their automatic pilot did not have an 'off' switch. They remained on edge, always expecting the worst, unable to trust or feel safe again."

Since you had to be constantly on the lookout for the ever-present danger of further abuse, your attention had to be focused outward so you would know what to do, how to act. This is where the co-dependent characteristic of "external referencing" comes from—having to scan the environment so you could minimize the risk of abuse or abandonment. Like reconnaissance by the soldier on the battlefield, scanning the environment lets you know what the situation is so you can act accordingly. Unfortunately, this means that you have to pay less attention to your own feelings.

Hal gives a good example of hypervigilance in his description of what it was like living with a physically and emotionally abusive mother. "Whenever I walked home from school, the closer I got to my house the more tense I got. I'd walk in the door and never know what to expect. Some days she wasn't even home. If she had been drinking that day, she'd usually start right in yelling at me. I felt like I always had to be on the lookout, always watchful, always so careful. I still do this today, always watching others to see what their reaction is so I know how I'm supposed to react." Hal's attention had to be directed outward in order to protect himself the best he could from his mother, which left him little time to pay attention to what was going on inside him.

Today Hal and his wife are seeking counseling after 24 years of marriage. Hal can't put his finger on it but thinks that Virginia may be getting ready to leave him. "She's been so busy, going to this meeting, to that meeting. She hardly has any time for me. I'm beginning to wonder if she isn't having an affair.

I called an attorney just in case. Which is what triggered us to come and see a counselor."

Virginia states that although she is frustrated by the intensity of Hal's reaction, she is not having an affair and has absolutely no intention of leaving. She has simply realized that she can't sit at home anymore but needs to get out and develop a life of her own. Since the children are adults and live away from home, she is feeling the need to start on her own career. Hal is understandably threatened by this and is constantly "keeping an eye on me." Thus his hyper-vigilant stance has contributed to the current dilemma in the relationship. Hal is beginning to understand how his history with his mother has directly contributed to his present co-dependent relationship with his wife, and how his suspiciousness and mistrust are based on faulty conclusions about what he observes.

A third major symptom of PTSD—and the one that is most crucial to understanding why emotions are so difficult in relationships for the Adult Child—is *psychic numbing*. This is internal shutting down, a natural response to unnatural degrees of trauma. Cermak says: "During moments of extreme stress, combat soldiers are often called upon to act regardless of how they are feeling. Their survival depends upon their ability to suspend feelings in favor of taking steps to ensure their safety. Unfortunately, the resulting 'split' between one's self and one's experience does not heal easily. It does not gradually disappear with the passage of time. Until an active process of healing takes place, the individual continues to experience a constriction of feelings, a decreased ability to recognize which feelings are present, and a persistent sense of being cut off from one's surroundings (depersonalization)." It is hard to relate on an intimate level with anyone since your feelings are locked away, encased in walls of protection built during the original childhood trauma.

This one hits home. In my first marriage, to Beth, who was also an Adult Child, there was a huge emotional and spiritual vacuum. I suspect we both felt this void but didn't know how to acknowledge it, let alone do anything about it. Although we shared some wonderful times together, keeping our feelings buried became the standard upon which we based our relationship. I had turned my feelings off some time ago in childhood, as she most likely had, too.

A sad commentary on just how afraid we both were of our feelings was the way we dealt with our affection for each other. The first time she told me very tentatively, "I love you," I countered with, "You'll get over it," attempting to laugh away my discomfort. She laughed right along with me. This became a standing joke as a way to respond when one of us told the other those three simple words.

In time I recognized that we couldn't go on like this, that there was a deep sense of something vital missing in our relationship. I took a backpacking trip by myself to think things over. I had to figure out on my own (of course) whether to stay married. I came home from my trip and nervously announced that I thought it would be better if we separated. To my surprise, Beth promptly agreed, and I felt a great deal of relief that we didn't have to deal with a lot of "messy" feelings. We calmly and rationally discussed our strategy for the breakup of our five-year marriage. We agreed that she would move out and that I would stay in the house and fix it up so we could sell it. It was painfully sad, but I was so regrettably numb to my feelings at the time I didn't know any better than to keep them buried and maintain the pattern of psychic numbing that had been familiar to me since childhood.

In most of us, the patterns begun in childhood continue into our adult relationships. The wounded spirit of our child is buried under symptoms of the repression and denial that were so important to our survival during childhood. Now, as an adult, until you start and stay with recovery from the original trauma, the spirit you knew in childhood will remain buried under the debris from your abuse. In order to successfully overcome the symptoms of PTSD and deal with your emotions, you must wake up and become acquainted with this aspect of your experience—your Inner Child.

LAUGH AND PLAY AND CRY: AWAKENING YOUR INNER CHILD

Your Inner Child is the part of you that feels emotions. Your Inner Child is naturally spontaneous, experiencing and expressing life with all the playful innocence that only a child can possess. She contains all the qualities you admire in a child, plus everything about being a child that is scary and intimidating—feelings.

For the emotional development of your relationship, awakening your Inner Child is a must. Otherwise you'll find yourself in a relationship that is serious and emotionally distant, with little room for the liveliness, vitality, and humanity that your Inner Child can bring. This is not to say that there aren't serious things to which you have to pay attention in a relationship. For instance, in any relationship there are maintenance needs to be taken care of, such as laundry, cleaning, shopping—the "business" of the relationship. Yet even these practical things can be done with more energy, spontaneity, and enthusiasm when your Inner Child is present.

The key here is spontaneity: to spontaneously experience whatever emotion is present—anger, sadness, happiness, fear. But when you've practiced most of your life being controlled and rehearsed, it's hard to be spontaneous. Your Inner Child was buried long ago and may now be trapped inside you, terrified at the prospect of expressing herself. After all, it was never safe being a child before, why should it be any different now?

"When I first heard the idea of an Inner Child," Walter says, "I was disbelieving and suspicious. My first reaction was to think, 'I'm a grown man. I can't go around acting like a child.' Then I realized that I'd been acting like a grown man since I was five years old. Seems like it's about time for me to loosen up a bit and learn how to laugh and play and cry. I haven't done that for years."

Awakening your Inner Child and learning "to laugh and play and cry" will make your relationship that much more rewarding and fun. If you want to learn how to do so, you need to work in two major areas: grieving and playing.

Grieving

Grieving is a way to unlock the feelings that are frozen inside you. Frozen feelings are the emotions of anger, hurt, pain, and sorrow that you could never feel or express when you were a child. They are there, however, buried inside you, contained within your Inner Child. One of your main tasks in recovery is to unbury these feelings, to undo the psychic numbing of Post-Traumatic Stress Disorder.

It's common in our culture to hide our true feelings. It would be such a treat if there were greater support for appropriate expressions of natural feelings. Grieving reminds me of a movie I once saw of an Italian funeral: women dressed in black cried out in anguish and readily shed tears over the loss. It's a rare sight at most modern funerals to see someone really unleash true feelings of anger and sorrow. In our dysfunctional culture, repression and "toughing it out" are valued above being honest and real. I recall how stoic Jackie Kennedy was when she had just lost her husband to an assassin's bullets. Most observers at the time expressed admiration of how well she was handling things.

That's exactly the problem. Like most Adult Children, you learned to "handle" yourself by repressing the spark of life that showed up as honest feeling. You saw it as a choice between doing that or risking abandonment.

Mark describes it thusly: "I learned quickly to stuff any feelings I had. My mom knew how to say things that would cut like a knife, but if I said anything back or acted like it hurt, she'd get on me about being a crybaby. One time when I was about nine years old, she got really angry over some clothes that were lying on the floor in my room. She started throwing everything out of my closet, saying, 'You little bastard! You're just doing this to aggravate me!

You're a slob and I'll teach you to keep your room picked up!' I was stunned. I started to get angry with her, and she threatened to send me to live with my dad. That really stung, and when I started to cry she said, 'Don't pull that one on me! You don't have to fake the tears just to get me to feel sorry for you. You're just like your father!' I couldn't win with her. The best thing to do was just to keep my mouth shut. I still have a habit of keeping my mouth shut about my feelings. If you don't believe me, just ask my wife."

Like Mark, not only did you learn to stuff away your feelings, you concluded that *you* were the cause of the abusive or neglectful behavior. Whenever a parent is mad or sad, the child always thinks it's his fault. The child usually takes it one step further and concludes that he is somehow "bad." When there's no one there to take you off the hook, to tell you that you're not bad and that it was not your fault when your mom or dad abused you, a layer of shame forms over your naturally childlike qualities. With persistent abuse of any kind, you form several layers of shame over your Inner Child and carry this into adulthood. The shame forms a further veil over your emotions; you believe that something's wrong with you because you have the feelings you have.

What's necessary instead of feeling shame, guilt, or blame is to grieve, to mourn. As Alice Miller writes in *For Your Own Good*: "Mourning is the opposite of feeling guilt; it is an expression of pain that things happened as they did and that there is no way to change the past." There is no purpose in blame or shame except to perpetuate the effects of the abuse. Instead, it's much more useful to take an attitude of grieving.

Opening up your senses.

Grieving helps you open up the sensory channels of your body that may have been shut down for a number of years, so the anger and hurt that you could not safely feel when you were a child are now experienced in adulthood. The psychic numbing is gradually lessened through your acknowledgment of the child inside the adult. It's through opening up your senses that you can rediscover the core of your being, your Inner Child.

As you remember things from your past, ask yourself how you actually feel about those memories. If you notice any sensory cues, such as holding your breath or your heart pounding, these may indicate that you are reexperiencing the trauma. Be particularly aware of your anger and sadness. Ask yourself what's going on in your body. Pay attention to subtle physical cues that you may have typically ignored in the past. Paying attention to these will open the door for your grieving, and thus open the door for experiencing feelings.

Gina talks about how she started her own healing process. Note the cues, italicized here, that set off her emotions: "I always thought there was something wrong in my relationship with my stepfather, but I never knew what it was. *I never felt comfortable around him,* and was always *on guard.* Last year *I was looking at some old pictures* one day, and suddenly *it struck me.* I *flashed on a scene* when I was about ten and my mother was gone. He got me drunk and molested me. I just sort of pushed it out of my mind all these years. I was confused, angry, hurt, and so ashamed that I didn't know what to do. It took me a lot of tears and a little help from my friends to realize that it wasn't my fault." This realization for Gina was the start of awakening her Inner Child.

Gina recognizes how over the years her discomfort around men to whom she was close, her suspiciousness, and her lack of trust were all related to this childhood incident. The way she had dealt with it most of her adult life was to go through a series of superficial, sexualized relationships with men, typically leaving any relationship after several weeks when issues of intimacy and commitment would come up. This insight has set Gina on a course of understanding her behavior and discovering how to let herself feel her emotions in greater depth and intensity.

A little help from your friends.

Gina mentions "a little help from [her] friends." A way to open up your shut-down emotions is to share your anger and sadness with someone who will be there for you, someone who can encourage you to shed your childhood shame and release your feelings. The other person might be your therapist, your sponsor in a 12-step program, a friend, or even your mate. The first and most important qualification is that this be someone with whom you feel *safe.* While your mate is not your therapist, he or she may be willing to offer support as you awaken your Inner Child and do the necessary grieving.

Beverly speaks with gratitude about how her lover has been there for her throughout her healing: "Jay doesn't always understand what's going on with me, but he gives me lots of room to feel whatever I'm feeling. Boy, is that ever different! Once, after a particularly rough therapy session where I opened up a lot of my pain about my mother's coldness and meanness, I walked home, sat down, and just cried. He walked in and saw me crying. He didn't say a word. He just put down his things, came over to the couch, and sat next to me and held me. I *really* started sobbing then, just letting the little girl inside me be sad without criticizing or judging her." Opening up her feelings through this grieving brought Beverly a great deal of relief and brought her closer to Jay.

In my therapy groups there is considerable emphasis on safety, support for one another, and opening up feelings. Through various exercises, participants experience their anger and pain in the safety of the group setting. One time in a group, Jody was retelling in very matter-of-fact terms how her mother used to beat her with various objects since as far back as she could remember. As she described a particular beating that took place when she was six years old, her face bore no emotional expression.

Another member of the group, Martin, was becoming increasingly restless and broke in, saying he was feeling angry—which in itself was a breakthrough for him. Jody's description of her abusive mother had aroused some genuine anger in him. I put some pillows on the floor in the center of the group and invited Martin to kneel in front of the pillows, cup his hands together in one large fist, close his eyes, and start hitting the pillows, saying "I'm angry." He did so, rather tentatively at first, but after a few soft strikes and with some encouragement he was bringing his fists down full force on the pillows, screaming, "I'm angry! I hate you! I hate you!"

After a few minutes of this, he let up and the tears started flooding. The other group members were either crying or frozen with fear in reaction to the intensity of Martin's anger. Martin acknowledged that he had at first been angry at Jody's mother, then at Jody, and finally at his own mother for the severe beatings she administered whenever she drank. As a group we talked about how this was a necessary step in the process of grieving the loss of your childhood. You can't change what happened, and it does absolutely no good to blame yourself or your parents, but it does help to acknowledge your anger at such mean treatment and your sorrow that it happened at all.

To experience an intensity of joy, you must know the intensity of your pain. Grieving is how you start feeling your emotions intensely. Grieving helps you let go of the past. It is the path to awakening and reclaiming your Inner Child, not only her pain but her love, joy, and creative expression. As she awakens you can acknowledge her as a vital, living aspect of your experience. In the innocence that lies beneath the layers of shame, you can discover the spirit of life itself showing up eagerly, playfully, and spontaneously through you, the adult.

As you bring this to your relationship, you expand your options for enjoying all the various creative dimensions of emotional expression with your partner. A second avenue to awakening your feelings is learning to play with your partner.

Playing

The emotional neglect of Danielle's childhood had taught her that it was dangerous to express feelings in any spontaneous fashion. "My husband, Todd, teases me about being so uptight, but the truth is that I really don't know how to play. He told me a joke the other night that he thought was hilarious, but I didn't get it. Then he got angry and told me that I'm just not fun, that I need to loosen up. I agree with him, but all I keep thinking of is how when I was little my mother kept getting headaches every time I would laugh out loud or play or just generally act like a child."

Like Danielle, you may have become a "little adult" when you were quite young. If so, perhaps you have forgotten how to play or were never allowed to play. The inhibitions that resulted from having to control your feelings and bury your Inner Child make it hard now to play as an adult. The emotional and psychic numbing of PTSD has left your body and your senses attenuated, and this has made it difficult to loosen up and play in your relationship.

To loosen up emotionally and play, you may have to challenge a core co-dependent attitude that says you must create a good impression on other people. To play means relaxing this attitude and being willing to *risk*—to risk embarrassment, to risk someone else's thinking you're acting silly or childlike (which is hopefully true!), to risk other people's disapproval and displeasure. Keep reminding yourself that it really doesn't matter one iota whether or not someone else approves of you. You are quite capable of living your life without anyone else's approval!

To bring play into your relationship requires all of the above plus a willingness to be spontaneously expressive with your mate. If you're timid about doing so, start with small things first. Get some Play-Doh and model animals together. Go roller skating. Build sand castles. Go fly a kite at the beach. Take an art class together. Be willing to try some off-the-wall kinds of activities, like body painting. Once again, the key is spontaneity.

Angie and Bill have been together for eight years. Angie giggles about what happened one day when they were on their way home from a family get-together: "Bill and I were riding along, worn out from the tension of being around my family all day. I kept thinking that I wanted to just play. We drove by a park with a playground, and I turned to Bill and said, 'Bill, let's go play at the park.' He pooh-poohed it at first, but this time I decided to be persistent. I really got up about the idea the more I thought, and I was determined to not let his reaction make me change my mind like it's done in the past. Finally he stopped the car, we got out and went over. I climbed the jungle gym, went on this neat wooden bridge, and played on the swings. Bill was reluctant at first, because I think it's harder for him, but eventually he played on the swings with me. I could tell he enjoyed it. There were a few people around, but that didn't matter. The few kids that were playing there didn't seem to bat an eye, and in fact seemed to enjoy seeing two middle-aged adults playing on the playground toys."

There's one version of adulthood that says once you are 21 years old you are an adult and have to start acting like one, that adulthood is serious business. Another version says that the child inside never dies, and it's up to us to coax her out to play. As Eric Sevareid has said, "No child has an adult inside, but every adult has a child inside." Through grieving and playing, you can recapture the lightness and the spontaneity of this Inner Child.

HOW DO MEN AND WOMEN REALLY FEEL?

Robert Bly, a poet who works with men's issues, suggests in "A Gathering of Men," a PBS interview he did with Bill Moyers, that men are simply not as good as women at putting together words and feelings. I agree. I'm often amazed at how women are able to identify and express their feelings so easily. I was in a relationship some years ago with a woman who was consistently able to articulate the deepest currents of emotion that she was experiencing. I, on the other hand, did not always know exactly what I was feeling. Sometimes I had to spend time thinking about how I felt before I could clarify my emotions.

With some practice we men can get better at putting words and feelings together, yet based on my own experience, women will always be in the lead on this count. If you're a man, it's important to respect that fact. You'll usually be a bit slower than your lover at processing your feelings. If you need time to think it through, give yourself the time. It doesn't mean you're incapable of feeling, just that it may take you longer. A relationship is not a contest about who is better at feeling (or anything else, for that matter).

If you're a woman, respect the fact that you're better at feelings. Honoring and respecting these differences will allow each of you to have more room to grow in your recovery and in your relationship.

There are some things you can do separately and together to lessen the effects of your "shell shock," to awaken your senses and emotions, and thus awaken your Inner Child. By working with these ideas and exercises, you can enrich the emotional dimension of your relationship.

SOLUTIONS: HOW TO FEEL BETTER

Let me make it clear that I don't mean how to feel good all the time, but how to *feel* whatever emotions you have in a responsive and natural way. As Alice Miller has said, the opposite of depression is not happiness, it's vitality. One of the main tasks of recovering from your childhood trauma is to encourage the vitality, the life energy, to move *through* you in whatever feeling form it takes.

The following exercises encourage you to open your senses to this vitality and to communicate your feelings with your partner. The first exercises are designed for you to do on your own, although you can certainly share your experience with your partner. The last two bring the focus of feelings into your relationship.

To start, you must be able to identify your feelings. In order to do so, you must teach yourself to listen to your insides rather than reacting to what's outside your own skin.

Making Sense of Your Feelings

To get acquainted with your emotions, you'll first get acquainted with what goes on inside your body. At first, it's useful to simply pay attention without responding to the information. As you're reading this, perhaps you can become aware of your breathing. Perhaps you are aware of areas of tension, possibly in your neck, shoulders, or stomach.

If your body was mistreated in some way by your childhood caretakers, perhaps through beatings or sexual abuse, or if it was not lovingly touched and caressed, then your sensory mechanisms have been shut down to some degree for a number of years. It will take practice and patience to reawaken this marvelous barometer of sensations and feelings. To get to know your feelings, do the following simple awareness exercise, adapted from *Adult Children of Abusive Parents*, at least once a day for the next 21 days. Tape the exercise, then play the tape back while doing the exercise. It's important to do this exercise in a place that's quiet and free from distractions. Although you can do this exercise alone, your partner can join you if you choose.

EXERCISE: Sit back in your chair and close your eyes. Notice your breathing. Pay attention to the steady rise and fall of your chest as you first inhale, then very slowly exhale. Notice how your breathing gets deeper each time. With each breath you exhale, feel yourself relax a little more. As you breathe in, say to yourself silently, "I am . . ." and as you slowly exhale, say the word, "relaxed." "I am . . . relaxed. I am . . . relaxed. I am . . . relaxed.

Now, pay attention to your skin. Notice its coolness or warmth, the differences in temperature on different parts of your body. Feel the weight and texture of your clothes against your skin. Feel the pressure of your body upon the couch or chair. Notice anything else about your skin that comes to your attention.

Now, notice any areas of muscle tension. When you notice any tension, breathe it out when you exhale, letting your muscles relax. Start with your head and face and slowly move your awareness down your body, through your neck and shoulders. Now, notice your upper arms . . . chest . . . then upper back. Now, your lower arms . . . hands . . . stomach . . . lower back. Be aware of any tension in your buttocks . . . genitals . . . anus. Now, your thighs, both front and back. Then your knees . . . calves . . . shins. Now, notice your feet, both tops and bottoms. Then your toes. Next, return your attention to your breathing.

Next, listen closely to the rhythms of your body. Hear your heartbeat and breathing. Feel the blood pulsing through your veins and arteries. Notice any other internal sensations. Return your attention to your breathing.

Now, gradually bring your awareness back into the room. Be aware of sounds, sensations, and lights around you. When you're ready, slowly open your eyes.

Ask yourself the following: What was the most noticeable area of tension in your body? Were you able to relax? Were any areas numb? Did you experience any sensation? Look for the smallest noticeable sensation when you first begin doing this exercise. Don't dismiss any sensation. If you do this with your partner, it will be useful to share your answers to these questions, plus any other observations you may have. If you do this alone, you may want to write out your comments in your journal.

Christine did this exercise with her husband, Ray. Some of Christine's comments: "This is one of the most relaxing exercises I ever did. Ray taped it with his voice, and we sat out in the patio on our easy chairs, turned the tape on, and took off. I could feel Ray with me throughout. I was aware that I carry a lot of tension in my stomach and my throat, and the first time we did it, it was hard to let those areas relax completely. Each time since, it's gotten easier."

What's in a Name?

When it comes to feelings, everything. There is considerable value in naming these internal sensations we call feelings, especially when you haven't had a lot of practice in discriminating amongst the various emotions. In *Adult Children: The Secrets of Dysfunctional Families*, John and Linda Friehl write, "Inability to identify feelings and inability to express them are two of the key diagnostic features of dysfunctional families or individuals." For Adult Children, the bridge between identifying feelings and expressing them is naming these feelings.

If you don't have a name for your feelings, you are at their mercy. Anne Wilson Schaef writes in *When Society Becomes an Addict,* "That which goes unnamed may exert considerable influence over us, but because we have no words for it we cannot address it directly or deal with it." When you learn to name your feelings, it helps reduce their hold over you. When you remain in denial about feelings or simply don't know what to name them, you may feel a sense of powerlessness. Naming feelings gives you a basis for communicating your innermost experience to your partner.

Helen recalls how in the earlier stages of recovery she "couldn't tell the difference between sad, scared, and angry. I had been beaten up so much that I was in what you would call your basic shut-down mode most of my life. I knew when I was too cold or too warm, but beyond that I couldn't tell you too much about how I felt. Mostly I was depressed, and I tried to cover that depression by being funny, even though it was no laughing matter. There was no way I was ready for a relationship until I started feeling things. That would have been just too awesome."

Like Helen, you have to discover your feelings first through attention to your internal sensations and, subsequently, to the emotions associated with these sensations. As you pay closer attention to the sensations in your body, it will be useful to practice naming feelings that you can associate with what you are sensing internally.

Identifying the four basic feelings.

Given that there are so many ways to identify feelings, it's astounding to realize that there are only four basic feelings: *mad, sad, glad,* and *scared*. All variations and intensities are rooted in these four basic feeling words. To discover what you are feeling, pay attention to your physical and sensory cues and give what you are feeling a name. For instance, if your heart is pounding, your stomach muscles are tight, and you feel like withdrawing, you are probably feeling scared or mad. If your eyes feel heavy, your shoulders are drawn downward, and you are frowning, you probably feel sad.

One approach is to go ahead and name your feeling out loud and see whether it seems to fit. If you notice a tension in your lips and eyes, your heart pounding, and your fist clenched, try naming this feeling anger. Does that feel right to you? Initially it will be helpful to categorize your feelings by one of the above four names. Practice the simple exercise below for the next week or two, and you will discover that you are able to name the majority of your feelings.

The purpose of the exercise is to systematically draw your attention to your feelings and to encourage you to give a name to them. It's also useful when you are in a supportive relationship to share with your partner what you are doing. If the two of you are working this program together, it would be useful to share your daily discoveries. If you are doing the program alone, share your results with someone in your 12-step group or any other friend. The point of sharing with someone is to further validate your naming of your emotions.

> EXERCISE: Across the top of an index card or a plain piece of pa-
> per, write down the four feelings plus a category of "don't know."
> Carry it with you at all times. Pause for a few moments once every
> hour throughout the day and ask yourself, "What am I feeling?"
> Start with when you first get up. Make a mark under the appropri-
> ate heading each time you recognize a feeling; when you're not sure
> what you're feeling, make a mark under "don't know."

Ruthanne tried this for two weeks and was surprised at the results. "For the first two or three days I got really discouraged, because I kept writing down a bunch of 'I don't know's.' I couldn't get a handle on whether or not I was feeling anything. But the next day I remember waking up feeling mad. I was mad at one of the other accountants at work because she kept asking me to do more and more work that was really her responsibility. From there I started marking my feelings down more easily. Boy, was I surprised at how much anger I was really feeling!" Ruthanne went on to discover that real hurt was associated with this anger, hurt that had its source in the humiliation she frequently experienced with her mother's fits of screaming and verbal abuse.

It's not uncommon for Adult Children to discover other feelings—particularly fear or sadness—lurking nearby when anger is present, whether or not the anger is expressed. Sometimes anger can serve to protect us from being too vulnerable with our other feelings. If you frequently identify anger as your feeling, see if you can identify any other emotions beneath the anger.

Variations and intensities of feeling.
As you are reawakening your senses, you may at first notice grosser sensations and feelings rather than more subtle feelings. For instance, you may have the expectation that for anger to be present, it must be a very intense feeling. Thus you may ignore any experience of anger short of rage. Or you may confuse sadness with depression. Whereas sadness is an active emotional state, depression is more the blocking of emotions, indicating some sort of emotional repression. Because you are more familiar with how to block emotions and to

shut down, depression will be a more familiar experience to you and so will be more recognizable.

Often the cues from your body will be so subtle that they will go unheard unless you remain very quiet for a few moments and listen to what your body is telling you. To name the differing intensities of feelings, being still is a must. Acknowledging and naming your feelings goes against all your training in your abusive upbringing, so it's necessary to be very patient with yourself as well. By naming your feelings, you're breaking a lot of family rules. As much as your Inner Child wants to emerge, you have a lot of fear about doing so. It will take time not only to make room for this Inner Child to come out and to reawaken your senses but also to learn how to put a name on those reawakened sensations and feelings.

Since each of these four basic feelings can occur in a variety of intensities, it may prove helpful to develop a vocabulary of feelings to help name the subtle differences in emotional states. The following is such a vocabulary.

Mad	Sad	Glad	Scared
angry	disappointed	happy	afraid
irritated	depressed	pleased	nervous
outraged	hurt	ecstatic	panicked
resentful	unhappy	joyful	anxious
annoyed	discouraged	comfortable	terrified
hateful	blue	excited	concerned
pissed off	lonely	peaceful	guilty
livid	forlorn	content	insecure
frustrated		exuberant	worried
peeved		thrilled	uncomfortable
offended		loving	

This list is not exhaustive but suggestive. Perhaps you'll discover other feeling words to add to it. You can also describe the intensity of what you are feeling with words like "really" or "a little" or "very," such as "really worried" versus "a little worried."

EXERCISE: Now that you've had some practice in acknowledging and naming your feelings, the next step is to outwardly express the names of those feelings as you are experiencing them. To do this, work with your primary partner if he or she is willing to be supportive. If not, then work with a friend or your sponsor. Your feeling of safety is the first priority in working this exercise with someone.

> Make a copy of the list of feelings above. With your partner present and available for listening, choose three of the emotions named. One at a time, describe to your partner a recent experience wherein you felt the chosen emotion. Your partner's response is to simply listen without correcting, advising, or criticizing. Repeat this exercise three times a week for three weeks.
>
> At first it may feel a bit awkward (there's a feeling!), but stay with it. Remember, this is new territory for you, and to change you must stretch yourself into new territories even if it feels uncomfortable.

Phil was pleased with the results of doing this exercise. "Wendy, my wife, has been getting after me for years to express my feelings more. It's only since our working in therapy that I can see the sense in that. I tried the naming exercise, and I found out that I have a hard time with some of the milder feelings—especially hurt feelings. I guess it was just too dangerous for me to feel those kinds of feelings. I'm just so grateful for Wendy—her toughness and her patience."

Feelings Talk

Communicating your feelings in a relationship is vital to the life of the relationship. Two people can have a relationship without communicating their feelings (I've done it), but the relationship is bound to have a big empty space, an emotional vacuum. That's why it's so helpful to learn to acknowledge and name your feelings and to discover ways to communicate those feelings on a continuous, dynamic basis.

The following exercise is one I use frequently in counseling couples. It is best done with your primary partner, but if you are not in a relationship it's possible to do this with a close friend. This is called the "Incomplete Sentence" exercise. Do this twice a week for the next three weeks, spending no more than 30 minutes at each session.

> EXERCISE: To begin, sit comfortably facing your partner. Next, take turns finishing each of the incomplete sentences below in as honest and straightforward a manner as possible, starting each by saying your partner's name. You may complete each sentence up to three different ways, but it's important that you alternate with your completions. If one of you has nothing more to add prior to three completions, you may pass. Move on to the next incomplete sen-

tence and follow the same procedure. The partner who is listening is *not* allowed to respond. There will be time for that later. Either partner can stop the exercise at any time for any reason. If you do stop, take a time-out, then return to doing the exercise if and when it's agreeable.

For example, if John and Mary are doing this exercise, John might go first and say, "Mary, I feel annoyed when you . . . don't come to bed when I do." Mary would simply listen to this statement without editorializing or commenting at all, then it would be her turn. She might say, "John, I feel annoyed when you . . . pressure me into having sex." Then, John would repeat the same incomplete sentence but this time would add a different ending. They would alternate until each has had an opportunity to finish the first sentence three different ways, then move on to the next sentence until all are complete.

Once the entire sequence is finished, you and your partner can spend some time discussing what the experience was like for each of you and what your various responses meant. However, it's important that you do *not* discuss any of this while you are actually doing the exercise. Save your comments and reactions for later. When your partner is speaking, do your best to simply listen. If the discussion gets bogged down or either of you gets defensive, refer to the listening exercises in chapter 5 on intimacy.

Here are the sentences (be sure to start each completion with your partner's name):

1. I feel annoyed when you . . .
2. I feel sad about . . .
3. The time I was most disappointed in myself was . . .
4. I feel pleased when . . .
5. I worry a lot about . . .
6. I feel disappointed when you . . .
7. I feel scared . . .
8. I feel most angry when . . .
9. I feel hurt when . . .
10. I feel alone when . . .
11. I am glad when . . .
12. My greatest fear is . . .
13. What I like best about you is . . .
14. I feel closest to you when . . .
15. I appreciate your . . .

When you have gone through the entire sequence, take a few minutes to share what you observed in yourself and to discuss what was said. As you're doing so, keep in mind two important points about feelings: First, having a feeling about something doesn't mean you are right and your partner is wrong. Second, just because you feel something, it doesn't mean your partner has to change his or her behavior. It simply means you are having a feeling!

When Chris and Roger did this exercise, it generated a lot of material for them to discuss and to work out. Chris observes, "One thing I learned is that when I go to Roger to talk about feelings, he usually thinks something is wrong and tries to fix it. Now I realize this isn't unusual for men to do when a woman wants to talk about things. I realize that Roger will tend to do this, and I just have to let him know when I am talking to him just to communicate, rather than problem-solve."

Roger comments, "I'm getting the idea that there are times when Chris just needs to talk to me. Because of my job [as an engineer] I'm used to fixing things and solving problems, so it's a natural for me to do so, even with Chris. I don't completely understand why Chris needs to just talk sometimes, but I'm willing to give it a try if it will help the marriage."

Come Play with Me

As described earlier, one of the two methods for accessing frozen feelings is play (the other is grieving). I don't mean play as in competitive sports, but play as in theater. This type of play requires cooperation and the willingness to take some risks with your partner and let your Inner Child express himself without censorship or judgment—not an easy task when you've been used to repressing yourself most of your life. In play the conscious, rational mind, the part of you that asks why and tries to figure things out, needs to take a break. In play, as in actual theater, your body becomes an active agent of your expression. If you have any doubts about what play is, watch younger children at play and observe how easily they move with one another as if in some kind of unfathomable dance. An even better way to tackle any doubts is to actually experience play, particularly in cooperation with your partner.

The following exercise can add playfulness to your relationship. Adapted from a description by Robert Lawlor in *Earth Honoring: The New Male Sexuality,* this type of exercise originated in the Stanislavsky method-acting technique as well as the ancient Eastern Tantric and Taoist traditions. When you first try it you'll undoubtedly feel somewhat self-conscious. I would suggest that in spite of your apprehensions and inhibitions, you and your partner should agree to do the exercise once a week for a total of six weeks. It's extremely important that you do not criticize, tease, or put down your partner during this process, but instead be fully supportive. It will thoroughly enhance your ability to play together as well as create greater intimacy. It can potentially enhance your sexual relationship as well.

> EXERCISE: Mirroring: The first step is to create a comfortable setting. Both of you should wear comfortable, loose-fitting clothing and put on some soft, pleasant music. You might place some brightly colored flowers around the room. It helps to spend some time getting connected before the actual exercise, perhaps through light conversation or even by dancing together.
>
> From here the exercise is very simple. First you agree on who will initiate and who will respond. Then you and your partner stand facing each another, and whoever is responding mirrors every movement made by the one designated to initiate the movements. One partner moves, the other matches the move. One partner makes a sound, the other echoes that sound. A gesture, a facial expression, an emotional act—whatever the initiating partner does, the responding partner imitates as quickly as possible. After a few minutes, switch roles. Remember: this is not a contest to see if you can fool your partner, but very much a cooperative act. The purpose is to play and have fun.
>
> A variation is for the responding partner to quickly come back with a complementary rather than a mimicking response. For instance, if the initiating partner acts fierce and pounds his chest, the partner might cower in fear.
>
> Lawlor comments: "The conscious one-pointed effort to mirror another person first brings about a breakdown in self-consciousness; each partner learns that he or she can play out and divulge many roles and attitudes that were hitherto kept hidden, even from themselves. This newly found intimacy brings about an unspoken communication and harmonization that, in time and through practice, dissolves into a complete, spontaneous flow between the partners." That is what true play really is—a "complete, spontaneous flow" between you and your partner.

Lowell and Shelly gave this exercise a try. Lowell describes his experience: "I felt pretty stupid at first. Shelly was the instigator or initiator or whatever, and I was the follower. I kept thinking that I was going to somehow blow it or that I wasn't doing it right. We both giggled and laughed a lot, which felt pretty good. I wanted to quit after a couple of minutes, but Shelly kept coaxing me to keep with it. After a while, it was just like dancing, and we moved back and forth from being silly to being serious. Finally she put both hands up and moved toward me really slow, and our hands touched very lightly, then we stopped. It was great!"

No-Fault Feelings

A final point on expressing feelings: Take responsibility for your own feelings. What this means is that you do not blame your partner or anyone else for your feelings. One way of showing an attitude of blame, often unconsciously, is in the way you state your feelings. Whenever you start a sentence with, "You make me feel . . . ," beware! You are undoubtedly blaming your partner for how you feel. Instead, use "I" statements, such as, "I feel shut out when you don't talk with me," or "I feel annoyed with you."

While it's true that the partners in a relationship obviously influence each other, that doesn't mean your partner *causes* you to feel something. For instance, while you may feel irritated if your lover likes to talk on the phone for hours, and you may need to problem-solve this issue, it's *not* true that she is *making you* irritated. It's best if you acknowledge ownership of your feelings from the start rather than blaming your partner for your feelings. Blaming will only fuel the fire and lead to conflict. Nor is it necessary to blame yourself in order to take responsibility for your emotions. It simply means acknowledging that the source of the emotions is within you rather than external.

Try this simple exercise with your partner or a good friend. Later you may repeat it once a month as a reminder.

> EXERCISE: Sit comfortably facing each other. Say to your partner, "You make me angry," while your partner listens without comment. Your partner then says the same thing to you. Notice how you feel while saying this statement as well as while hearing it said to you. It's not necessary to be actually feeling anger at this time, just be aware of your reactions to speaking the phrase and hearing it said back.
>
> Repeat this process, this time saying, "I'm angry with you" to each other. Pause, and consider how you experience this way of stating the emotion and how it compares with the first. The third and final step is to say, "I choose to be angry with you." Note your reactions. Share your observations with your partner.

There is no right or wrong way to respond to this exercise, so trust that your experience is just right for you, and your partner's experience is just right for him.

Now, repeat the entire sequence with the feeling words "hurt," "afraid," and "happy" in place of "angry." After each sequence, take a few moments to share your observations.

Jackie did this with a close friend and reports that "it was like a big light bulb. I can see why I'd get so infuriated with my ex-boyfriend Tom because he always seemed to be putting the blame on me for every little thing. Come to think of it, I was probably doing the same with him. I can't say I won't ever do that again, but it's nice to know there is a different way to talk about feelings."

Now that you have done some work with your emotions, you are "armed and ready" to move on to the next issues. You are now aware of your feelings and can identify and express them, which is vital to dealing with the other major areas of Adult Child relationships: control, boundaries, intimacy, conflict, and commitment. You can make giant strides in being able to reach out and communicate with another; remind yourself to *risk* with your feelings. As you can see, emotions are the key to any relationship.

So let's move on to the next major area that is usually problematic for Adult Children as husbands, wives, and lovers: control.

CHAPTER 3

CONTROL

*A*lice listened as Dave finished his phone call. "Lunch tomorrow? Fine. Drop by my office at twelve-thirty. Okay, bye."

"Honey, who was that?" Alice asked.

"Oh, that was Gary," Dave replied. "You know, my old friend from school. I haven't seen him in ages."

"Oh," Alice scowled. "Well, I was hoping you'd take *me* out to lunch tomorrow."

"You could join us if you want," Dave said.

"No, that's all right." Alice shrugged her shoulders. "I don't know that I belong in your conversation about football and old girlfriends."

"Sounds like you don't want me to get together with Gary."

"It's not that." Alice frowned. "It's just that I thought you were . . . well, past all that."

"Past that?"

"Well, you know, you've gone on, gotten married, gotten a career," Alice paused, "and Gary's still in the same old job at the local market. I just don't think he's ever going to amount to anything."

"So you think I shouldn't be friends with him, is that it?"

"Well, yeah. He's really not such a good influence."

"What about *your* friends?" Dave said. "Robin, who's always trying to marry rich men . . . or Barbara, who's drunk half the time? I suppose they're such good influences?"

Donald came into the house after washing the car and found Arlene watering the houseplants. "You know, Arlene, I've been thinking," Don said as he sat on the sofa and leaned forward, elbows resting on his knees. "I don't really want to go to dinner tonight with you and Patty. No offense, but you know I just don't care for her."

Arlene looked at him with disbelief. "But Donald, I already made plans with her. I can't cancel them now. I haven't seen her for a long time, and I was looking forward to it."

"Well, I just find her too opinionated," Donald countered. "I'd rather stay home tonight and read."

"Oh, come on, it won't be *that* bad," Arlene continued. "Besides, we'll have a nice dinner. I have reservations at one of your favorite restaurants."

"No, I've thought about it and I'm just not interested."

"Hmm." Arlene paused for a few moments, then set the watering can down. "Well, I'm disappointed, but that's your decision." She went off to the den and returned in a few minutes as Donald was preparing a snack.

"You know, Donald, I think I'm going to go ahead and have dinner with Patty anyway. I've been looking forward to it for a while."

He smiled. "I think that's a splendid idea. I'm sure the two of you will have a great time, and I really don't mind staying home alone tonight. In fact, I could use a little quiet time."

"Yeah, I am looking forward to seeing her," Arlene said. "The more I think about it, the better it sounds. She and I have a lot of catching up to do. I'll call the restaurant and change the reservations to just two."

Like everyone else, you desire stability and order in your life—this helps you feel secure. If you can predict with some certainty that things will basically be the same tomorrow as they were today, then you can sleep a little bit easier. Unfortunately, in an attempt to make life more predictable and secure, or when you fear losing any security you have, sometimes you try to control the people in your life, especially those you're closest to—your husband, wife, or lover— by trying to manipulate them into doing what you want or what you think they should do. Although control is an issue in every relationship, as an Adult Child you may find that it assumes an inordinate role in your relationships.

In Alice and Dave's relationship, for instance, there are some obvious control maneuvers. Alice attempts to control Dave's relationship with Gary by trying to manipulate him into feeling guilty for having the friendship at all. Dave makes his own attempt at control by his counter-criticism of Alice's friends. Each partner has expectations and demands for the other that can often lead to power struggles, whether the attempts are direct or indirect, passive or aggressive.

Donald and Arlene likewise are presented with a situation where their wants and needs differ. However, in their relationship neither partner ultimately tries to control the other. They recognize each other's individual preferences and honor each other's boundaries. Although Arlene is disappointed in Donald's choice not to go to dinner with her and her girlfriend, she not only respects his right to differ but also resolves the dilemma by going herself, without resorting to manipulation.

Even in the healthiest of relationships, couples will on occasion try to control each other. That's understandable, since most of us want our own way. But partners in healthy relationships respect each other's individuality. Rather than control and manipulation, there is negotiation and compromise. Rather than innuendos and intimidation, there is agreement and understanding.

This is not what you witnessed or learned in your family. To discover the basis for your overdeveloped need for control in your relationships, once again we must look to your childhood.

YOUR FAMILY: LESSONS IN CONTROL

As you were growing up in your abusive family, control was a major issue. You watched adults who were either out of control or rigidly in control. You were manipulated, and in turn you learned to manipulate. You learned your lessons in control well—lessons that are rooted in your instinctive need to survive your dysfunctional family.

Because of the abuse, because of the craziness in your family, your very survival depended on how well you could control yourself. You couldn't let yourself be a child—spontaneous, playful, emotional—for fear of being severely punished for such behavior. Rather than be destroyed, you took that part of you, your Inner Child, and buried her for safekeeping behind a facade of control—a facade that was necessary at that time.

Kimberly learned how to control herself in the face of her father's rage. "I could tell when he'd been drinking because when he first got home he'd be kind of happy. But within just a few minutes, he'd be yelling at my mom and my brother and me. One time he slapped me hard because I said something to him about his drinking. I started crying and sobbing and he looked straight at me—I'll never forget that look—with his hand raised and said with his stinky breath in my face, 'Stop your crying right now or I'll really give you something to cry about!' You can bet I stopped!"

Your Real Self Gets Under Control

Like Kimberly, you learned to deny and control your natural reactions. Out of the necessity of denying and repressing your Inner Child, your real self, you developed a false self, created so that you could survive the abuse. With practice, this false self became a role that served to control and keep hidden those parts of you that would be unacceptable. You may have taken on the role of the Hero/Heroine, the Perfectionist, the Invisible Child, Daddy's Little Princess, Mom's Little Man, or the Caretaker, to name a few. Whatever your particular role, it was designed to keep your real self protected and under control.

Gail provided emotional support for others in her family and put many of her feelings in the box marked "Caretaker." "My mother was always sick, and my dad just wasn't around. I was the 'good little girl.' I feel like I practically raised my two sisters. I remember one time when I was about nine years old, I got angry and threw a spoon on the floor, and my mom was just coming into the kitchen. She just stood in the doorway to the kitchen for the longest time, looking at me and not saying anything. Then she let out a big sigh, turned around, and went back to her room. She never said anything about it, and I never asked, but I learned to control my temper because I didn't want to make her any sicker than she was."

When Gail lost control of her temper in front of her mother, she showed a part of herself that wasn't acceptable and by so doing risked losing her mother's love. Gail feared that if she expressed her real self, she would be emotionally, and perhaps even physically, abandoned. To a child, that's a death sentence, and the child naturally does whatever she has to do to avoid it.

"I'll Do Whatever It Takes; Just Please Don't Leave Me!"

When you were a child, the thought of abandonment by a parent was absolutely terrifying. You knew how fragile and vulnerable you were; your parents literally held your life in their hands. You could withstand a lot of abuse, but one thing you could not withstand was to be left completely on your own to fend for yourself. You controlled yourself so you wouldn't be abandoned. If you were abandoned in spite of your efforts, you blamed yourself.

Teresa recalls an incident when she was about four years old. "My dad had just left. He and my mom had just had a fight. I was scared, sitting outside on the front lawn, and when he had left, my mother came out and just sat down on the curb. When I went to sit at her side she was sobbing, so I put my hand on hers. She pulled it away and acted like I wasn't even there. I sat next to her for a little while, feeling scared and helpless, then quietly went back to my spot on the lawn. I decided that I had best not be a problem for her, because she might go away too, just like Dad did." Teresa's way of being "good" and controlling herself was to withdraw and "not be a problem" for her mother.

Like Teresa and Gail, by controlling yourself, by keeping your real self hidden behind your role, you came to believe that you could control others, particularly your parents. By "being good," by performing your role, you thought you could get your mom or dad to feel better, to stop yelling at you, or to not abandon you. The only trouble is that it didn't always work. Even if you were "good" all the time, you couldn't stop your parents from abusing you or blaming you or abandoning you. But still you kept trying.

Antidote for Powerlessness

You kept trying because if you stopped trying you might have been overwhelmed with a sense of powerlessness. Besides, your efforts to influence your parents were sometimes successful; they did not abuse you all the time. If you were extra quiet, or if you did all your chores, *maybe* this time they wouldn't abuse you, *maybe* this time they wouldn't leave.

Since children are naturally self-centered and tend to think that they are the cause of events around them, as a child you came to believe that your behavior could magically control your parents' behavior. When your efforts seemed to work occasionally, your victory stirred you to maintain your efforts at playing out your role, thus reinforcing your belief. By maintaining this illusion of control, you could more readily cope with the underlying sense of frustration and powerlessness.

I always felt a great deal of responsibility for my mother's happiness and was told on more than one occasion that I could make her feel better. She looked to me to take care of her emotionally (and sometimes physically), and I carried a sense of obligation to do so. I felt guilty when she was unhappy or sick, as if I was somehow at fault. One time, when she was upset at the fact that my older brother had joined the Marines, she got drunk on cherry brandy. I stayed with her while she rambled on, and I cleaned her up after she vomited. I felt powerful and in control because I was there to comfort her in her time of need—yet continually lurking beneath the surface was the sense that, when it came right down to it, I was at her mercy and was ultimately powerless.

"NOW THAT I'M GROWN UP . . ."

This underlying sense of powerlessness didn't just go away when you grew up. Your continued attempts to control others are often compensation for it. If you can be powerful over another person, if you can somehow maintain an illusion of control over that person, then you don't have to face your own feelings of powerlessness.

"I know I was abusive with my first wife," Marshall confesses. "I'd yell at her and call her names. One day she was trying to tell me her feelings about the car I wanted to buy, and I got pretty upset with her and started getting mean and—déjà vu! I flashed on how my mom used to yell at my dad, and I'd get so angry because he'd just sit there and take it. I remember thinking at the time that he was really a wimp, and I never wanted to be like him. I think a lot of the reason I treated my wife that way was because I was afraid if I let go then *I* would be a wimp, too."

Although controlling your mate will make you feel temporarily powerful and perhaps even give you some sense of security, it will never totally ease the deepest fear of your Inner Child—that you might be abandoned. This fear touches a profound chord in you and makes you continue to believe that any kind of abandonment by your mate would be emotional suicide—it feels as if being left or leaving would be a life-and-death issue. So you take your childhood role into your adult relationship, continue hiding your real self behind it, and try to secure the relationship in any way you can to avoid being abandoned. It's ironic that your anxious, controlling behavior may in fact instigate the very thing you fear.

Jacqueline reflects on how this worked with her last boyfriend: "Keith was a great guy. I guess inside I always wondered what he was doing with me. We lived together for about a year and a half. I kept hinting about commitment, about marriage, and he would usually change the subject. I didn't want to press him on it because I was afraid he would leave, so I'd put the whole subject back in the closet. But finally, after a conversation with my mom—she kept talking about how old I was, about having children—I decided to push for it. Wrong! I told Keith that night that either we get married or it was over. He took a deep breath, looked at me, and said, 'Then I guess it's over.' I was crushed! Anyway, I moved out, and we dated for a while, but it was never the same after that."

Whether because of a sense of powerlessness, a fear of abandonment, or a combination of the two, you spend a lot of time and energy on controlling your mate. You do your best to make sure that life has no surprises. The trouble is, life is full of surprises. As John Lennon said, "Life is what happens to you while you're making other plans." As long as you try to maintain this illusion that you can control your partner, you must be prepared to carry a lot of tension and to have a fair amount of conflict in your relationship.

Denise is a person who thrives on predictability and has trouble when things aren't completely in her control. "My boyfriend, Dale, decided he'd be cute and throw a surprise party for my birthday. I was so mad at him I wouldn't talk to him for a week. My friends all showed up at my front door. I didn't have any makeup on, and I was in some old sweat clothes and I hadn't showered. I tried my best to smile and act happy through the whole thing, but inside I was boiling. I'm still mad at him when I think about it. I do *not* like surprises, and he knows that."

The Illusion of Control

It's important to recognize that all of your efforts at controlling someone else, whether through bullying or passive manipulation, are based on an illusion: the illusion that you can control another person. You may believe that by acting in certain ways—being nice, bullying, screaming, withholding—you may be able to control someone else's behavior, thoughts, or feelings, but it's simply not true. You can certainly influence your partner to some degree—that's true in any relationship—but you can't control your partner. Anne Wilson Schaef writes about this in *When Society Becomes an Addict*: "The illusion of control is only an illusion, because none of us can really control anything. We think we can, we think we should be able to, we think we ought to try, and we cannot. . . .

"For instance, a lot of people firmly believe that they can *make* someone love them. They forget that love is a gift that must be freely given. Instead, they get involved in saying the 'right' things, wearing the 'right' clothes, and behaving in the 'right' ways. They think that they have the power to change someone else's mind and arouse the desired feelings in that person."

This illusion of control is played out vigorously in your relationships, yet it remains an illusion. Your partner may adapt to your wishes, but at the cost of her own thoughts and feelings, at the cost of her being a real person. It's amazing what lengths you will go to in order to maintain this fantasy of control in your relationship, all because of the fears and anxieties generated by your childhood experience and the training you received in your family.

Let's look at how you play out some of your attempts at controlling your mate.

Strategies for Controlling Your Mate

Your need to be in control can wreak havoc in your relationships, especially with your mate. You hope that he will do what you want, be what you want, but he never acts exactly the way you want him to. Even if you could control someone all the time, you would not be getting a real person. Instead, you'd have a puppet with his strings tied tightly to your demands. Your mate has his own will, desires, plans, and these may not conform to yours.

Sherry recalls how her boyfriend, Jeremy, finally exploded one day: "We were walking in the park, and I was talking about how I thought he should get his hair cut soon. He suddenly clenched his fists and screamed, 'Stop nagging me!' I really jumped, because it's so unlike him to say anything. Then I proceeded to tell him how he was wrong for acting the way he did. As soon as I started correcting him, I caught myself, looked at him, and started cracking up. That broke the ice, and fortunately we both were able to laugh about it. I've got to admit, I've been watching how much I correct him or tell him what he's doing wrong. It's a lot like my mother used to do with my dad."

Another way to exercise control over your mate is through passivity. By taking the passive and submissive role initially in the relationship, you assume your mate will supply the control. After some time you find ways to use your passivity as a means of controlling your mate. Withdrawal, withholding, and silence are among the most powerful passive weapons in the control battle.

Although every relationship has some control issues, Adult Child relationships are especially susceptible. As the relationship progresses, the controlling strategies make their appearance. Let's identify some of these common controlling strategies, then we'll explore ways you can rethink the attitudes that support these strategies as well as learn some nonmanipulative ways of communicating with your partner.

Below are five common strategies Adult Children use in an attempt to control their partners.

Withholding.
A passive form of controlling, withholding means keeping your feelings and thoughts to yourself and not letting your partner in on what's going on. The classic scene of withholding is a husband noticing that his wife has her mouth

turned down, her brow furrowed, her arms crossed and that she is not making eye contact with him. When he asks her what's wrong, she sharply says, "Nothing!" Further prodding yields no further information, and eventually an argument breaks out.

Anna describes how her lover, Rick, one night spurned every effort she made at communicating with him. "He sat there with his eyes glued to the television. I got so mad, but I didn't know what to do. So I just sat there and fumed, and when it came time to go to bed, I slept on the far side, away from him." Here, Anna returned Rick's controlling strategy with some withholding of her own.

Withholding in the early stages of the relationship may not have been a control mechanism. It may have been simply the result of your inability to express your thoughts or feelings. Perhaps you were angry, and because angry feelings generally led to abuse or abandonment in your family, you learned to steer clear of anger at all costs. Thus when there was conflict with your spouse or lover, you withdrew.

Over time, you learned that this withholding had an effect on your partner. Perhaps she left you alone when you withdrew. Perhaps she felt guilty and remorseful and tried to make it up to you by trying harder to please you. Perhaps you were physically or verbally abused when you withdrew, which triggered familiar feelings of helplessness and powerlessness and thus re-created the traditional patterns originated in childhood. There is a certain comfort in familiarity, as painful as it might be.

Harlan describes how he would withhold from his wife: "She could be demanding, and when she was, I'd get real quiet. I didn't think I was mad at her, but I discovered that I really was—and scared as hell to own up to it! After she'd come at me with her laundry list of things to do, I'd steer clear of her for days. I remember she'd ask if I was mad at her, and I'd usually shrug my shoulders and shake my head no. I'd just spend a lot of time in the garage. Well, after a while it seemed like I was spending a lot of my time out in the garage. I got to know the garage pretty well." Harlan's method for dealing with his wife's demands helped protect him but did nothing for the relationship.

That's the point of withholding as a strategy: to protect yourself. It's a quiet and passive way to express your power and control. It's saying to your mate, "I'll abandon you so I won't have to deal with your abandonment." Unfortunately, withholding as a strategy keeps you in denial of what you are feeling and keeps your mate in the dark, having to guess at what's going on with you.

Always doing for others.
One of the roles a child can take in the family is that of Caretaker. This role, like any other, can follow you into your adult relationships. It gave you a

sense of purpose in your family and undoubtedly still does. This is prime co-dependent behavior and is motivated by a sense of shame and a belief that you are only worthwhile if you give to another.

The controlling trap of this role is that you give, and give, and give, yet your giving remains subtly conditional. Whether you consciously recognize it or not, you are keeping a mental scorecard and assume that your partner owes you something in return. You fantasize that eventually he'll see the light, and then he'll feel so much love for you that it will be impossible for him not to meet your needs. You secretly figure that it's what you are due from all your generosity. What you want or expect from your partner remains unknown to him. You assume that he should be able to interpret your hints or read your mind. You find that when your cues or thoughts are not heeded, you get upset and stew about it in silence or else turn your anger inward and get depressed. "Look at everything I've done for you!" becomes your refrain, whether spoken aloud or brooded upon silently.

Nick recognizes how he has played this out with his lover, Teresa. "I give a lot because I like giving, but I'm starting to see just how co-dependent I can be. Teresa has been telling me that I give way too much; she told me she feels guilty because I do so much for her, like she can never do enough in return. When she came back from a recent trip away, I decorated her apartment with flowers all over, got a big banner, a cake—I went all-out. She told me she liked it, but she felt really self-conscious since she had only been gone for three days. I was really hurt by her reaction and got pretty mad at her, too." For Nick, this feeling of not being appreciated is a common one.

Martyrdom is one version of this controlling strategy, whereby you take on everyone else's problems and then complain about how burdened you are. You "suffer in silence," letting your partner or anyone else know about your troubles from time to time through your sighs, frowns, and general unhappiness or, if you're more vocal, through constant complaining. Although you valiantly endure this distress, you let others know you are enduring it and continue to act selfless throughout.

"No one likes to think of themselves as a martyr," says Sheila. "Jack pointed it out one day during a heated discussion about the kids. I didn't like hearing it, but the more I thought about it, I knew he was right. I rarely buy things for myself. One time I was given some money for clothes by my Aunt Harriet, and I spent it on my children. When I told Jack about it, he said 'Good!' but I wish he had told me I should have spent it on myself."

By always doing things for others or martyring yourself you unconsciously attempt to control your partner through guilt. This may be a replay of how you were controlled by guilt and shame as a child. It's easy to understand why you would continue to play out this way of controlling in your present relationship.

The net effect of this strategy is that you have to suffer in order to manipulate, so you have to re-create your victim role. This results in your partner doing things for you not because she wants to but because she feels guilty if she doesn't. You have to ask yourself whether you want your mate to give to you out of guilt or out of love.

Acting helpless.

Not only is a sense of helplessness and powerlessness usually a result of growing up with abuse; in adult life it can become a means of controlling your spouse or mate. As a child you learned these feelings of helplessness because you had no sense of your own influence or power. Because of the unpredictability and inconsistency in your family, the periodic chaos or the rigid control and lack of involvement, you felt helpless to influence events or people. You had a sense that no matter what you did or said, it had no effect on how things turned out.

James Leehan and Laura Wilson describe this in *Grown-up Abused Children*: "The child learns that certain outcomes (e.g., abuse, neglect, violence) and responses (the child's behavior) are independent occurrences. If the child believes that others can control outcomes by behaving in certain ways, but he or she cannot, either because they lack the skills or do not know the effective behaviors, the child feels personally helpless."

For most of my life I believed that I didn't really have an effect on other people or events. The source of this belief goes back to when I was a child, witnessing the periodic chaos that happened in my family and feeling—no, *knowing*—that I could not stop the violence or make everything better in my family. I was resigned to the fact (at that time) that I could do little or nothing to influence the outcome of events. This sense of helplessness turned to passive behavior that showed up later in my adult relationships. I used my passivity to avoid confrontations and intimacy by keeping distant, playing dumb, and denying my true feelings. This is a good example of how the conditioned helplessness that developed in childhood can become a passive form of manipulation and control in adulthood, and how a sense of powerlessness can lead to an attempt to gain control.

By maintaining this attitude of helplessness you are accepting the false belief that both successes and problems are caused by external factors. In other words, you tend to think the same way you did as a child, that things and events happen *to you* without any direct influence. You deny your personal power and any responsibility for making choices, thus taking no action to bring about change. As long as you still think this way, you'll tend to treat yourself as a victim and see yourself as having no choices.

By denying that you have a choice in the matter, you let others make your decisions for you. In a relationship, while this control may be gratifying in some sense to your partner, ultimately it becomes a losing game. You have the illusion that your passivity and helplessness keep you safe. If you never take a stand or make any decisions, your partner will love you—or at least not abandon you. Unfortunately, your partner may get tired of your passivity and helplessness and leave. Thus, the very abandonment that you fear may actually happen, further reinforcing your sense of helplessness and belief that you have no influence on events around you.

Vicki elaborates on how this has been true for her: "When Jeff and I were first going out, I think he liked me because I was so easy to please. I would go along with whatever he wanted. What I wanted didn't seem important, and I really wanted him to like me. When we got married, I think he still liked the fact that I was so agreeable. And when he told me he wanted a divorce, all I could do was break down and cry. He just looked disgusted and walked out of the room. Six months later we were divorced."

The sense of passive helplessness that many Adult Children experience can be used as an indirect controlling strategy, and it has a quietly insistent quality to it. The objective in acting helpless is either to avoid unpleasant feelings or else to get your partner to take care of you—to make your decisions for you, to protect you, or to rescue you.

Paul and Colleen sought counseling because of marital difficulties. Paul came to realize that he had taken on a passive, helpless role with Colleen, similar to the role he had played with his mother. Paul would share with Colleen all of his frailties and uncertainties, in an unconscious attempt to get his wife to mother him or rescue him. At times this strategy succeeded, but at the cost of Paul's self-respect and of Colleen's respect for him.

Another consequence of maintaining this helplessness is that you don't express your feelings but instead internalize them, especially anger. This internalizing can lead to tension and psychosomatic illnesses such as headaches and ulcers. If these illnesses become chronic, they can further control your mate by discouraging intimacy and sex.

Lying.

You may be saying to yourself, "But I don't lie. I'm basically an honest person." While this may be true, it's important to understand that lying involves not only those big, grandiose tales you might tell to cover yourself but also "little white lies." Little white lies are those relatively small distortions of honesty—

excuses and fabrications—we make up when we don't want to tell the truth. You may justify little white lies by saying that you don't want to hurt another person's feelings.

The real reason you lie is to protect yourself. When you were abused physically, sexually, or emotionally as a child, this way of protecting yourself made sense. Since denial with a capital "D" was the primary unspoken rule in your family (don't feel and don't talk), you couldn't tell the whole truth because you might get hurt. Now that you are a fully functioning adult, it makes less and less sense to lie and pretend. In your relationship, it just keeps the denial going and creates mistrust.

In *Adult Children of Alcoholics,* Janet Woititz addresses those from alcoholic homes, but she could just as easily include Adult Children of abusive parents when she writes, "Lying as the norm in your house became part of what you knew and what could be useful to you. At times, it made life much more comfortable. If you lied about getting your work done, you could get away with being lazy for a while. If you lied about why you couldn't bring a friend home, or why you were late coming home, you could avert unpleasantness. It seemed to make life simpler for everybody."

"Ginny makes such a big deal anyway about my golf," Thomas says, "that half the time I don't tell her when I go to the driving range or play a round. About once every two weeks I and some of the guys in the office go out early. I usually tell Ginny that I have an early morning meeting, and since I keep my golf clubs in the car, there's no suspicion on her part. I just figure it's a lot easier if she doesn't know."

Since straightforward, honest communication is unknown to you and may be just too terrifying, you go to great lengths to try to control others' impression of you by lying. Anne Wilson Schaef coined the term "impression management" for this co-dependent characteristic. You shade or distort the truth just enough so that others won't disapprove of you, doing your very best to control their impression of you. Under the illusion that by lying you can get people to like you (or at least *not dislike* you), you deny your feelings, preferences, opinions. You protect yourself in many ways, such as telling someone you will call her back right away when you have no intention of doing so, or by not telling your mate that you don't like his way of touching. You may gain approval in the short run, but in the long run you just continue acting out of your childhood role and denying your real self. It takes a lot of energy to maintain this facade.

Frances has tried hard to create the "right" impression with Bill: "We've been dating for a few months now, and I still feel like I always have to look my best, wear the right perfume, the right clothes. I would *love* putting on some old sweats and going for a walk on the beach with him, but I can't tell him that. I don't think he would like it, because he said he always likes his lady to look sharp."

When lying becomes a standard way of controlling your mate, what results is a considerable gap between your real self and the false self you present to the world—especially to the one you love. As long as you continue lying to your mate, you will create increasing emotional distance. The main risk in being honest and direct with the one you love is that you would have to give up your illusion of control. To continue lying as a means of controlling your mate will only result in your having to hide your true feelings more and more, and in your mate becoming increasingly distrustful and distant.

Using your anger to manipulate.

Anger is especially a problem if you were abused as a child. In your family it was one extreme or the other: either your family expressed anger destructively and abusively or they did not express it at all. It became a frightening emotion with which to deal. In either case you find yourself now as an adult denying and internalizing your anger as a means of controlling yourself, or else using your anger as a means of intimidating and thereby controlling others, especially your mate.

There is no such thing as unexpressed anger. Even if you are denying your anger and your partner is going along with the denial, it will get expressed somehow, usually in a displaced fashion. We've all played out different versions of "kick the dog" with our anger. Perhaps you lose your temper with your children when it's your husband you're really angry with. Perhaps your anger is easily triggered by other drivers on the road after a disagreeable encounter with your mate. When you use this unacknowledged and unexpressed anger manipulatively to try to get your partner to feel guilty or afraid, or to intimidate her into giving you what you want, it becomes a problem of control. It is a potentially destructive way to compensate for the underlying feelings of powerlessness.

One type of covertly manipulative behavior, called *passive-aggressive behavior*, results from unexpressed anger. Passive-aggressive behavior is when you act as if you are not angry and have no problems at all, when you really are mad. All the while you're saying there's no problem, you are manipulating your partner into feeling guilty or frustrated and unsure why she's frustrated. If your partner feels guilty, then you've got her! If she gets frustrated and angry, you can feign innocence and assume that she is the one with a problem. Some examples of passive-aggressive behavior: "forgetting" to pick up the dry cleaning for the fourth time; being late for an important date; driving fast when your mate wants you to drive slower; procrastinating on a project you're doing with your lover; and giving "left-handed" or crooked compliments, such as, "You really do look good for someone your age."

Paula says, "When Howard and I were dating, he used to get so upset when I was late. I'd tell him each time that I would try harder the next time, but it never seemed to work. The truth is, I don't think it was as big of a deal as he made it out to be. Instead of telling him that, I would just be angry and be late the next time! I think the little kid inside was saying, 'There's no way you're going to tell me what to do!' and so I would be late. Of course, we don't see each other anymore. I guess I showed him!"

If you do express your anger overtly there is always the possibility that you can become physically or verbally abusive, unless you have discovered ways to contain anger and not to use it to control, intimidate, or abuse. It's always useful to acknowledge your anger, but it is not useful to vomit your anger all over someone else. If you're feeling intensely angry, the emotion probably has more to do with the past than with the present. Although on the surface it looks like you're incredibly angry with your husband for his lack of involvement, you're probably unconsciously feeling some old, unresolved anger—perhaps toward your alcoholic father who was never there. Whenever you feel anger that's extremely strong, be suspicious. Its source is likely in your childhood feelings, and it's worth asking yourself what your anger is really all about. It would be helpful to talk with someone else about it, or write down your thoughts in journal form.

If you use anger destructively toward your mate to try to control her, you may be unconsciously *identifying with the aggressor*. This term means that you're feeling and acting like the abusive parent you had, especially when you're dealing with someone you see as less powerful than yourself. Now you have someone else who serves as the scapegoat for your anger, much as you once served as a scapegoat for your parents' anger.

Earl discovered this about himself. "The other day Sally was trying to tell me something about what was wrong with the car, and I was having trouble understanding what she was trying to say. Well, things got pretty heated up, and after a while I was standing up and screaming obscenities at her. At one point she said, 'You're acting just like your father!' That really pissed me off, so I just took off for a while. But later, while I was cooling down, I thought about what she had said, and as much as I hate to admit it, she was right. My father used to yell and scream at me a lot of the time, usually for the littlest things."

One important note: If you become physically, sexually, or emotionally abusive as a result of your anger, you should seek professional help. You do not have to be bound by the patterns from the past. You *can* break the pattern of using your anger abusively and manipulatively, but you may need help to do so.

SOLUTIONS: LETTING GO OF CONTROL

When your whole life has been built around control—controlling yourself and therefore controlling others—it can be absolutely terrifying to even consider letting go of control. All sorts of fantasies surface at the mere thought: "If I say what I'm really feeling, my wife won't like me and she'll leave me." "If I tell my husband that I want to go back to school, he'll be upset." "If I stop trying to control my lover's drinking, she'll go off the deep end."

While these are potentially realistic outcomes, any of them may happen with or without your attempts to control and prevent them. Your wife may leave you, your husband may get upset, or your lover may go off the deep end with her drinking no matter what you do. If you operate your life on the premise that these feared outcomes are to be avoided at all costs and on the illusion that you can somehow control them by your actions, then you aren't living, you're just surviving.

This need to maintain control keeps you from risking, from expressing and acting on your own feelings and needs. Yet to live and to learn requires that you take some risks. For a relationship to grow and thrive and prosper, you must be prepared to take some emotional risks. If you remain frozen with the fear of letting go of control, your fear will be controlling you.

"In my first marriage," Marjorie says, "my husband—excuse me, my ex-husband—was always threatening to leave, telling me I was no good, that I was frigid. I figured that I just had to put up with him, because I was afraid that if I said anything he really would leave. One night he threatened to leave me, and I guess I had had enough, because I told him to go ahead and go. He really did a double-take on that one! He didn't go that night, but after that I started seeing that I could really live without him. It took a couple of years before we finally divorced, and during that time I started speaking out more and more."

Because of your tendency toward an "all-or-nothing" orientation, you may at first see letting go of control as *losing* complete control. As you'll see, letting go of control does not mean losing control. Letting go is a voluntary act. It requires that you learn to rethink your controlling attitudes, to let your partner and others be who they are, to more directly and honestly communicate your wants and needs without manipulating, and to trust that life knows what it's doing in spite of your judgments as to how things could be better.

Letting go of control does not mean you will feel powerless or helpless; it means that you recognize the limits of your power. Letting go means giving up your co-dependent habits of trying to rigidly control yourself in order to manipulate your partner. It means recognizing that you can make conscious choices for yourself, that you do affect others, and that you have very real, very human limitations. Letting go means that you stop trying to judge and then dictate how anyone else should be, think, or act.

To gain some fluency in letting go of control, let's look at some ways you can identify and change these controlling attitudes.

Changing Your "Stinkin' Thinkin' "

In Alcoholics Anonymous (AA), irrational and unrealistic thinking is called, rightfully so, "stinkin' thinkin'." This is thinking that is not based in reality, that leads to falsifications and distortions of the truth. It's thinking that reinforces the illusion of control. For example, maintaining the belief that if you just love and care for your wife enough she'll stop her drinking, leaves you living in fantasyland. As difficult as it may be to accept, in reality the choice is ultimately hers as to whether she stops drinking. The choice is yours as to whether you want to be around her as long as she's drinking. You have no control over her behavior or feelings. To recognize this fact requires you to challenge some basic co-dependent attitudes about control.

A simple but profound fact to appreciate is that it's not the situation itself—in this case, your wife's drinking—that makes you feel or act the way you do. It's what you tell yourself, what you are *thinking*, rather than the situation, that prompts you to feel and act the way you do. This is a powerful truth, because it suggests that nothing outside you can *make* you feel or act in any particular way. It's an inside job—your feelings and behavior are prompted by your attitudes and thoughts. If you can accept this as true, it becomes apparent that you in turn cannot control or cause anyone else to feel or act in a particular way. It's your partner's thoughts that cause her feelings and behavior.

Your experience of your wife's drinking will be far different if you rethink your controlling attitudes. You cannot *make* her behave or feel in the way that you'd prefer; although it may be unfortunate, if she continues drinking and if you separate because she refuses to get treatment, it will *not* be the end of the world. If you treat this possibility as horrendous, you're much more likely to try to control her behavior.

Two major types of "stinkin' thinkin'" contribute to your disturbing feelings and reflect your futile efforts to control the situation: *demanding* and *catastrophizing.*

Demanding: When "want" becomes "should."
Demanding thinking is treating preferences as if they were imperatives. For example, you might *prefer* that your husband agree with your vacation plans

completely rather than have his own opinions. Layered over the preference is an absolute, demanding thought that because you prefer it, he *should* therefore agree. Implied is that if he doesn't agree, he deserves to be damned or punished.

As long as you hold on to this demanding way of thinking, it can lead you into controlling behaviors. If you sincerely believe that another person *should, must, ought to,* or *has to* do what you want him to, you will have unrealistic expectations of him. You are judging how your partner should be. This can lead you to withholding, lying, acting helpless, or using your anger in order to manipulate your partner into giving you what you want. This type of thinking can also be part of the strategy of always doing for your partner, then expecting him to return in kind. It's a parental kind of thinking.

Demanding is vastly different from having preferences. You undoubtedly have preferences as to how your partner thinks, feels, or acts—ways you would "like" her to be. You'd prefer that she feel sexual tonight, that she never leave you no matter what, that she'll want to join the softball league with you. Yet these preferences do not have to lead to absolute demands. As long as you identify your preferences as preferences rather than demanding what you want, you are less likely to try to control your partner. By thinking in terms of preferences rather than demands, you face the risk of not getting your way, but you're also able to let go of trying to control your mate.

After eight years of marriage, Jerry and Joanne sought counseling for their constant arguing and belittling of each other. Together we looked at their expectations of each other and their demanding thinking. Jerry realized that he still thought that Joanne "should" stay at home for the sake of the children and not work, even though both children were now in school full time. When she tried to discuss her desire to go back to work, Jerry would either clam up and withhold or become defensive and argumentative, usually over some other trivial point such as the state of the housekeeping, thus using his anger to try to manipulate Joanne into feeling guilty for her desire to change. Joanne, on the other hand, believed that Jerry "should" see these changes as reasonable and "ought to" go along wholeheartedly without any resistance or objections. This belief led her to ignore or ridicule most of Jerry's objections, adding fuel to the fire. She also reminded Jerry of all the things she had done for him and told him he "owed" her his support. It was necessary for both Jerry and Joanne to challenge these unrealistic, absolute demanding ways of thinking about each other before they could resolve their conflicts.

First they went through the exercise below to identify the demanding thoughts they held toward each other in order to exchange them for preferences. For an opportunity to examine your demanding thinking and expectations as well, do this exercise with your partner.

EXERCISE: Make a list of 15 incomplete statements about your partner, each beginning with the phrase, "She/He should . . . ," then complete each sentence as truthfully as possible. If you are working with your partner, both of you can make this list, but do so independently of each other. Put down honest answers that reveal how you actually think about your partner; otherwise it will be just an empty exercise. A few of the ways Joanne and Jerry finished their incomplete sentences:

Joanne	*Jerry*
He should . . .	She should . . .
. . . support me in getting work.	. . . take better care of the house.
. . . listen to me.	. . . dress up in sexier clothes.
. . . not spend so much time at work.	. . . be more affectionate.
. . . understand how I feel.	. . . be more sociable.
. . . do more with the children.	. . . spend less money.

Next, do the same with "I should. . . ." Some examples from Joanne's and Jerry's lists:

Joanne	*Jerry*
I should . . .	I should . . .
. . . not get so angry all the time.	. . . remodel the kitchen.
. . . get more done during the day.	. . . not be so stingy.
. . . read more.	. . . tell Joanne how much I love her.
. . . spend more time helping our daughter with her homework.	. . . slow down and relax more.
. . . spend more time with other women.	. . . find a new place to work.

You may be surprised to find out that you have rigid expectations not only about your partner, but about yourself. If you are working with your partner, after you've completed both lists sit down with each other and alternate reading one item at a time from the "She/ He should . . . " list, then one at a time from the "I should . . ." list. Talk with each other about how you felt as you read your lists. This is not the time to debate your lists but to share your personal experience of reading them.

Next, reread your lists in a similar fashion, but this time substitute for "should" the word "prefer." As you read your lists to each other, it's best not to editorialize; instead pay close attention to what you are experiencing. When you have both completed your lists, take a few minutes to discuss your observations. At first you may feel awkward or silly, but it's important to do the exercise in spite of these feelings. During the discussion you may consider such questions as: How did you feel during the exercise? Were you completely honest, or did you hold back on telling the truth? What were your strongest "shoulds"? How do these absolute beliefs manifest themselves in attempts to control your partner? In attempts to control yourself? What happened when you changed each to a preference statement? Can you really let go of control by reminding yourself that all absolute beliefs, all demands, are really preferences in disguise, and that you may not get what you want?

Over the next few weeks, listen closely to what you say and to your internal dialogue. Whenever you catch yourself saying out loud or internally any statement with a "should," "ought to," "must," or "have to" in it, pause and restate it with "I'd like" or "I'd prefer." Talk about your discoveries with your partner, particularly in relation to control.

Demanding thinking is characteristic of childhood, when you thought in more black-and-white, all-or-nothing terms. As a child, this type of thinking helped you make order out of your world by supplying rules about how you should and shouldn't act, and it gave you some sense of control. It served the purpose of internalizing parental dictates for self-control. Now as an adult, the main purpose served by demanding thinking is to keep you rigid and inflexible and operating from the illusion of control. It's more practical and much easier to operate from preferential thinking, without imposing your demands and expectations on your partner. It requires you to let go of control, but it can help you become much more relaxed about your relationship.

Next we'll consider a second type of thinking that reinforces the idea that we have to hold on to our control: catastrophizing.

Catastrophizing: Blowing things out of proportion.

Catastrophizing, simply put, means making mountains out of molehills, blowing things way out of proportion. It's telling yourself that the worst possible outcome is the one most likely to happen, and that if it does happen it will be terrible—the end of the world. When you were a child and did not have the advantage of adult perspective, many things seemed to be catastrophic, and in fact they were. When viewed from the child's perspective, rejection and abandonment are horrible things to face, since they can literally be a matter of life and death. Your parents' anger could be catastrophic to you, since their wrath could not only be scary and painful, it could literally kill you.

Now as an adult, you have greater latitude of choice. If you're rejected, it's not a life-or-death issue. If you're abused you have the choice, although it may not be an easy decision, of not staying around for more. Yet your Inner Child still carries with her this deeply ingrained fear that's based on thinking that awful things might happen if she were to be abandoned or were to lose control of herself.

It's because of this type of thinking—catastrophizing—that you try so desperately to control things. If you try to control your partner's reactions by lying, you won't have to face the dreadful possibility of his being upset with you. If you're always "nice" and doing things for your mate, perhaps you can ward off (control) his leaving you. If you indirectly express your displeasure by withholding, you can avoid the catastrophic possibility of more directly expressing your anger. You may avoid a relationship altogether because you can picture disastrous consequences of getting involved, such as losing complete control of yourself. Based on the illusion that you can somehow control these outcomes, you imagine the worst possible scenario and then further imagine that if it were to actually happen, it would be absolutely horrendous and you couldn't stand it.

Many Adult Children catastrophize about rejection or abandonment by their partner. By assuming that you couldn't get along without your partner, you will try to control her to such an extent that you may end up creating the very thing you fear. For example, by continuing to act helpless, by being passive and submissive, you find yourself tolerating abuse from your partner to such an extent that you lose your self-respect as well as the respect of your partner. The end result is that your partner does leave you—and you survive!

Marlene describes how this happened with Howard over a 12-year marriage: "It wasn't until I read an article in a magazine that I realized how much I had been letting Howard verbally abuse me. He would call me names and put me down a lot and I just accepted this as normal. After all, that's what I saw in my parents' marriage, only my dad would also beat my mom sometimes. I figured that since Howard wasn't beating me it wasn't all that bad. Plus I think I was petrified at the prospect of living without him. The article maintained that wives often put up with this because they're afraid they'll lose their husbands if they stand up for themselves. The description fit me to a T, and that's when I decided that I had had enough."

It was after this that Marlene sought counseling with Howard. One of the things she worked on was changing her catastrophic thinking. She really didn't want to break up her marriage, but she started to think of that as a possibility. She realized that if things came to this pass, she would be sad but she would survive. By thinking this way, she could deal with her feelings about Howard in a more realistic manner and assert herself more in her marriage. The risk of loss and abandonment, while still fearsome, was no longer so overwhelming that it stopped her from speaking up for herself.

Although the first part of the counseling was a struggle for both of them, eventually expressiveness actually became attractive to Howard. As he stated to Marlene in one of the counseling sessions, "I want you to talk to me, to tell me what's going on." Much to Marlene's surprise, Howard actually began to encourage her to tell him what was on her mind and what she was feeling. Marlene's courage in taking risks with Howard increased as she continued to challenge her catastrophic thinking and let go of trying to control herself so much and in turn control Howard's reactions. That, plus Howard's supportive attitude, has helped make the relationship more solid.

To help challenge your catastrophizing, ask yourself three questions: First, how likely is it that the feared consequence will happen? You may worry and worry about some feared outcome only to discover that you've wasted a lot of time and energy. As Will Rogers said, "I've had a lot of problems in my life— and most of them never happened." A friend I know has continually worried about the possibility of her husband's leaving her—worried throughout the ten years of their marriage!

Second, even if the feared consequence did happen, would it really be the end of the world? Although it would be unpleasant and undesirable if your spouse left you or if your boyfriend got upset with you, you would survive. Trying to control an undesirable outcome because you think it would be catastrophic causes you to create a lot of unneeded tension in your life.

Third, how much misery are you causing yourself as long as you focus on this kind of thinking? Although the kind of hypervigilance that results from anticipating catastrophes served a purpose when you were younger, now it simply creates undue strain in your life as an adult. The physical and psychic tension that result from habitually catastrophizing can literally make you ill.

As a way of bringing your catastrophizing back into perspective, do this next exercise with your partner or on your own.

> EXERCISE: Independently, each of you think of some area in your relationship where you might feel a loss of control that you imagine would be catastrophic. For example, Gary decided that he would feel

vulnerable and out of control if he shared his hurt or fearful feelings with Maureen. He thought this would be catastrophic.

Write out this situation at the top of a sheet of paper, then ask yourself, "What's the worst that can happen if this feared situation actually takes place?" Write down a feared outcome. For example, Gary wrote, "If I told Maureen how scared I felt about my new job, she might get upset with me."

The fun begins when you *escalate the catastrophe,* writing out all possible disastrous consequences, taking it to absurd proportions one thought at a time. For example, Gary escalated the catastrophe about his situation: "If I shared my fears, not only could she get upset, but she'd think I was a real wimp. She'd probably laugh at me. She'd probably start yelling at me, too, and all the neighbors would hear. Of course, how could she live with a wimp? She'd probably move out. Because she was so upset, she'd pass out a flyer to all of our neighbors, telling them that I couldn't handle my new job. She'd call my boss and tell him that I was a scaredy-cat, and probably call the newspapers. A story would appear in the Sunday paper, describing how incompetent I really am. At that point, I'd have to leave the state." And all because he took a risk in sharing with Maureen his fears about his new job!

Thus when you escalate you can see the absurdity in your catastrophizing. Once you have gained some perspective on your catastrophic fears of letting go of control, the next step is to ask yourself what *realistically* might happen. Then note that even if this consequence did occur, it's unlikely to be as disastrous as you had imagined. For Gary, the worst appeared to be manageable: "Actually, the worst that might happen would be that Maureen would be upset because she looks to me for being 'the rock' in our relationship. She might try to convince me that I shouldn't be afraid, that I really am competent."

From here, write out some thoughts that would support your taking the risk. Gary went on to write, "Even if she did get upset, it wouldn't be the end of the world. We've managed to get through upsets before. It also would be something I could survive. I don't have to hold back from telling her how I feel just because she might be upset. We both agree that we value emotional honesty, so here's an opportunity to practice it. And it's perfectly okay for me to be afraid. It doesn't mean that I'm not doing a competent job. I have a right to be afraid, and she has a right to her feelings too."

It's useful to remind yourself that even if your mate leaves you, gets upset, doesn't agree with you, or whatever, it isn't the end of the world—you will survive and probably learn something in the process. If it truly is a life-and-death issue to express yourself in this relationship, the more pressing question would be, what you are doing in a relationship where you are not treated with respect?

If you are working with your partner, it would be useful for you both to do this exercise, then spend some time discussing your thoughts and feelings. It's important not to invalidate what you feel, but to recognize that you can influence your feelings depending on what you are telling yourself. If you are catastrophizing, you will create feelings of extreme upset, misery, depression, helplessness, and rage. If you rethink some of these catastrophic assumptions, you will find that you will still have some feelings but they won't be paralyzing or self-defeating.

Further, by rethinking your demanding thinking and catastrophizing, you lessen your need to control yourself or your partner. This does not mean that you are helpless or powerless to influence your partner, just that you are not insisting that things be any certain way. You still have your preferences, and it's useful to identify and express those preferences. It's also useful to consider letting your mate be himself or herself.

Let Your Partner Be

Be what? Be himself or herself! What a revolutionary concept—especially for us Adult Children, when the models we grew up with represented much the opposite. To have a successful relationship, you must eliminate *all* efforts to control your partner. You must consistently shed your habitual attitudes and strategies of control. Sure, you'll find ways to justify and defend your attempts at controlling your partner— "It's for his own good." "He needs me." "I'm not going to change until she does!" That's exactly what these attitudes are: justifications for your ingrained habits of co-dependency and your deep-rooted fear of abandonment. As long as you continue to think that abandonment would be catastrophic and insist that your partner think, feel, and behave the way you want him to, you will continue to play out your controlling games, ones that neither you nor your partner can win.

Love is not something you can control. It must be generously donated for it to be the genuine product. Otherwise it's just need and addiction. Anne Wilson Schaef writes about it pointedly in *Escape from Intimacy*: "Frequently, much of our reality is based upon subtle control. We believe if we act a certain way we can make our partner love us and want to stay in the relationship. Love does not work like that. It cannot be controlled. It is a gift. We must respect that even if someone has promised to love us forever."

It's fear that will keep you trying to control; it's love that will help you let go. Harold Bloomfield in *Lifemates* sums it up: "You must learn to accept your lover exactly as he or she is; not as you hope or wish him or her to be. A change that you think is in your love partner's best interest may not seem that way to him or her. Certainly you can be candid, make requests, and give feedback, but manipulation of your lover to meet your needs is a prescription for disaster. Change only comes about because your lover wants it. Mature love means accepting your lover's flaws and respecting that which is unique and lovable."

With these thoughts in mind, try the following simple exercise with your partner. I'm sure you'll find it quite powerful.

EXERCISE: Sit comfortably facing your partner and establish eye contact. Be aware of any discomfort—don't say anything, just make a note of your experience. Determine who will go first. This person will be called Partner A; the other, Partner B.

Partner A, as you're looking in your mate's eyes, say, "I love you, (Partner B's name), and accept you exactly as you are." Partner B then slowly responds, "Yes, (Partner A's name), you love me and accept me exactly as I am."

Pause for a few moments, and both of you pay close attention to your reactions—thoughts, feelings, and actions. Initially you can expect to feel uncomfortable doing this exercise. There's a lot of built-in resistance both to stating this unconditional love and to hearing it said back to you. Just note these reactions without analyzing them.

Repeat this exact sequence up to 10 times. Stop, and for no longer than five minutes talk about the reactions you observed in yourselves. Then change roles and repeat the process, this time with Partner B going first and Partner A restating the affirmation. Once again, spend a few minutes describing to each other your personal reactions.

This can be a subtle yet powerful affirmation process, so treat it accordingly. Repeat this once a day for the next three weeks and watch what happens in your relationship.

Nora and Phil did this exercise. After her first experience, Nora said, "It was hard to do, both hearing it said to me and saying it to Phil. When Phil was saying it to me the voice in my head kept saying, 'How could he love you just like you are—you have too much wrong with you. You're overweight and you're bitchy today and you had a fight with him just yesterday.' Then after that, I started questioning his judgment! At first I laughed, and then I got quieter. After a few times I could finally let it in. When it came my turn to say it to him, I kept wanting to qualify it—you know, 'I love and accept you exactly as you are except when you tell me I'm doing something wrong.' Once I stopped that, then I could really feel my love and appreciation for Phil."

Phil's comments: "At first when Nora was doing this I felt like Mr. Rogers was talking to me, like at the end of his program when he says 'I like you just as you are.' It was hard to take it seriously at first, but then it's usually hard for me to express my softer feelings without making a joke. I think it was a great opportunity for us to do something like this together. After Nora and I did this together, we tried it with our son, Chris. He squirmed a bit at first, but I could tell that he liked it. One thing is that I'm sure that every now and then Nora and I will look at each other and be able to say that and really mean it."

Now that you've explored some attitudes that can help you loosen your grip on control, let's look at two ideas that can help you communicate in a non-controlling way.

Communication Without Manipulation

You can influence your partner without trying to control her. There's a big difference. Influence means you *affect* someone else, while control means you try to *make* her do what you want. When you're trying to influence someone, you may be trying to get your preferences met, but without the insistent, manipulative quality that is there when you try to directly or indirectly exert control. When you try to influence someone, you are more willing to accept that the other person has a choice as to how to respond. If I want my lover to go with me to the movies, I can suggest or ask, and from there it's up to her whether she wants to go. On the other hand, if I'm trying to manipulate and control her, I can act as if I would suffer if she didn't go, or get mad at her and pout to try to make her feel guilty.

In order to influence your mate, it's useful to learn how to communicate without manipulating. There are ideas on this throughout the solutions section of each chapter in this book; here we'll focus on two main ideas that will enhance your ability to let go of control and communicate more directly. These ideas are *asking for what you want* and *communicating consequences*.

Asking for what you want.

An effective alternative to the controlling strategies (withholding, always doing for others, acting helpless, lying, using your anger to manipulate) is the simple idea of asking for what you want. To do so requires you to challenge your demanding and catastrophic thinking and truly let your lover make his own choices. It also requires your willingness to accept no for an answer. If you give yourself the right to ask, be sure to give him the right to refuse.

In fact, that's the main risk—that you may not get your way. If you receive a refusal and then catastrophize about it, you are more likely to move from direct nonmanipulative communication to your familiar controlling strategies. Remember, it's not the end of the world if your request gets turned down. Maybe the timing was poor, the request was too large, or your partner simply didn't feel like giving you what you want. Giving you what you want is not a test of his love for you anyway, so go ahead—take some risks and ask for what you want.

Asking for what you want should be simple and straightforward, although it's easy to complicate it with catastrophic fears about what might happen. Here are some examples of ways you could ask for something from your lover.

> "I'd rather you just hear me out without offering solutions. I know you want to help me, and I appreciate that, but I mainly need you just to listen, okay?"
>
> "Tonight can you just hold me for a while? I really don't feel like having sex."
>
> "I know you're really busy, but I'd really like to spend some time with you during the week, even if it's for just a couple of hours. How does that sound to you?"
>
> "Will you give me a backrub?"

By asking in ways such as these you can learn to further relax your control. Below is an exercise you and your partner can do together.

> EXERCISE: For the next three weeks, make it a point once each day to ask for something from your partner. Keep it simple to start with and only increase the size of your request when you are comfortable doing so. Do not monitor each other, but instead pay attention to your own process of making requests. Making this a part of your daily communication diet will help you become more direct at asking for what you want rather than relying on manipulation. After the three weeks of practice, talk with your partner about what it was like for you to make the requests.

I personally like this simple idea of asking for what you want. Having been in the role of Caretaker in my family and later in my adult relationships, it was against my training and principles to ask directly for anything I wanted from my partner. In the first place, to ask for anything might suggest that I was needy, and of course, I operated within a role where I didn't "need" anything from her. To fulfill my role completely meant I had no needs and could take care of myself completely. Second, my lover was, of course, supposed to be able to read my mind so that I wouldn't have to ask.

Over the years since I've been in recovery, I've come to see how valuable it is to simply ask for what I want. I remember with one girlfriend a few years ago, I was feeling especially burned-out and felt like being taken care of. Being direct in asking for what I wanted was relatively new territory, so I thought that this would be the perfect opportunity. When we got together I asked her if she would wash me down as I took a bath, then give me a massage. I recall feeling that it would be okay if she refused, but to my pleasant surprise, she agreed. And I thoroughly enjoyed it!

Communicating consequences: When/then.

Rather than controlling your partner, another option you can consider is communicating the consequences on you of his behavior—in other words, how you are affected by what he does.

There is a consequence to every behavior. If I smile, most often the consequence is that others will smile back. If I let go of an apple, the consequence is that the apple will fall to the ground. If I am in a relationship and I say I am going to be home at a certain time but show up late consistently, the consequence is that my partner will soon learn not to trust me.

Communicating consequences is a much healthier way to work with each other than trying to control each other's behavior or judging what the other has done as wrong and in need of correction. Often it's useful to communicate with your partner about how his behavior is affecting you. This is best done by using a "When . . . then . . ." type of statement.

For instance, "When you are late and don't call, then I get scared and have trouble sleeping"; or, "When you speak to me so loudly, then I find I shut down and withdraw and don't hear you"; or, "When you act angry when I don't want to have sex, then I end up having sex with you anyway but resenting it." This doesn't solve all of the problems of control, but it presents you with an opportunity to open up some dialogue without trying to control your partner. You can always follow this type of statement by asking for what you want. If all this fails, turn to the chapters on boundaries and conflict (chapters 4 and 6) and study them thoroughly.

Below is an exercise that will help you and your partner practice communicating consequences.

> EXERCISE: Take a sheet of paper and divide it into two columns, labeled "Behavior" and "Consequences." Under the "Behavior" column write a few of your partner's behaviors that you don't like. Then in the "Consequences" column, describe how you are affected by these behaviors. The effects can be tangible ones or can be described in terms of your feelings. Lonnie wrote out the following about her lover, Fred:
>
> | *Behavior* | *Consequences* |
> |---|---|
> | 1. Not answering my questions | I feel left out. |
> | 2. Leaving his stuff in the living room | I trip over it, and the living room looks messy. |
> | 3. Threatening to leave | I don't feel safe, so I close down. |
> | 4. Working at home most of the night | We don't have any time together in the evenings. |
>
> Once you've written down your lists of behaviors and consequences, share them with your partner using the "When . . . then . . ." technique of communicating. Spend some time discussing your responses. Over the next few weeks, practice communicating consequences to each other consistently in this manner.

Lonnie reports: "When I talked to Fred this way, rather than my usual method of telling him what to do, he seemed to listen. Like the other day when I was trying to tell him something about my work, and he kept interrupting me, giving me advice. I paused for a moment and very carefully chose my words, then said, 'Fred, when you keep interrupting me, then I lose my train of thought and I feel like you don't think what I'm sharing with you is that important.' He stopped doing it, and I went on to tell him about the prospect of a promotion for me at work."

No More Struggle

One final note to put this control issue in perspective: I've noted throughout this section that control is an illusion, that you really don't have as much control as you would like to believe. Yet it seems so tempting to continue trying to control your partner, your children, your friends, yourself, and even the environment around you. I find myself smiling whenever the television commercials for Honeywell conclude with "Honeywell: helping you control your world." It's absurd to think that our efforts at control do not have ultimately destructive consequences.

Attempting to "control your world" is usually counter to the movement of life and therefore results in a lot of unnecessary struggle and discord. It's like trying to swim upstream rather than moving *with* the river. By swimming against the current, you'll eventually wear yourself down and ultimately make little progress. In your tired, worn-out state, you'll ultimately be swept up with the current anyway. How much simpler and easier to move with that current in the first place! By moving with life you can give up the struggle.

Trying to control your partner also invites a lot of struggle, tension, and contention. There will be times when he doesn't want the same thing you do, and when he doesn't act as you think he should. Spending your time and energy getting your partner to align with your version of how he should be is like swimming upstream. It's possible to do it, but there's a price to pay. Rather than control, however, you can learn to ask for what you want, negotiate, compromise, set boundaries, and make agreements. Although it takes practice in letting go of your familiar habits of control and some training to acquire these new attitudes and skills, you can benefit by a much more relaxed type of relationship.

Now you have some ideas and some tools for letting go of control, and I'm sure these will help you improve not only that one special relationship, but other relationships in your life as well. Now that you can loosen some of your controlling tendencies, we will move into the next major issue that is common to Adult Children as husbands, wives, and lovers and is an important replacement for control: setting boundaries.

CHAPTER 4

BOUNDARIES

*D*ick sat down on the couch next to Barbara, who was watching television, and studied the *TV Guide* for a few moments. He picked up the remote control and switched the channel. Barbara looked at him incredulously. "Dick, I was watching a movie."

"There's a rerun of 'Columbo' on I want to see," he said. "It's a lot better than your stupid movie."

Barbara crossed her arms, almost in tears. "Last night you told me I could watch it, and now you're . . . "

"Quit your bitching and whining!" Dick barked. "You've been watching the tube since you got home. It won't hurt you to miss your movie."

Barbara sat back on the couch in stony silence. As she started to get up a few moments later, Dick glanced at her and asked, "Where are you going?"

"I don't know. I guess to the bedroom. I don't care for that program."

"Aw, c'mon, sweetheart," he pleaded. "Stick around. I miss you. I haven't seen you all day."

"Yeah, okay," Barbara muttered. She sat down sullenly, staring into the television.

Georgia stood at the front door for a few moments, took a deep breath, then opened the door and stepped into the house. Immediately, Justin and

Mindy, Georgia and Mike's nine- and seven-year-olds, charged toward her, jabbering away, obviously eager to see her.

"Mom! Mom!" Mindy squealed with excitement, "look what I made at school today!" Mindy held up her drawing for Georgia's approval.

"That's great, Mindy," Georgia responded, giving Mindy and Justin a hello hug.

"Mom, Mindy's being a brat!" piped in Justin.

"No, I'm not!" Mindy countered. "You're just being mean!"

"Hold on just a minute. Both of you." Georgia looked squarely at Justin, then at Mindy. "I just got home. I need a few minutes to settle in. After that, I'll spend some time with each of you." Both children scowled and groaned, but soon went about playing with each other.

"Hi, honey," Mike said as he came into the living room. "Boy, am I glad you're home. You're a lifesaver. I'm having trouble with the new word-processing program, and I have to get this damned newsletter ready for the printer tomorrow. Can you give me a hand right away?"

"Not right now, Mike," Georgia stated. "I just got home, and I've had one of those days. I need to take a few minutes for myself, then I've promised Justin and Mindy some time."

"But I need your help. I've got to get this newsletter done today."

"No, not right now, Mike. I know it's important to you and I do want to help, but first I have to have some time to myself. How about later tonight, after the kids are in bed?"

"Well, okay," Mike said. "If that's the way it has to be."

"Thanks, Mike. It really is important. I'm going to go to the bedroom and flake out for a while. I'll be out in just a few minutes."

Boundaries in a relationship are critical for your health and the health of the relationship. They tell you where you end and where your partner begins. Without clear boundaries you can't have a clear sense of yourself. Without a clear sense of yourself you either feel consumed by the relationship or else feel distant and isolated from your partner much of the time.

In unhealthy relationships like Dick and Barbara's, both partners lack defin-able boundaries. It's hard to tell where one person ends and the other begins. Dick treats Barbara as if she were an extension of himself, and Barbara acts as if she has no rights as a person. Barbara easily loses herself in the relationship and doesn't define her limits or claim her rights. Dick in his self-centeredness often treats Barbara as if she were there mainly to accommodate his needs.

In a healthy relationship such as Georgia and Mike's, each partner has a much better sense of his or her own boundaries, and they share mutual respect for these boundaries. Each person has a reasonable sense of self and is able to set limits as needed. Georgia is able to define her needs and set her limits with her children and with her husband. Even when Mike tests her limits, Georgia stays firm.

YOU, YOUR LIMITS, AND YOUR FAMILY

Webster's defines a boundary as "any line or thing marking a limit; a border." When it comes to personal boundaries this has a couple of meanings. First, knowing your boundaries means that you are aware of your own tastes, preferences, and needs; you are aware of yourself as a separate and distinct individual.

Personal boundaries also address specific physical and psychological limits, defining what is yours and what is another's. When you set your boundaries you are describing your bodily and emotional borders and letting others know what and whom you will let into these borders and what and whom you will keep out.

Your physical boundaries relate to your body and your property. By these physical boundaries you determine how you want your body to be treated and whether or not someone else can use your possessions. Your psychological boundaries relate to the kind of treatment you will accept from others. Knowing your psychological boundaries helps you fend off emotional and verbal abuse and helps you decide when and how you will share your time and attention with someone else.

Having clearly defined boundaries gives you much greater personal freedom. Without boundaries, you waste a lot of time and energy defending yourself, feeling resentful and victimized, and avoiding situations where you risk being stepped on or feeling used. With boundaries, you can choose when to let others cross the line and when to keep them out. Knowing that you have this choice, you feel much more confident in all your relationships.

Georgia is a good example of someone who is reasonably clear about her boundaries. She seems to have a reasonable sense of self, a respect for her limits, and she claims her own needs with a quiet authority. She has a good sense of her preferences and draws the line when her husband and children want more of her than she is willing to give at the time.

On the other hand, both Dick and Barbara are lost in their relationship, tied into an unhealthy co-dependency. Barbara has not set any boundaries with Dick, nor does Dick have any clear boundaries. He has no sense of where he ends and Barbara begins, so his boundaries include her. Dick grew up with physical and emotional abuse, and Barbara grew up with sexual abuse; the patterns that started in their childhoods persist in their relationship.

Chances are that growing up in your family didn't give you much of a head start when it came to boundaries. It was a case of too much or too little: either the boundaries between family members were too loose or too rigid or gravitated unpredictably between the two extremes. It was difficult for you to clearly define your personal boundaries and thus define any clear sense of self.

Enmeshed Boundaries, Confused Roles

If the boundaries in your family were too loose, this led to enmeshment and role confusion. Enmeshment occurs when the boundary rules in the family are lacking or unclear and subject to change on a whim. You could not count on anyone to honor your limits. Your body was not yours, and your possessions were not truly yours. Mom would come into the bathroom when you were using it. Your sister would take your toys without asking, and your objections went unheeded. Dad would keep tickling you no matter how much you protested. In the case of sexual abuse, your personal physical boundaries were clearly violated. You dared not whisper the word "no" to your parents, nor by any other means declare yourself a separate human being with feelings and thoughts that differed from theirs.

Ellen's relationship with her mother typifies this sort of enmeshment: "She never went anywhere out of the house without me. I think now she was deathly afraid of being outside the home, so she took me along to comfort her. At the time I sort of enjoyed it, because I felt very special. But as I got older, it got to be burdensome. If I went out on a date, she acted like a lost puppy dog. After a while it was so painful to see that expression on her face that I stopped dating for the longest time."

Enmeshment of boundaries may have occurred with your siblings as well. "My family didn't have any boundaries," declares Daryl. "Both my sisters used to really take advantage of me, especially the oldest one. From the time I was about five years old, she would come into my room at night and molest me. She would also tease me, telling me that something was wrong with me, that I was bad and evil. She would taunt me, saying I had a little penis. My parents never did anything about it. I'm not even sure they knew, and I wasn't about to tell them. I was too ashamed." Daryl is 32 years old and has never been in a relationship. He feels a lot of hostility toward women. It's no wonder he has difficulty forming relationships, given the lack of boundaries in his family and particularly this distorted sexual relationship with his sister.

Another result of loose boundaries is role confusion. When role definitions in your family were not clear, adults often acted like children and as a result the children had to act like adults. You were raised by six-year-olds in grown-up bodies. You may have been Mommy's Little Hero and been treated more like your mother's rescuer and protector than her son. If you were Daddy's Little Princess, you felt you had to be your father's emotional blanket and, in the case of incest, his sexual partner as well. There was probably some role reversal in your family. Even as a small child you may have had to take care of one or both parents physically and/or emotionally.

One of the most vivid memories I have is of myself at 13 or 14, performing the role of marriage counselor with my parents. We had just moved from Iowa to California, and things were pretty rough. My dad was drinking, my mom was feeling helpless, and they were fighting a lot. I remember taking charge and sitting down with them, advising them on how to make their marriage work. It's astounding to me now that I was doing this, but there I was— hiding my own fears, my own depression, and my own need for parental guidance from them, trying to act so adult, so strong, pretending I knew what I was doing. This is the kind of role reversal that results from unclear boundaries. It led me to do the same thing later in my adult relationships—trying to act strong, as if I knew what I was doing when I didn't, and denying my own vulnerability and needs.

Each of Us in Our Own World

At the other extreme, you may have come from a family where the boundaries were very rigid and led to isolation. There was little or no physical or emotional contact between family members, and everyone lived in his or her own little world. If this was the case for you, rules in your family were extremely strict and you learned to obey very well. Religion may have been the justification for these inflexible personal and psychological boundaries.

"The outstanding memory about growing up in my family was the intense loneliness," John says. "My family was church-going, and my parents were upstanding citizens of the community. However, I do not once remember my mother giving me a hug. It was like she and my dad and my sister were just stick figures—and so was I. Most of the physical contact I got was when I was getting a beating. My father would invoke the name of the Lord as he was administering his beatings. One of the worst beatings came because I asked him why God let him hit me like he did. As he proceeded to beat me he kept quoting Bible verses."

In his recovery, John is attempting to break some of his own perfectionist habits. Maintaining such rigid personal boundaries has made it difficult for him to relate intimately with his wife, and for a number of years in their marriage his fear of intimacy was masked with his intense addiction to his work.

Lydia recalls, "My mother was such a clean freak—she insisted the house be in order all the time. She even kept plastic covers on the lampshades and on the couch, and we had to walk down the side of the stairs so that we didn't wear down the carpet in the middle. I thought something was wrong with me because she ignored me a lot, and I don't ever remember her touching me or holding me. I can see from Grandma where she got it. At least now I know it's not my fault."

Boundaries Were Anybody's Guess

When they reflect upon their childhoods, many Adult Children recall a great deal of inconsistency when it came to boundaries. Boundaries would fluctuate between being too rigid and too relaxed. Living in this type of family made it difficult to predict which boundaries would apply at any particular moment. Sometimes Mom would let you play at your friend's house; sometimes, for no particular reason, she wouldn't. Sometimes she would be affectionate and loving, and then turn unpredictably distant and angry. Sometimes Dad would be cold, sometimes affectionate, and sometimes the affection would turn sexual. You were involved in a constant guessing game about boundaries, and trying to outguess your parents was a no-win proposition. You never knew what to expect. As a result you learned to guard against the unexpected by creating rigid personal boundaries for yourself, thus seeming to reduce your risk of getting hurt.

This type of fluctuation is characteristic of alcoholic families. My family was a typical alcoholic family, where the boundaries often fluctuated wildly between being quite rigid and very loose. Periods of quiet were punctuated suddenly by fighting, usually triggered by one or both parents' drinking. There was unpredictability and intermittent chaos. Boundaries between family members and rules changed on a whim.

I recall one time having saved a lot of money from my allowance. I was so proud of myself. I had a whole coffee can full of coins collected over a period of several weeks. One day without warning, my mother in a fit of anger made some vague accusation that I was becoming overly concerned with money. I guess I had counted my coins one too many times. She took the coins away without any further explanation, and I never saw them again. I was confused and upset. In retrospect this was a clear violation of boundaries, and it took me a long time to get over it. This is one example of the unpredictable violation of boundaries that was characteristic of my home, and it is typical of the boundary fluctuations in a dysfunctional family.

NOW THAT WE'RE ADULTS

Growing up confused about your boundaries—your sense of self and your ability to set limits—you carried over into adulthood whatever lessons you learned from your family. Since the question of boundaries only surfaces in relationship with others, you're ripe to reexperience these issues in your closest relationships, especially with your spouse or lover.

For me this earlier training in my family clearly showed itself in later relationships, especially in my second marriage. I maintained rather rigid barriers that kept me safe but distant and lonely. Since I wasn't secure in my ability to establish my own boundaries, I erected walls that served to keep everyone out. Unfortunately they also kept my wife out—the very one I yearned to be close to. I had such a fragile sense of self that I dared not risk losing *me* in the relationship. There was no way at that time that I could have experienced any true, lasting intimacy.

At times Susan tried to tell me that I was unreachable, inaccessible, but I didn't know how to hear what she was saying. Even if I could have heard or understood, I doubt there was anything I could have done about it at the time. I was too locked into my private castle. One time after we had made love, she commented with a note of sadness that we didn't look each other in the eyes during our lovemaking. I muttered something to joke it away, but I was struck by the truth of what she said. Still, I continued to avoid eye contact much of the time because it was just too scary. If she really saw me I'd have to let her in. If I let her in I might lose myself, and if I lost myself I would be vulnerable. If I was vulnerable and loved her too much I might lose her. Maintaining these rigid boundaries kept my risks low.

If, on the other hand, your boundaries remain so loose that they are extremely permeable, then as an adult you find it easy to feel lost in your relationships—to lose any sense of your own feelings, needs, or limits. Kathy had a great deal of difficulty distinguishing her feelings from her husband's. As she puts it, "Jack would walk in the door and I could feel what he was feeling before I even saw him. If he was angry, I'd feel it and then feel scared and tippy-toe around him. It's like I knew whatever he was feeling, whether he knew it or not.

"You get so caught up in the other person that you don't know who you are. Whatever Jack wanted, I wanted. Whatever he said no to, I agreed with. I'm an intelligent woman, but I lost my ability to discriminate for myself. It was like I was his shadow, staying in the dark all the time but always attached."

Boundary Issues in Your Relationship

What you saw and learned from your family shows up in particular areas of your relationship with your husband, wife, or lover. Boundary issues in particular show up as difficulties in creating and maintaining intimacy, expressing your sexuality, taking time for yourself, and especially in saying no to your mate.

For genuine intimacy to occur, the ability to set boundaries is crucial. Melody Beattie explains this well in *Beyond Codependency*: "To momentarily merge with another in the experience we call intimacy, we must be able to emerge again. Otherwise it's not intimacy and closeness—it's fusion and dependency. We need a healthy sense of self so we can count on ourselves to take care of ourselves." To "emerge again" requires that we have a reasonable sense of our own boundaries. In the example above, Kathy could not "emerge again" with Jack, but instead would lose her sense of self.

As for sexuality and sexual expression, the first boundary you need to address is whether to allow sexual contact. If the answer is yes, then boundaries further help you define the when and how of your touching and sexual pleasuring. If your partner is touching you too firmly or too softly, it's up to you to explain what you don't want and what you want instead. If you have sex at times when you don't feel like it at all, you are violating a personal boundary. As Wayne Kritsberg says in *Healing Together*, "Being in a sexual relationship does not mean that either partner has unlimited access to the other's body. When a partner sets limits on the amount or kind of touching they want or on their sexual availability, they are setting a personal boundary. Setting a boundary is not the same as creating a barrier to intimacy. . . . They signal our preferences and desires."

Karen, a victim of sexual abuse as a child, was not able to define her sexual boundaries with her husband. "The first night of our honeymoon, he raped me. It really set the stage for our sexual relationship. After that night I did my best to avoid having sex with him, but that was hard to do. Mostly I just let him do it to me. It was really painful most of the time, but I didn't know how to stop it. Plus all my training said that you're supposed to please your man."

Sex can be one of the most intimate acts two people can share, or it can be entirely mechanical and heartless—even, as it was for Karen, downright abusive. The degree to which it is an intimate act depends in part on whether the two people involved can define their boundaries, as well as relax their boundaries and let go. To relax your boundaries you need to feel safe. To feel safe you need to feel reasonably secure about your ability to set boundaries when appropriate. Sharing sexually is certainly a time when boundaries can soften, yet it is still necessary during sexual play to be alert to the more subtle requirements for boundary clarification, such as letting your partner know what feels good and what doesn't, how you want to be touched and held and how you don't. In the next chapter, we'll explore these considerations more thoroughly.

Another vital boundary issue is taking time for yourself. It's so tempting to get caught up in the flurry of day-to-day business, in activities involving the children, or in your relationship that it's easy to forget to take time out for yourself. Many people who do take time alone to recharge their batteries note how restorative it can be. Private, personal time is vital for reducing stress and "finding yourself." In the context of a relationship, you must make it a point to schedule time for yourself.

One of my friends, Charles, has worked out an arrangement with his wife, Leanne, where he intentionally takes an assignment away from home once every three or four months and is gone for the weekend. Charles asserts, "It's necessary. It gives me time to clear my head, to record my thoughts and just be away from everything and everyone. I take along a little tape recorder and talk into it about all sorts of things. I feel much better after a weekend like this, and Leanne and I get along better as a result." This is a workable arrangement that gives both spouses a chance to have their own time apart from each other.

Last but not least, another boundary issue is the ability to say no in order to set limits between yourself and others. In a sense all of the above described areas are ways of saying no. In fact, the core of setting boundaries is the crucial ability to say no. It isn't all there is to boundaries, but it is the foundation.

Hugh describes the experience of saying no to his girlfriend: "I guess I've spoiled Christine. I'd usually let her have her way, but too often I'd end up feeling angry and resentful. So I decided I would get honest with her and tell her when I didn't want to do something instead of going along with it. She asked me the other day to move in with her. I told her no, I wasn't ready. She pushed a bit, but I stood my ground, in spite of feeling guilty and scared. She was really miffed and didn't talk to me for two days. But I'm glad I did it. It would have been a big mistake to have just gone along with it. Eventually Christine admitted that she respected me for being honest with her even though she was disappointed with my answer."

Do What You Want; Just Don't Ever Leave Me

Marsha is typical of many Adult Children. She married when she was 16 to "get myself out of the house." She wanted to get away from a cold, tyrannical mother and from the constant verbal battering of her father. Her husband, Ron, came from a household where he took care of a younger brother and sister in the frequent absence of his single mother. His father abandoned the family when Ron was eight years old, and what Ron remembers is mostly his father's savage temper and how he would frequently whip Ron and his brother and sister for the slightest reason.

The first year of their marriage was fairly smooth, but then Ron started drinking more and more. He became increasingly aggressive in his demands on Marsha and became sexually abusive with her. Marsha became more and more passive, acceding to Ron's demands time and again but never able to please him fully. The more she tried, the more he demanded, calling her all sorts of degrading names.

Marsha became terrified of making a wrong move, so for much of the early part of the marriage she did nothing and became increasingly depressed. When she showed up at my office at age 34, she had two children, little support, and complained of depression and marriage problems. Ron refused to attend any of the sessions, implying that it was Marsha who needed to change. According to Ron, Marsha needed to stop complaining and learn to like sex more.

Although there were other factors involved, Marsha exhibited a lack of clear boundaries. She had no sense of self and did not know how to develop personal "rules" that would help her define herself. She let Ron walk all over her, as both her parents had done. For instance, even though Marsha was working and contributing money to the family, Ron continued to control the checkbook. When Marsha asked for money, it was "like pulling gum off a hot sidewalk." Like her mother, Ron was cold and tyrannical. Like her father, he used words to intimidate her and to hurt her. Marsha felt as she had when she was a child—helpless, frustrated, enmeshed, and with no sense of her own power or of her own self. Marsha felt totally consumed by Ron and the marriage.

A similar sense of helplessness and frustration is no doubt familiar to you. It results from a deep-rooted childhood fear of abandonment. You were emotionally abandoned as a child, and in some cases physically abandoned as well. Your parents simply weren't there for you. They were nonrecovering Adult Children themselves and were preoccupied with their dysfunction. They couldn't be there to meet your emotional and developmental needs. They may have ignored your needs altogether.

Or perhaps in your case your parents directed all their attention to you because it was too painful to deal with themselves or with each other. They tried to meet their needs through you. This was another version of emotional abandonment, one in which their behavior toward you was overwhelming. In either case—whether they ignored you or overwhelmed you—they were not there for you emotionally.

As I've stated, for a child, even worse than any abuse is the prospect of not having a parent there, since as a child you depend on your parents for your very life. In a child's mind, to be abandoned means plunging into darkness, into the unknown, being completely alone. This primal fear of abandonment stays with you into adulthood and manifests itself in myriad ways, particularly in how you deal with your boundaries in your present-day relationships.

In *Healing Yourself*, Wayne Kritsberg identifies two distinct dysfunctional relationship patterns that offer a refreshingly different way to look at a relationship. As a mate, you become either *engulfing* or *abandoning* with your partner. Both of these opposing patterns result from problems with boundaries.

Engulfing your mate.

Because of your fear of abandonment, you may find that boundaries between you and your mate become murky and your behavior toward your partner becomes engulfing. When you feel threatened you move toward your partner, desperately clinging all the more. Your boundaries become so enmeshed with your partner's that you lose any sense of yourself. You become extremely jealous—you have to know your partner's whereabouts all the time, you demand constant attention and never want to be left alone. You feel threatened much of the time about the prospect of losing your mate and of being alone. Sometimes your behavior is passively engulfing, such as self-martyring, illness, and depression, and sometimes it's more actively engulfing.

Julia mentally relives a tumultuous first two years with her husband, Dennis: "I couldn't let him out of my sight or mind. When he was away from me I'd get real suspicious, even if he was at work. I remember one time grilling him for most of his lunch hour about some remark he had made the day before, something about the girls at work wearing shorter and shorter skirts. That had set my mind spinning, and I imagined all sorts of things were going on when he wasn't with me. When he came home that night we had a huge fight. He told me that I didn't give him enough slack to have an affair even if he wanted to. That wasn't very reassuring. Now I'm not sure what to do. I still get panicky and suspicious."

Abandoning your mate.

Another pattern based in the fear of being "swallowed up" by your partner is one in which your behavior is abandoning toward your mate. Whenever you feel threatened you move away from your partner. You keep rigid boundaries around yourself because you fear being engulfed and overwhelmed, or because such rigidity is all you've known. You feel so uncertain about your ability to establish and maintain boundaries that you keep yourself hidden behind thick psychological walls, and it becomes extremely difficult if not impossible for anyone to cross these boundaries. You are terrified of losing yourself if you were to let anyone in too close.

Ironically, it's because you're not sure of how to set boundaries that you maintain such rigid ones. If you knew how to set boundaries and felt assured that, once you merged with someone intimately, you could emerge intact by reestablishing your personal boundaries, then you would not feel the need to keep your partner at such a distance.

You may use various means to keep your distance: acting angry much of the time, leaving the relationship (especially after periods of closeness), being unwilling to touch or hug, withholding feelings, and being emotionally or sexually unavailable. You erect all sorts of physical and emotional barriers because you're afraid that if you get close you'll lose your individuality.

Rick's fear of being engulfed showed itself in relationship after relationship. "I can see now how when I would start getting close it scared the dickens out of me. Girlfriend after girlfriend, I'd maneuver my way out of the relationship after a few months. It was what my last girlfriend said that hit me between the eyes and made me go and get help. She noticed that I started using my sense of humor more and more as a shield, and that I got more and more distant the more she loved me. It makes me sad now, because I really think she did love me."

Three Pernicious Pairings

In your relationship you tend to be either abandoning or engulfing toward your mate. The pattern depends not only on your background, but also on the unique combination the two of you create when you pair up. You may have found yourself behaving in more of an abandoning way in one relationship, while in another you became more engulfing. There are three possible combinations of these dimensions in a relationship, each with its own distinct form of expression.

Abandoning-Abandoning.
If you are abandoning with your mate and find yourself in a relationship with someone who also acts this way, your relationship will be very distant and your interaction will be unemotional and uninvolved. Unless there is some intervention, you'll probably drift apart. Neither of you is willing to relax your

boundaries because of your apprehensions about being engulfed, which are rooted in the deep-seated childhood fear of being abandoned. To let each other in means being vulnerable and heightens fears of abandonment. If you don't invest much of yourself, you figure you have less to lose.

My first marriage was like this. Both Beth and I had mothers who could be controlling and smothering and fathers who were alcoholic and distant, so we were both ripe to act in an abandoning way toward each other. I really loved her to the degree that I was capable of loving, and I'm sure she loved me as well, but we had emotional walls a mile thick. In a conversation one night after we had been married two years, we both acknowledged there was something missing in our relationship. After a short discussion we agreed that we could practice an "open marriage" as a solution to whatever it was that was missing. George and Nina O'Neill's book *Open Marriage* was the rage at the time, and we had both read it. The spirit of the book was to encourage a more open attitude in marriage, but in a narrower interpretation we took it to mean opening ourselves to having sexual relationships with others. What a joke! This experimentation turned out to be just another maneuver to maintain emotional distance from each other. We both took the position of abandoning each other and the relationship in order to feel safe.

Abandoning-Engulfing.

If you are the abandoning one in the relationship and your partner is engulfing, this will feed your fears of being engulfed. The more your partner tries to engulf you, the more distant you become. You'll find increasingly creative ways— anger, withdrawal, addictions, or passivity—to fend off your engulfing partner and to keep yourself distant and unavailable. As the abandoning partner, you have to erect increasingly rigid boundaries to keep your fragile sense of self intact and avoid your own fear of abandonment.

If you are the engulfing partner and are with someone who is abandoning, you will be continually anxious and apprehensive about his emotional disappearing act. Since he seems emotionally and spiritually unavailable much of the time, this will trigger unconscious childhood fears of abandonment and loss. The more distant he is, the more anxious and engulfing you become. You lose all sense of yourself as you do what you think your partner wants from you, with the objective of not losing him. Needless to say, you don't have any clear sense of your own boundaries.

When Frank and Rita came for couples counseling, it became apparent in the initial interview that their style of relationship was abandoning-engulfing. Both expressed the desire to stop the continuous fighting that had been going on for nearly the full year of their marriage. Rita complained of Frank's fanatic interest in golf and of his unresponsiveness even when he was around. She saw him as being more and more distant and accused him of using golf as a way to avoid the relationship. She found herself "getting bitchier and more demanding all the time" and feeling greatly disappointed in the outcome of their marriage.

Frank was eager and willing to work out their differences, but by his own admission he found closeness with Rita difficult. He felt inadequate to fulfill her demands and didn't feel she gave him much room. He began to see that the more she pressed, the more he withdrew, using golf as an escape. They both could see that the more Frank withdrew, the more Rita became anxious and fearful and the more she pressed for his time.

Rita and Frank present a fairly classic picture of the abandoning-engulfing couple. They are both contributing to their present dilemma by their behavior styles in the face of their particular fears. As they worked through the exercises that appear below in the solutions section, they came to understand each other's styles of dealing with the underlying fear of abandonment, and they could communicate more clearly about it. Some of the initial work involved boundaries, in working out a way whereby Frank could have his golf yet Rita could share some quality time with him.

Engulfing-Engulfing.

In this type of relationship, neither of you has a sense of your own boundaries and so you become enmeshed in each other. You are stuck together psychologically because of your fears of being abandoned. It's hard to separate each one's needs and preferences from the other's—it's as if you've become fused into one unit.

While this may look like an ideal relationship to outsiders, the truth is that you are suffocating each other. The relationship operates on the fear that one of you may leave, so it tends to stifle change and risk-taking—if one partner changes, the other is threatened.

Jim and Hillary, who have been together three years, represent well this engulfing-engulfing dynamic. They are totally absorbed with each other; except for going to their jobs, one rarely does things without the other. One time Hillary's company offered a retreat for all its employees, and Hillary had told her boss that she would attend even though it meant going without Jim. When she told Jim about it, he was so upset that she canceled her plans.

With these descriptions of some of the problems you can encounter in the arena of boundaries, let's move on to specific skills and ideas you can use to work out boundary issues in your relationship.

SOLUTIONS: SETTING AND MAINTAINING BOUNDARIES

However you deal with your fear of abandonment, whatever the style of your pairing, the central problem is your difficulty in defining and maintaining adequate physical and psychological boundaries. You have come to believe that you have no right to say no. This has led you to either become a yes-person or to isolate yourself behind rigid personal barriers for fear that you might lose yourself altogether in the relationship.

Learning to set boundaries in your relationship will help you feel better about yourself. You can gain a tremendous amount of self-respect as you define your limits and express them to your partner. Your partner may initially react with attempts at control and manipulation but is likely to respect you more as you express your boundaries more and more clearly. If you and your partner can work on boundary-setting together, your relationship will grow stronger as a result.

Eric was nervous at first about setting boundaries with his long-time girlfriend, Betty, but as he started to do so he gained respect—for himself and from her. He describes one of his first experiences with this endeavor: "Betty wanted to go on a houseboat for our vacation, and I didn't think we could afford it. I told her I didn't want to spend that much money, and she kept saying we could charge it, that it's only money, that we only live once, and so on. She even started acting angry. I got very adamant but remained calm about saying no. She didn't talk to me for a whole day. The next time we talked about it, she admitted that when she thought about it, I was right. We couldn't really afford to spend that kind of money for our vacation."

Further, you can develop a stronger sense of yourself while being in a relationship. This helps you develop a stronger sense of your own identity apart from the relationship yet included within the relationship. This is not an ability you witnessed in your parents, but it is something you can learn to do for yourself now as an adult.

As you're learning to set boundaries, it's important to remember that they are not permanent and inflexible. A boundary you set today may change after a while as dictated by your preferences, new information, your partner's needs, or the developmental needs of the relationship. Today you may say no to taking dance lessons with your wife but in six weeks decide to do so. Today you may feel okay about visiting your in-laws each weekend but later decide to limit those visits to once a month.

In the following section you'll find ways to help you set and maintain your boundaries. First you'll learn how to prepare yourself for setting boundaries.

Preparing the Way for Boundary-Setting

Most Adult Children have some difficulty setting and maintaining boundaries simply because they are not accustomed to doing so. Go easy on yourself and realize that you are not the only person who has difficulty with this issue. Start with identifying simple boundaries, such as what television shows to watch, where to sit in a restaurant, or taking time out for yourself. To set the foundation, it's important first to consider how to know when you need to set boundaries.

When do you need to set a boundary?

There are times when you can set a boundary in advance, but there are also many times when you have to set boundaries at the time the situation presents itself. Either way, it helps to do some homework so you can know more clearly when it's right for you to set a boundary. The first step is to be able to identify these times.

There are three ways to find out whether you need to set boundaries.

1. *Listen to your feelings*. Certain feelings will suggest you need to set a boundary. If you're feeling resentful, victimized, used, worn-out, or crowded, these are good cues.

   Physical cues are also good indicators that you are not taking care of yourself in the area of boundary-setting. If you're aware of a persistent tension in your body, especially in your stomach, back, neck, chest, or jaw, these symptoms may suggest you need to set limits and take better care of your needs. Frequent illness also indicates that you should look at your life and note the areas where you need to set limits. If you repeatedly get headaches or have stomach problems, these may be clues that you are feeling victimized in your relationship.

2. *Check it out*. When in doubt, check it out. One way to check is to observe how other people act in their relationships. How do they deal with their children? How do they show physical affection in public? How do couples act when they are shopping together? How much do other couples do things together and do things apart? While observing other couples you will witness a broad range of ways of setting (or not setting) boundaries. Not all will necessarily be healthy, but from the range of what you've observed you can get a better idea of how others handle boundary issues.

   In addition to observing, talk to others. You can ask a friend, sponsor, or counselor about a particular boundary issue or ask other couples how they handle their boundary issues. As an Adult Child, you did not have much reality testing of boundaries when you were growing up, so be willing to ask others' opinions about boundary issues.

3. *Be prepared*. Consider areas in your relationship where boundary-setting is applicable. This can help you focus your awareness on some potential limits that aren't being acknowledged. Although certainly not an exhaustive list, here are some areas to consider, with questions you can ask yourself.

Sex—How often? How do you want to be touched or not? When do you want sex? When don't you want it? What kind of things do you enjoy when you make love? What are some things your partner does that you like? That you don't like? What other things would you like your partner to do?

Money—Who is in charge of the spending? Of the budget? Who pays the bills? How is the money to be spent? How do you account for the spending?

Child-rearing—How do you set boundaries with your children? How do you and your partner differ in your boundary-setting with the children? Do you have time with your partner away from the children? How do you handle child care?

Maintenance—How are the household duties handled? Who cleans the house? How do you deal with household repairs?

Time—How do you spend your leisure time? How much quality time do you spend with your mate? How much quality time do you spend on yourself? How much time do you spend working? Playing?

EXERCISE: Write out answers to the above questions in as much detail as possible. Be specific! The purpose is to help you identify areas where you can begin applying boundaries. As you are considering each area and each question, pay attention to your physical and emotional feelings for further cues. If you get a tightness in your stomach as you think of visiting your in-laws, this is a good clue that there's some boundary work to be done. It isn't necessary at this point to take action on every area. The ability to set boundaries is something that you can learn over time. The main purpose here is to identify problem areas.

You can talk with your partner about what's on your list, but do not present the list as a way of demanding change. Read through the rest of this chapter before talking with each other about changes so that you can be more prepared to work with your specific boundary issues. Don't worry about settling up on everything right away. Right now, it's more important that you clarify those areas in which you have boundary issues. If you do share this exercise with your mate, the main objective should be to explore with each other the whole issue of boundary-setting.

Mark did a survey and discovered some interesting facts: "I found that I was much more of a yes-man than I thought. I try to please my boss by always working overtime, and my wife is upset with me. My wife tells me that I'm working way too much, so I cut back on my work hours, and my boss is upset. I keep trying to please my boss, please her, and I'm not too pleased with myself! I realize I have to start setting some boundaries with both my boss and my wife. Frankly, it terrifies me to even think about it, but at least it's a start."

You have a right.

In your relationship, consider that you have a right to your boundaries. Your partner does not own you, and you don't have to treat your partner as if he were some omnipotent authority figure. As much as you've learned to obey your parents, you are an adult now, and your role is not to obey your spouse. The word *obey* has been removed from most marriage ceremonies. Love, cherish, and honor your mate, but rather than obey, communicate and negotiate. If you're a woman, this is particularly true for you, since the tradition in our patriarchal culture has been to treat the father's authority as sacrosanct and inviolate.

It's crucial to acknowledge your rights internally again and again as you work on setting boundaries with your mate. It's also crucial to recognize that as you assert these rights, there will be consequences. Your partner may not like it or may be upset since he's used to your acting in a certain way. One way to remind yourself that you have rights is to work with affirmations that proclaim specific rights and boundaries. The following list of rights and boundaries will be useful in affirming and confirming your right to have boundaries in your relationship.

> I have a right to decide what I do with my body.
> I have a right to spend time and attention on my recovery program.
> I will set aside an hour a day just for myself.
> Because I love myself, I will maintain my boundaries with others.
> I have a right to take time to relax and enjoy myself.

I have a right to keep my home drug and alcohol free.

I have a right to not work overtime.

I will spend at least an hour a day with my child.

I will not allow anyone to abuse me in any way at any time.

I have the right to say no.

I have the right to be the ultimate decision-maker regarding what's right for me.

I have the right to not justify or explain my boundaries.

I have the right to let others find solutions to their own problems.

I have the right to slow down and take time to think about my answer before responding to someone's request.

I have the right to change my mind.

I have the right to not rescue others.

I have the right to tell the truth about my limits and boundaries.

I have the right to walk away when I am being mistreated.

I have the right to decide who I spend my time with.

EXERCISE: Choose two to five of the above affirmations. For at least the next 21 days, spend a few minutes each day repeating these to yourself. When you are alone, state the sentences out loud, saying your name immediately after "I"; for example, "I, Marie, have a right to decide what I do with my body." Repeat each affirmation 10 to 12 times, pausing after each to let yourself feel your body's reaction. If the affirmation is an effective one for you, you will initially notice some sort of physical sensation or emotional response; or you may notice some specific internal chatter that negates, discounts, or denies the affirmation. As long as this reaction is not too overwhelming, simply notice it without analyzing or defending or caving in to it. These reactions that are stirred by your stating positive affirmations are merely the conditioned habitual feelings and thoughts of your Inner Child. At one time they served to help you survive, but now they can only hold you back. Rather than get upset or criticize yourself for having these thoughts, let them go and move on.

Continue repeating the affirmation, each time pausing briefly to notice your physical, emotional, or mental reaction. You will probably notice that the more you work with it, the more potent the positive effect of the affirmation becomes. You are introducing new ways to think about your boundaries, and as you affirm these rights and boundaries, your belief in them grows stronger. It will take a few practice sessions until you begin to feel the effects of the affirmation, so stay with it. It's worth it. This way of thinking is instrumental in allowing yourself to set boundaries.

Marie worked with a few of these affirmations for the 21-day period suggested. "I felt good about them, especially the one about having the right to say no. I've never thought about the fact that I have a right to say no. With my boyfriend, Robert, I have usually just gone along with things. But lately I've been speaking up a little bit more. The other night we were out, and he asked me if I wanted to stop and get some ice cream. I told him no, I didn't think so. It was fine with him, and no big deal. But it was a big deal to me, because I spoke up instead of just going along with what he wanted."

You may be left, but never abandoned.
In preparing the way for setting boundaries, it will be useful to reevaluate your catastrophic thinking about abandonment. By continuing to believe that to be left alone would be the end of the world, you perpetuate your original childhood fears of abandonment. The truth is, while it would be disappointing and inconvenient if your partner were to be upset with you or even to leave you, none of possible outcomes would be catastrophic. Even though you might not believe this at first, when you consider it realistically I'm sure you'll agree it's true. You would survive. You might very well find love with someone else. This doesn't mean that you should deny your feelings. It does mean that instead of upsetting yourself about potential abandonment, you can change your catastrophic thinking.

One way to rethink your catastrophic beliefs is to ask yourself two questions: First, if you do set a boundary with your mate, what's the worst that could happen? Then ask yourself, if this worst case did in fact happen, would you survive? By considering these questions, you'll see that, short of situations in which your partner would physically harm you, you will survive. Although this sounds very simple, it takes some practice to rethink deeply held beliefs. These beliefs came in handy for your survival during childhood, so your Inner Child is probably hesitant to give them up. With some consistent and gentle persuasion on your part and with some experience in setting boundaries, your Inner Child will relax. She will come to see that you will protect her and will not tolerate her being abused ever again.

This raises another important consideration that will help you build a foundation for boundary-setting behavior: the idea that, as an adult, while people may come and people may go in your life, *you can never be truly abandoned*. You do not have to rely on others to feel okay about yourself. As I noted in *Adult Children of Abusive Parents*: "The truth is that now, as an adult, you can only abandon yourself. As long as you give someone else the power to declare you okay or not okay, you risk potential feelings of abandonment when this other person does not approve. When you *know* you're okay and do not need someone else's approval to feel okay, then you cannot truly be abandoned."

Jennifer, who has been married to Bob for 13 years, details how this realization occurred to her. "I used to be so terrified of Bob's leaving me, particularly the first few years we were married. Sometimes when Bob would get angry, he'd threaten to leave me or get a divorce. Lately, I have come to realize that if necessary, I could survive on my own. It would be tough, but I could do it. The last argument we had, Bob said something about leaving me, and I reacted very differently. I looked at him and told him that if he felt he had to leave, I wasn't going to stand in the way. I was surprised to hear myself say that! And I know Bob was surprised as well. He stayed, and later confessed that when I told him that, he realized he really did have a choice about staying or going."

> EXERCISE: Imagine a boundary that you would like to set with your mate. Perhaps you'd like to take Wednesday nights for an activity by yourself, such as going to an evening class or joining a Toastmaster's club. Take a piece of paper and write out all the possible catastrophic things that could happen if you told your mate of your intentions. Particularly note your fears of abandonment. For instance, she could be angry; she could accuse you of infidelity; she could leave you; she could decide to go out every night of the week and get involved in her own activities. Then write out the answers to these two questions: First, how likely is it that the thing you fear would actually happen? Most of the things we imagine happening never materialize in spite of our worrying. Second, even in the unlikely event that the thing you're most afraid of does happen, will you survive? In other words, would it really be a catastrophe? Most of the time you will see that while the feared outcome may be unpleasant, you would in fact survive.
>
> Next, write out some realistic, supportive statements to remind yourself that it is okay to set your boundaries. For instance: "I have a right to take time for myself, and although my lover may be upset with me, it won't be the end of the world. We do spend time together to balance out my time away. Even in the worst possible

instance, if she did leave me, I may be lonely for a while, but I would get through it intact." In particular remind yourself that if she were to leave you, it would not mean that you'd be alone and abandoned as you may have been when you were a child.

Setting Boundaries

Now you're ready to actually set boundaries. If at any point you get stuck, go back and review the previous section to reinforce your practice of setting boundaries. Here we'll look at setting boundaries ahead of time, negotiating boundaries with your partner, and getting support.

Setting boundaries in advance.

When possible, set your boundaries in advance. Although many boundaries are set "on the spot," it helps to anticipate boundaries. Consider what some of your general ground rules are. Examples might be:

I will not permit drug or alcohol use in my home.
I will not allow *anyone* to abuse me in any way.
I will reserve at least 30 minutes each day just for me.

By setting these in advance, you can anticipate and practice what you will say if these boundaries are ever challenged. It also encourages you to establish within yourself the inherent rightness of permitting yourself to have boundaries. It's useful to write these ground rules out and keep them posted where you can easily see them. In doing so you are actually developing and using affirmations that will support your acting on these boundaries.

> EXERCISE: In the previous section you did a lot of work on identifying areas in your relationship where you need to set boundaries. Pick out those areas where you can set your boundaries in advance. Make a list of these and put it where you can see it every day. From this list, create affirmations and work with those affirmations daily for the next 21 days. This work will continually reinforce your right to set boundaries. This consistent self-encouragement and reinforcement will make it easier for you if and when you must confront your partner or anyone else with your ground rules. I can't stress enough how vital it is to remind yourself again and again, in general as well as in very specific terms, that you have a right to have boundaries.

> By identifying and setting in advance those boundaries that can be anticipated, you make your life and your relationship that much easier.

Negotiating a boundary.

Although it would be nice to anticipate all your boundaries and set them in advance, obviously this won't always be the case. In many instances you will be called to set boundaries "on-the-spot"—for example, when your partner wants to have sex but you don't; when your partner wants time with you but you have an important project to complete; when a discussion gets heated and you don't want to end up in a fight.

In other instances, either "on-the-spot" boundary issues or ones you can anticipate, you will want to negotiate boundaries with your partner. Issues of time, attention, money, sex/affection, and others will come up for review from time to time. Here is a simple four-step process for negotiating a boundary, adapted from *Lifeskills for Adult Children* by Janet Woititz and Alan Garner.

Define—Define your boundaries as specifically as possible. Identify what is acceptable and what is not.
Express—With your partner, tell her what your concerns are and what your absolute boundary is.
Listen—Once you have stated your limits, listen to her considerations and feelings. Determine what boundary she thinks is best.
Act—Develop and agree on a plan of action. This will undoubtedly involve some compromises for both of you.

John used this approach to working out his time on his home computer. Ellen was upset that he was spending so much time with the computer, yet John knew it was important to him, so he decided to talk it over with Ellen.

Define—John wanted to spend 30 minutes each day on the computer for the next six to eight weeks so he could learn the system. He was willing to take Sundays off from doing this; after some consideration he decided he could also take one week night off. (Notice he was specific and identified what would be acceptable and what would not.)
Express—John expressed this to Ellen, stating how important it was for him to learn to use the computer.
Listen—In this all-important third step, John encouraged Ellen to express her feelings and thoughts and asked her what she wanted. She

wasn't happy about his decision and admitted that she wanted to trash the computer. She also recognized that it was important to John and felt relieved that he was showing some concern about working this out. She did want to have a night during the week where they could spend some specific time together, and John was willing to do this. They chose Wednesday nights as a time to have dinner together, followed by some activity such as going to a show.

Act—John and Ellen worked out a schedule together for the next six weeks.

Although it took some discussion, John and Ellen were able to follow these guidelines and come to some resolution. This particular process is useful because it takes into account your needs and limits and those of your partner. (If you find this process leads to greater conflict, use the six-step problem-solving formula in chapter 6.)

Support for your boundaries.
Since you did not have support for boundary-setting behavior as a child, you need to get that support as an adult. What this means is that you must find a friend, or use your sponsor or therapist, as backup for boundary-setting. As you begin to establish clearer boundaries, you may get some resistance from your mate. After all, he is used to your acting in a certain way, so as you change and set some limits, expect to get some reactions from him. Unless your mate is also recovering from his co-dependency or is very supportive and understanding, he will try to manipulate you into staying the same.

As she moved further into her own recovery, Amy met with some resistance from Nathan, her husband of nine years. "He'd give me lots of flack whenever it came to the day of my ACoA [Adult Children of Alcoholics] meeting. He'd be late home from work so I wouldn't have anyone to watch the kids. He'd complain about the house—just about anything to get in my way. But each time I showed him I wasn't going to back down. I talked a lot to my best friend Sandy when I first started going and Nathan was giving me so much trouble. She would listen, and once or twice she watched the kids for me. I'm really grateful that she was there, because there have been a few times when I'd just as soon have given up, and she would encourage me to go on."

Maintaining Your Boundaries

Once you have communicated your boundaries, it's helpful to have a way to back yourself up. If you don't have a supportive mate, you will encounter some resistance and testing of your newfound limits. For this reason, it's handy to have a couple of extra tools to support your initial boundary-setting.

Broken record.

This skill is particularly useful when you are first practicing setting boundaries, because it can give you an added dimension of confidence. It's also helpful when you are dealing with a lover or mate who is persistent in his attempts to get you to soften or back down on your boundaries.

With the Broken Record technique, you repeat your main point (in this case the boundary) over and over again, like a broken record. You may acknowledge your partner's feelings or objections, but it's important not to get into a debate or argument over the fact that you are taking this stand for yourself. Once you acknowledge his feelings or objections, follow up by reiterating your boundary statement. Say the same words over and over in the same firm tone of voice. Remember: You don't have to justify your boundaries unless *you* choose to do so. It's important not to get sidetracked when you are using Broken Record to establish and maintain a boundary. For example:

ROB: Hey, Teri, let's go to bed and cuddle, okay?
TERI: Oh, Rob, I'm not in the mood tonight.
ROB: Ah, c'mon! It's been a long time since we made love.
TERI: I know, but I'm really not in the mood tonight.
ROB: You're never in the mood. How about just this once doing it even though you're not in the mood?
TERI: That's true, I wasn't in the mood last night, but I'm still not in the mood tonight.
ROB: I'll give you a backrub.
TERI: Thanks, but no, I'm not in the mood tonight.

Notice how Teri responds to Rob's feelings and objections but stands her ground and honors her own feelings. Rob may not be completely happy with her, but Teri stays with what is acceptable for her. Using Broken Record won't necessarily make everything better, but it gives a tool that can be useful in maintaining your boundary.

Another noteworthy point is to pay attention to your body language and your voice tone when you are setting boundaries. If your voice is soft and hesitant, you are stooped over, you have a false smile and a pleading look on your face, and you avoid eye contact as you keep repeating, "George, I really don't want to make love with you tonight," George is not likely to take you seriously! When you are using Broken Record, or at any time when you are making a boundary statement, it's important that your body language and your voice match your message. Deliver the message in a firm yet relaxed manner. To do so, pay attention to these aspects:

Voice: Steady yet relaxed, clear, and loud enough to be heard.
Eyes: Straightforward, consistent eye contact with your partner.
Body posture: Standing straight but not rigidly erect, hands at side, chin up.
Facial expression: Matches your message. Avoid the false smile but be pleasant.

> EXERCISE: With your partner or with a friend, do a brief role play using Broken Record. It's helpful to have practiced this ahead of time so that when an actual situation turns up, you'll be more prepared. You can use the example above or any other example of boundaries that you've worked with up to this point.
>
> Once you have run through the role play, ask your partner for feedback. Have her tell you what was strong and what needed improvement. Perhaps your voice tone, posture, and statement were strong, but you were smiling all the while you said it. After listening to your partner's feedback, try the role play again and this time work on improving your delivery. Once again get feedback. If necessary, try it a third time.

George tried Broken Record with a friend before he tried it with his girlfriend. "I wasn't willing to spend more than thirty dollars apiece on tickets for a Janet Jackson concert," George said, "no matter how much we both like her. But the tickets were all sold out and the only way to get them was through scalpers, and they were charging outrageous prices. Trish has been bugging me all week, and I needed to tell her no. Michael and I sat down and practiced it, using Broken Record. I felt a bit silly doing it, but it really worked. Michael pointed out that I crooked my neck and looked down when I said no, and that wasn't very convincing. I went and tried it with Trish, and it worked. She isn't bugging me anymore."

"If . . . then . . .": When boundaries are violated.
It's also important that you consider what the consequences will be if your boundaries are violated. These boundary violations and the resulting consequences are called *If . . . then . . . contingencies.* For example, you could say to your partner, "If you ever hit me, then I will leave you." Other examples would be, "If you don't leave me alone and let me read, then I will go into the

other room" and "If you aren't home on time, then the rest of us will go ahead and have our dinner."

Contingencies are not threats and need not be stated in a threatening manner. A contingency is merely stating matter-of-factly what you will do if your mate behaves in a certain way. It puts the choice back in your partner's lap as to whether she continues the undesirable behavior, and at the same time makes clear how you will react if she does continue. If your mate then does violate the boundary, it's critical that you follow through and do what you said you were going to do. Otherwise she will not take you seriously in the future. Once again, it's important to pay attention to your body language and voice tone.

Carrie set a boundary in advance with her boyfriend, Paul, when she told him that if he were to drink, she did not want to be with him. She soon had to put the if . . . then . . . contingency into practice. "We went to this party and about half of the people were drinking. When Paul went and got a glass of wine, I froze for a few moments. I was really surprised, but I decided I had to stick to my guns. So I told him if he was going to drink, that was his choice but I would find a ride home. He got upset with me, but I stayed with my boundary. He chose to drink, so I asked one of the women there to drive me home. I was a little shaky, but somehow I knew it was important to do what I did. When I saw Paul the next day, he was mad at me, but I didn't feel the need to justify what I did. I just used Broken Record with him, telling him I had a right to do what I did. Paul still drinks, which is his business, but he doesn't do it around me."

Again, a contingency should not be used as a threat. If you do use it as a threat, you are merely trying to control your partner rather than letting him be and establishing your own boundaries. The following exercise will be useful in helping you identify more clearly how you can further protect your boundaries.

> EXERCISE: Take a sheet of paper and write out any of your partner's behaviors that you find difficult to deal with. Then think about possible contingencies for those that are most disturbing. For instance, in the above example Carrie found Paul's drinking objectionable and decided that her response would be to not be around him if he drank. Other examples: "If my lover ever calls me names again, then I will leave the room and take a time-out." "If he is not here on time, then I will leave." "If she doesn't want to go see the new Arnold Schwarzenegger movie, then I will go by myself or with a friend." From here, it would be fair to let your partner know what your decision will be if he acts in the particular objectionable way.

Now that we've discussed how to set boundaries, let's take a look at how you can relax those boundaries and draw closer to your partner. (You can't break the rules until you've set them up!) In the next chapter we'll explore how you as an Adult Child can experience greater intimacy with your mate.

CHAPTER 5

INTIMACY

*P*auline sat across from her husband, Ben, at a booth in a local restaurant. About once a month they rounded up a babysitter for the children, went to this particular restaurant, ordered the same meal, then sat together over dinner with only occasional, somewhat forced, conversation. After years this had gotten to be quite a routine—just like their marriage. After 14 years together, everything seemed a little stale. In spite of an increasing restlessness, Pauline kept telling herself that this is the way it's supposed to be. Most couples weren't all that happy, so why should their marriage be any different? After all, her parents had stayed together for 35 years, and they had never seemed particularly happy. Besides, she had made a commitment, and they should stay together for the children's sake.

"I called the carpet company about fixing the tear in the new carpet," Pauline told Ben. "They said they couldn't make it out until next Tuesday."

Ben grunted an acknowledgment, then went back to his steak and french fries. He felt really burned out. He was tired of his job and had been passed over for promotion twice in the last year. He felt locked in, afraid to make a change to another company because he had built up seniority. Besides, the money was decent, and with three children, he couldn't afford to take many risks. He loved his family, but sometimes felt as if they were a burden. He felt a vague sense of shame that he was somehow letting them down, but he couldn't really articulate it. How could he tell any of this to his wife? She would never understand.

Both of them kept looking out the window and only once in a while made nervous, furtive eye contact. They both yearned for closeness, for comfort and affection from each other but didn't know how to express this yearning. Although both were starved for intimate contact, their fears kept them at arm's length from each other. So they kept on eating, and in spite of their inner turmoil, only Pauline's occasional sighs gave any outward hint that there was anything wrong.

Jerry grabbed his jacket from the closet and stopped at the end of the staircase as he was putting it on. "C'mon, Sheila! It's getting late and I'm hungry."

"I'm coming," Sheila replied as she descended the stairs. "I know it's late and I know you're hungry and I also know you want me to look my best."

"Wow!" Jerry stopped with his jacket halfway on. "You look gorgeous! I'm a lucky man to be going to dinner with the likes of you."

Sheila blushed slightly but gave Jerry a smile that said she didn't at all mind this kind of attention. "Oh, Jerry. I think we're both pretty lucky. I've been looking forward to this all day."

"I have, too," Jerry said, "but first, sit down and close your eyes."

Sheila did as requested, wondering if she had forgotten about this being some special day or anniversary. Perhaps, she thought, Jerry had gotten a raise or a promotion. Then she heard him say, "Now open your eyes." Before her in a beautiful crystal vase was a single yellow rose.

"Jerry!"

Yellow roses had a very special meaning. They had first met when Jerry came to San Francisco on a business trip and were immediately attracted to each other. After a couple of long-distance phone calls and two letters apiece, he had sent her a half-dozen yellow roses as a surprise. One thing led to another, and now after 10 years of marriage he was still full of surprises.

"I just wanted to remind you of how much I love you," he said, "and how much I appreciate your loving me. It's been a joy sharing the last ten years with you, Sheila."

"Jerry, you're just an amazing man," Sheila said as she stood to give him a hug and a loving kiss. "Let's skip the show after dinner. I've got a better idea." Sheila smiled slyly and took Jerry's arm as they eased toward the door.

Intimacy is the experience of sharing your innermost feelings and thoughts. It's a closeness that happens when you allow the boundaries between yourself and another to dissolve. Unlike co-dependency, where you lose yourself in the other person because your boundaries become enmeshed, with intimacy you *consciously* let the other person in, merging yourself with another for moments at a time. Rather than lose yourself, you volunteer yourself. With a healthy sense of your own boundaries, you can then separate once those moments have passed until the next opportunity for intimate sharing. An intimate relationship, then, consists of a series of intimate moments accumulated over time.

For Pauline and Ben, it's painfully evident that intimacy is missing in their marriage. Their relationship lacks vitality and freshness as a result. Everything has become routine and tedious and there's no communication of their deeper concerns and fears. They exchange little tenderness or affection. Neither one feels safe being real and honest in the presence of the other, and so they hide their most personal thoughts and feelings.

In contrast, Jerry and Sheila freely show their love and affection for each other. In their willingness to do so, they generate intimacy and closeness. They genuinely admire each other, and their bond is creative rather than constrictive. Theirs is not a perfect marriage—they've had their conflicts and disagreements in their 10 years together—but in spite of this they actively try to create an atmosphere of intimacy as much as possible. They are attentive to each other without being possessive and provide support for each other's feelings and needs without denying their own.

THE FIVE INGREDIENTS FOR INTIMACY

The desire for closeness and connectedness is what drives most people to become husbands, wives, and lovers: a deep yearning that stems from the basic human need to love and be loved. Even though everyone has this need, many things can interfere with experiencing intimacy. As an Adult Child, your earlier training did not teach you how to be close to another person. Instead it taught you how to be guarded or how to lose yourself in another person. Yet to develop and sustain intimacy in a relationship, certain essential qualities must be present in that relationship, at least to some degree. These five qualities are trust, vulnerability, clear boundaries, empathy, and appreciation.

Trust

Trust is the first and most fundamental requirement for intimacy—the prime ingredient. When there is a reasonable degree of trust in the relationship, the door is opened for emotional safety. When there is safety, there is room for your real self to emerge in that relationship. Genuine intimacy can occur only when you and your partner are operating from your real selves.

Trust is not something you can make happen; it develops over time as a result of sharing your innermost feelings and thoughts and finding that they are received in an atmosphere of safety and respect. In the example above, Jerry and Sheila have this sort of safety and trust in each other.

As you were growing up, your sense of basic trust was violated time and again. How could you trust when there was so much unpredictability, so much inconsistency, in your family? You couldn't count on your parents being there for you when you needed them. Without a consistent and safe adult being there to validate your feelings and acknowledge your presence, you experienced little or no emotional safety. Your conclusion was clear: Don't trust. Don't trust your own thoughts and feelings—they will just be denied by others—and certainly don't trust other people. This is the conclusion you have taken with you into your adult relationships.

Not having a foundation of trust makes intimacy difficult. As you learn to be more trusting, and especially as you learn to trust yourself—your inner wisdom, your intuitive sense—you set the stage for increasing intimacy.

Vulnerability

To let yourself be vulnerable, you need to feel safe. Vulnerability means being open, being willing to communicate your tenderest emotions as well as to share the parts of yourself that even you may find less than acceptable. Being vulnerable requires you to have a way of checking in with your own feelings and a willingness to be honest about what you find. Intimacy requires risk-taking, and in taking risks you will be vulnerable. It means that you are willing to be who you are, especially during those times when you are acting much less like your ideal self than you'd like to be.

At one time for you vulnerability seemed a death warrant. It simply wasn't safe to be open with your feelings while growing up—you'd either be abused or abandoned if you did. So instead you erected defenses at the time to keep from showing your vulnerability. You had to play your role, to act through your false self rather than reveal your true self, thus denying parts of you that were unacceptable to your parents.

In the example above, it's apparent that neither Ben nor Pauline is willing to be vulnerable with the other. Ben is feeling a lot of frustration and sorrow and keeping it all to himself. Pauline is feeling a vague uneasiness about something missing in the relationship but is afraid to say anything to Ben. Being vulnerable with each other feels too dangerous, and so each remains self-contained even in a situation that looks intimate on the surface—a romantic restaurant dinner.

The task in your present relationship is to increasingly take risks with your vulnerability when and where it's reasonably safe to do so. Many of the exercises in this book are designed to help you with this. As you find out that you can take care of yourself, you will become more willing to take risks with your vulnerability.

Clear Boundaries

As noted previously, you must have both a strong sense of your own ability to set boundaries and an ability and willingness to soften those boundaries in order to create intimacy. The paradox is that the more confidence you have in your ability to be clear about your boundaries, the easier it can be to relax those boundaries.

These all-important abilities were difficult or impossible to learn from your family. Because the boundaries in your family were either very rigid or very enmeshed, you learned either to be extremely distant from other people or to lose yourself in relationships, or to fly back and forth between these two options. Although other influences can contribute to this polarization, the fragile sense of personal boundaries that you learned growing up makes it hard for you to sustain intimacy.

Rita recalls the unpredictability of her mother: "There were times when she could be so warm and loving, and other times she'd be so mean. The problem was I didn't know what to expect on any given day. Once when I was about nine we had just spent time together cleaning the house, and we had been laughing and joking. She found some streaks where I had cleaned the windows, and all of a sudden she hit the roof, calling me all sorts of names and hitting me with the broomstick. I was crushed because I had felt so relaxed with her. I learned to keep my guard up around her." It makes sense that Rita would not want to relax her personal boundaries with her mother, so it's no surprise that she has this difficulty with her lover.

As you feel more at ease and confident in setting your boundaries, you will feel a greater ease in relaxing those boundaries. As you discover that you can not only merge with your mate but can emerge again with your separateness and your individuality, then you can discover greater depths of intimacy with your partner. As long as your boundaries don't become rigid and encasing, this fundamental quality can serve to free up your ability to love.

Empathy

Another quality necessary for intimacy is the ability to empathize with your mate. Empathy is not sympathy. Sympathy is feeling sorry for someone; empathy is feeling *with* someone. It's the ability to walk in another's moccasins, to resonate with his or her feelings. When you empathize with someone, your attention is primarily directed to the other person, although you simultaneously use your own sensations and feelings as indicators about what the other person is experiencing. For example, if you're talking with your spouse and she is describing how well her interview for a new job went, you not only see her delight in her body language and hear her happiness in her voice but also notice your own happiness in response to what she's sharing with you.

Empathy differs from co-dependency in that you do not become a sponge to your partner's feelings. When you empathize, you step into your mate's feelings, then step out again into your own skin. You do not take your mate's feelings on, and you can distinguish between his feelings and yours. This is a skill for which you may have a head start. If you tended to be the caretaker in your family, then you've learned well to direct your attention to other people's feelings and have developed a genuine compassion for others. The problem is that you didn't learn to pay much attention to your own feelings, so instead of empathizing you have ended up continuing to caretake, perhaps getting lost in another's emotions at the cost of denying your own.

In Tim's relationship with his mother, "I think she just saw me as an extension of herself. She didn't show much concern for my feelings, but I always felt it was my duty to be concerned about hers. One time she got so upset at a bank teller because of some delay that she was practically yelling at him. I was really embarrassed, and when we left the bank I told her so. Boy, did she ever turn on me. She slapped me and told me I should have been angry, too! Then when I got upset, she started teasing me because I was upset. I couldn't win with her."

Empathy breeds empathy, and in your family there wasn't much. A child learns empathy when there is a mother who is there to mirror the child's feelings, to help her sort out, identify, and label those feelings. This sort of mothering gives you the tools that help you draw a map of your interior. This type of mother also shares with the child her own interior. It's unlikely you had this from your mother or father.

In your relationship, you can practice empathy in some specific ways, as you'll see in the solutions section of this chapter. This, plus your willingness to remain close to your own feelings, will enhance your ability to empathize.

Appreciation

Another ingredient that opens the door for intimacy is appreciation. Appreciation is expressing your positive, tender feelings both in word and deed. It's saying "I love you" when you really feel it and mean it, not just as a routine. It's pausing in the middle of conversation and saying specifically what it is at that moment you appreciate about your partner. It's complimenting your partner for things that you might otherwise take for granted. Appreciation is not only saying things, it's doing things for your partner that express your love. It is giving with love and without expectation rather than giving to get something in return. A good example of this would be Jerry's simple gesture of giving Sheila the yellow rose.

In a relationship, it's so tempting to get caught up in what's wrong and what's lacking, to look at your partner and notice the flaws. This negative focus interferes with any intimate connection. The negative atmosphere in which you were raised undoubtedly contributed to your tendency to focus on what's missing rather than on what you can appreciate. In your family there was little or no honest emotional expression. Rarely if ever did anyone express tender, loving feelings. If *you* did, perhaps you got back sarcasm or teasing. Naturally you'd think twice about ever expressing warm feelings again.

My former wife Susan had always described her family as being negative. There was genuine warmth between some of her family members, but it was rarely acknowledged or expressed openly. Teasing or joking quickly followed any expressions of affection. Most everyone in this large family of nine children had learned to cover his or her feelings behind a smile.

When I met the entire family for the first time at Thanksgiving, I felt warmly received. At the dinner table before the feast began, I raised my glass and offered a toast, saying that I felt very close to everyone there and thanked them for the way they had welcomed me so generously into the family. It was a risk for me and a sincere expression of appreciation. Everyone toasted with me, but when I finished there was an awkward silence. No one seemed to know what to do with what I had said. No one looked directly at me. I don't think they were used to hearing this sort of expression. After a pause I sat down, and within a few moments the clatter of activity at the table resumed. As the plates of food were being passed around, one of Susan's sisters leaned over to me as she handed me the mashed potatoes and murmured, under her breath, "Thanks."

I realized from this experience how important it is to express appreciation without concern for results. In spite of the lack of a more general acknowledgment, I felt good about what I had said and I think most of the family members were positively affected. Appreciation as a bridge to intimacy requires you to take risks in showing your heartfelt gratitude. It requires you to notice what's right rather than what's wrong. Sincerely expressing appreciation in word and in deed not only makes you feel good, but enhances intimacy in your relationship.

YOUR FAMILY: TRAINING GROUND FOR AVOIDING INTIMACY

As has been noted, your family gave you a poor start in learning about intimacy. The way you dealt with abusiveness was to isolate yourself, shut down your inner feelings, and become extremely sensitive and reactive to others. Adapting to the craziness in your family left you little room to learn about intimacy, since you had to hide your real self to protect it from the assaults of your guardians. To be intimate with someone, you have to be fully available.

Humans aren't designed to feel pain and pleasure at the same time, so if something was painful, you learned to avoid it. It hurt to be close. Being close often meant that the pain of abuse would follow, or emotional or physical abandonment. If your dad was affectionate with you, he may have followed it by yelling at you or perhaps sexually abusing you. Mom may have been emotionally unavailable or physically abusive. As a child you had to erect barriers to cope with this sort of interaction.

Being intimate requires you to be truly present with another person. Because of the abuse, you were split off from yourself much of the time, putting on a role as a way to protect yourself. When you do so, you cannot be completely present.

My role as the Invisible Child in my family provided me a great deal of protection from the violence going on around me. It was much easier to just "disappear" when my mother and father would fight and my older brother would somehow get involved in the fighting. I'd get lost in whatever television show happened to be on, or would just wander off to my room. I learned this disappearing act so well that it became a habitual way of dealing with any discomfort with the people around me. It just wasn't safe to be anything less than guarded. While this disappearing act helped me get through my childhood, it was destructive when it came to creating intimacy in my adult relationships.

Another significant factor in your avoidance training was watching your parents relate—or not relate. Children learn about relationships in part from watching their parents and modeling their behavior. Since you had poor models, you lack accurate ideas as to how to carry on an intimate relationship. My friend Tom once defined intimacy in a way that struck home: "Intimacy? I don't have a clue. I thought intimacy was when the fighting stopped!"

Communication between your parents was either distorted or nonexistent, and there was little or no emotional honesty. You learned to deny very well. If your family did not talk much, you had to guess what everyone else was feeling. If there was communication, much of it was loaded with angry and hurtful feelings. If open fighting occurred, it's unlikely you ever saw a resolution to the conflict.

"One time my mom and dad had one of their biggest fights ever," Wanda says. "I got my sisters to bed and made sure they were as quiet as they could be even though they were sobbing and crying a lot. I heard a door slam, which turned out to be my dad leaving. My mom looked in, and I think she thought we were all asleep because we were so quiet. I heard her go into the bathroom for the longest time. I kept thinking that maybe she was going to kill herself. Finally she came out and went to her room. Dad must have come home real late because I don't remember hearing him. What was strange was the next morning it was like it had never happened! Nobody said anything! And I knew I'd better not mention it, because it was kind of an unspoken rule that you never talked about the fights."

For Wanda, the conclusion was clear. Never talk about conflicts, and never resolve them. She says she still has a habit of clamming up when things get tough, much to the irritation of her husband.

With the kind of training ground for intimacy you had, it's no wonder you have difficulty in your relationship with your husband, wife, or lover. Your past continues to affect your present in both obvious and subtle ways.

PAST DECISIONS, PRESENT BARRIERS

The decisions you had to make as a child just to survive continue to haunt your efforts at intimacy today. In my case, all of my childhood training as the Invisible Child came to focus in my second marriage. I went about doing my disappearing act in the marriage. I figured a marriage was something I had to endure and a woman was someone I had to "handle." After all, this is how I related to my first woman, my mother. I handled her various physical and emotional complaints and did my best to ease her pain. Why should it be any different with my wife? This kind of distancing left little room for any sustained intimacy.

There were some real moments of intimacy, especially in the first two years, but these faded into history as the challenge of staying involved and close with someone I deeply loved became increasingly trying. Much of the time I felt a gnawing, unidentifiable fear that made me feel trapped in my own system of denial and pretense. I wanted to be intimate, but I kept bumping up against barriers of which I was barely conscious, barriers based on lifelong habits of fear and avoidance.

Like me, you learned many attitudes and behaviors that protected you from being hurt as a child and now get in the way of intimacy. Below are a few of the more common ones.

Lack of Trust

As we've already seen, trust is the prime ingredient for intimacy. It is so crucial that the lack of trust can be the most significant barrier to intimacy. Trust begins with first trusting yourself—your feelings, your thoughts, your intuition. This may be difficult since you received little validation of your feelings and responses from your family. In order to learn self-trust, a child needs mother (the primary caregiver) to be there for him and to reflect back to him his fragile yet growing sense of self.

Alice Miller describes this validation process in *The Drama of the Gifted Child*:

> Every child has a legitimate narcissistic need to be noticed, understood, taken seriously, and respected by his mother. In the first weeks and months of life he needs to have the mother at his disposal, must be able to use her and to be mirrored by her. This is beautifully illustrated in one of Winnicott's images: the mother gazes at the baby in her arms, and baby gazes at his mother's face and finds himself therein . . . provided that the mother is really looking at the unique, small, helpless being and not projecting her own introjects onto the child, nor her own expectations, fears, and plans for the child. In that case, the child would not find himself in his mother's face but rather the mother's own predicaments. This child would remain without a mirror, and for the rest of his life would be seeking this mirror in vain.

If you are still "seeking this mirror in vain" as an adult, you find yourself always looking to others for validation of your feelings and thoughts. It's difficult to trust your own sense of self, of *you*. This puts you in the precarious position in a relationship of not being able to trust your own senses. You must either keep your senses shut down or rely on your partner to tell you who you are in an extreme pattern of co-dependency, like Melissa.

"I drove Joe crazy sometimes. I kept asking him to tell me I was okay. I wasn't always blatant about it, but I'd be asking just the same—does this dress look all right, am I too fat, did I do the right thing? One time he exploded and told me to handle my insecurities, that they were driving him buggy. Then I really got insecure and wouldn't let him out of my sight."

The second aspect of trust is trusting others. When you can't trust someone, intimacy is impossible. If the someone you can't trust is not in fact trustworthy, you get an "A" for your judgment of character; but in many cases your judgment is clouded by habitual all-or-nothing patterns of dealing with trust and in turn intimacy. As an Adult Child, you may find that you go into a relationship trusting your partner 100 percent, only to be eventually disillusioned and then pull back your trust completely. Or you may be with someone who is basically trustworthy, yet because of your extreme wariness and all-or-nothing attitude you are always on the lookout for him to prove that he is not. When you do find some proof, which you most likely will, how easy it is then to withdraw your trust completely.

"When Adam and I were first going out together," Muriel recalls, "I was really impressed with him. He called when he said he would, showed up on time, treated me well—I wasn't used to that from a man. Then I caught him in a lie. He had told me a couple of months in advance that he was going away for a weekend. Then as the time got closer, it turned into a week's vacation, then ten days. He kept complaining about how tired he was of work and how much he needed the break—he really sounded like he was suffering—and I kept encouraging him to go ahead and go. Two days before he left he let slip that he had gotten the tickets for this trip well in advance. It turns out he had been planning it all along, and of course I was furious. He apologized and said he didn't tell me the whole truth because he was afraid I'd be upset. I lost all trust in him for a while and even began to question my judgment about trusting him earlier in our relationship. But he pointed out that while he had slipped this time, his track record was excellent. He had a good point, but it still has taken me a while to gain back the trust."

Trust is not an all-or-nothing proposition. To build trust with someone takes time and experience to see how the other person operates under a variety of circumstances. As a friend of mine said, "If you want to trust me, hang around for two or three years and let me get to know you."

Control

This is one of the most destructive characteristics you carry over from your abusive childhood and one of the greatest barriers to genuine intimacy. As described in chapter 3, there are several different ways control can manifest in a relationship.

Some attempts at control are obvious—bullying, criticizing, acting angry—but many others are less blatant. If you are trying to control another person, the attempt will interfere with the open sharing of deeper feelings that is necessary for intimacy. Whether you control through aggressive demands or by acting helpless, through lying and dishonesty or through placating behaviors, you limit the degree of vulnerability both you and your partner are willing to assume, and therefore limit the degree of intimacy.

Dishonesty

Dishonesty is an obvious barrier to intimacy. You can be dishonest about little things—what we typically call "little white lies"—or you can be dishonest about almost everything. Some people think that little white lies don't interfere with intimacy, but I think that in itself is one big white lie! I'm not suggesting you express everything that's on your mind—it really is okay not to tell everything about yourself—but honesty is the only policy that works for creating genuine intimacy. If you are feeling angry, why not acknowledge it instead of lying about it? It doesn't have to be a big deal that you're feeling angry, but denying or repressing anger leads to even bigger blowups or else leads to withdrawal.

Your childhood training, however, suggested that honesty is not the best policy. You learned to cover up and deny the truth with your parents for fear of abuse or abandonment. You continue to cover up because it's what you learned to do. There are times when you're dishonest about your feelings, about your wants, your needs, your opinions—perhaps even about being dishonest.

It's hard after all those years of training in denial to come out and tell the truth about who you are. To do so involves risk. You risk rejection and abandonment. You risk your partner getting to know you and learn about you, which is particularly threatening if you don't like who you are. You also risk letting go of the image of yourself as a victim to which you have been bound for many years. Genuine intimacy can only be experienced when you release all of your facades and let your real self—"warts and all"—shine through.

After two years of recovery, Lana began to realize how her facade of "niceness" created distance with her husband, James. "I've always been considered a nice person, starting with the days my mom and dad raised me to be a 'nice little girl.' James could do no wrong. I was always trying to please him, and when he was upset I instantly realized that it was probably my fault. I was constantly saying, 'I'm sorry.'

"In my therapy, I began to notice how I often denied what I wanted, for fear of upsetting the apple cart. One day it really hit home how dishonest I was by denying what I wanted or what I was feeling. James and I talked about staying a weekend in Palm Springs, and I got really excited and started thinking of all the fun things he and I could do together. Then he told me he was inviting the Taylors to join us. Instead of telling him, 'No, I just want to be with you,' I kept my lip zipped and said nothing."

Lana's continuing dishonesty led her to feeling angry and resentful, but burying these feelings was the tradition for her. It resulted in her being unable to feel close and intimate with James or with her friends, and therefore having only a marginally tolerable weekend.

Blaming

This is one of the leading preventers of intimacy. When you blame your partner for your feelings or behavior, you are perpetuating the victimization begun in childhood. By pointing fingers and blaming, you are saying that someone or something (your partner) has power over you to determine your feelings and behavior. Blaming says that you have no choice, that it's someone else's fault that you got the speeding ticket, were late for the luncheon, or started the argument. It puts the locus of control outside yourself. Blaming your partner puts the power in her hands.

Although this may be one of the hardest habits to break, it's important to pay attention to this attitude of blame and the associated victimization. Your judgments and condemnation of yourself and your partner will interfere with closeness. If you are blaming your partner, you'll likely carry a grudge or a load of resentment and ill feelings that will cause you to remain distant and removed. Like other Adult Children, you'll have all sorts of reasons to justify the blame, but this only alienates your partner all the more.

I remember how easy it was in my second marriage to find reasons to remain distant and alone. It hurts me to think how alone I was in that relationship, and I can now appreciate how alone my ex-wife must have felt. I could come up with a number of reasons, usually having to do with lack of affection or not enough sex or her bitchiness, to justify being off in my corner. I can see now that these were convenient excuses for not dealing with the truth that I had only a glimmer of at the time: that I was terrified of being abandoned if I let myself get too close. By blaming her I could settle cozily into my self-righteous justifications, even though at the same time I would feel the coldness and loneliness that came with an all-too-familiar sense of isolation.

By blaming I not only removed myself from any responsibility for my choices, I stood in judgment and condemnation of my wife. It's as if I were playing God, saying I knew what was right and wrong and what should or shouldn't be. Blame has beneath it a thick blanket of shame, and that's what I ultimately needed to deal with. Blame is shame turned inside out. When I blamed my wife for not paying enough attention to me, there was a deeper sense of shame about some inadequacy on my part—otherwise why wouldn't she pay attention to me?

Shame

This is the key ghost from your past that blocks intimacy. Shame is a fundamental experience for all Adult Children, and it is at the core of most of the other ghosts that continue to haunt you and prevent you from enjoying full intimacy with your partner. In *Healing the Shame That Binds You*, John Bradshaw graphically describes the effects of this kind of shame:

> Toxic shame, the shame that binds you, is experienced as the all-pervasive sense that I am flawed and defective as a human being. Toxic shame is no longer an emotion that signals our limits, it is a state of being, a core identity. Toxic shame gives you a sense of worthlessness, a sense of failing and falling short as a human being. Toxic shame is a rupture of the self with the self.
>
> *It is like internal bleeding*. Exposure to oneself lies at the heart of toxic shame. A shame-based person will guard against exposing his inner self to others, but more significantly, he will guard against exposing himself to himself.

It's evident that shame (what Bradshaw calls toxic shame—I think *all* shame is toxic) is a damaging emotion, so pervasive that it is like a fabric that runs through all other emotions and experiences and contaminates them. It's what you experienced in your shame-based family as a reaction to virtually any of your most human, childlike responses. Whenever your parents abused you, you felt shame. Whenever you got no response from your mother or father, you felt shame. Because you had to develop a false self in order to protect your real self, you felt shame. Aside from all of this, you carry the weight of your family's shame. It is deeply ingrained, and only through a commitment to your recovery will you release this shame. As long as you are ruled by shame, it's difficult to be intimate with others.

The connection between shame and difficulty with intimacy makes sense to Debra, a friend of mine. "I see how I've messed up relationships most of my life with this shame thing. I started getting close to this man, started liking him, and then I got all anxious and worried about whether or not he liked me. I got very demanding, and that just drove him away. I know that fear and shame are behind that kind of behavior. I worry that I'm not pretty enough, sexy enough, or just plain good enough, and I drive myself crazy. I just think there's something wrong with me. This is a pattern that's haunted me my whole life." Fortunately, Debra is beginning to identify this pattern and understand the shame that's behind it.

Caretaking

You took on the role of Caretaker in your childhood to fulfill your family's need for empathy as well as to shield your Inner Child from pain. You turned your focus to others, at the cost of your own feelings, wants, and needs. It was the best thing you knew to do, but it left you with your insides shut down.

One of the primary requirements for intimacy is the ability to pay attention to what is going on inside you. If your focus tends to be fixated externally, as it is in caretaking, you cannot resonate with what is going on within. Caretaking has moved you in the right direction to empathize with others, but you need to be able to tune into your internal processes as well.

Melody Beattie in *Beyond Codependency* describes coming to the realization that her caretaking had kept her from closeness: "I can recall walking into the living room one evening and having the sudden and profound awareness that I was too frightened and nervous to be close to my children. I knew how to stay in the 'Mom' role. I knew how to take care of and control them. But I didn't know how to relax and be close."

If you, like Melody Beattie, find yourself in the Caretaker role, underlying this role are undoubtedly some deep childhood fears of closeness that keep you from experiencing intimacy.

Addictions

I like Anne Wilson Schaef's definition of addiction in *When Society Becomes an Addict*: "An addiction is any process over which we are powerless. It takes control of us, causing us to do and think things that are inconsistent with our personal values and leading us to become progressively more compulsive and obsessive. A sure sign of an addiction is the sudden need to deceive ourselves and others—to lie, deny, and cover up."

There are two broad categories of addictions: *substance* addictions and *process* addictions. A substance addiction is an addiction to anything you ingest. This includes alcohol, drugs, and food. A process addiction involves an activity, such as gambling, work, sex, religion, or a relationship. The purpose of any addiction is threefold: First, to avoid dealing with uncomfortable and seemingly unmanageable emotions; second, to cover for low self-esteem; and third, to somehow try to fill a deep sense of void, of something missing. This sense of void stems from a person's alienation from the deeper source of life within, from the spirit. These three aspects are present in all addictions and are keys to understanding the addictive process.

Addictions interfere with the full blossoming of intimacy in your relationship because they become more important than the relationship itself. In most cases the addiction becomes something that soothes any discomfort you may feel at the prospect of closeness, yet it also creates an emotional numbness that makes you even more distant and unavailable. In *I Don't Want to Be Alone*, John Lee describes how addictions can interfere with intimacy:

> I realized that as a very young child I turned to or was given sugar to comfort and nurture me at times when my parents could not. Later in adolescence and adulthood, sugar became one of my main sources of emotional sustenance. So the substance that comforted in childhood became an adult addiction. If I was beginning to feel sad or lonely or scared, sugar helped me survive. But I realized that sugar takes me out of the world of feeling and into the world of depression—and thus away from my essential self—in a round-about, very indirect, seemingly harmless and legal way. I abandoned myself very much like I was abandoned as a child. The very things I used, whether sugar, caffeine, or sex to try to numb out the pain and comfort the captive child trapped inside me, became that which perpetuated the feeling of abandonment.

Thus when you are addicted, you always move toward the addiction and away from closeness. If you are actively addicted you keep yourself out of intimacy.

One of my clients, Denise, identified some of the difficulties she has had in the past two years dealing with intimacy now that she no longer resorts to alcohol and marijuana to escape her discomfort: "I've never known how to say no to a man, especially if he's very romantic and acts like he really wants me. There's this one fellow at work who has been really attentive, calling me all the time, sending me cards. I'm really attracted to him, but I just finished with one relationship and I'm not ready for another. I'm trying something new with him, which is to get to know him and be friends with him without going to bed with him. He's really pushy, and that scares me. I like him a lot, and there are times I feel really close to him, but I just have to watch myself, because I know I could get really involved and get addicted to him. If I did, I feel like I would lose everything I've worked for so far."

Now that we've identified some of the major barriers to intimacy that are holdovers from your upbringing, let's move on to some ideas and practical skills that will help you develop your capacity and abilities for intimacy.

THE TRUTH ABOUT INTIMACY

Most Adult Children harbor some unrealistic ideas about intimacy. We need to challenge these and replace them with truth. There are three fundamental truths that can be most illuminating in dealing with intimacy.

Truth # 1: You must first know yourself intimately before you can be truly intimate with another person.
In doing research for this book I asked people what they thought was required for intimacy. Many of them stated unequivocally that in order to be intimate with another person, you must first know yourself intimately.

Socrates said, "Know thyself." Perhaps he was the first expert on intimacy! "Knowing thyself" in this sense requires a willingness to continuously discover what is going on inside you moment to moment. It requires honesty, sensitivity, and a willingness to love yourself unconditionally, so that you can acknowledge and embrace fully whatever it is you discover—even the shadowy parts of you.

To know yourself intimately, you can have no denial or pretense, no falsification of what you feel inside your own skin. Your internal boundaries must be permeable. As my friend Joanna says, "You can't have any walls up. You can't keep any secrets from yourself, and all channels are open for discussion." By knowing yourself intimately, you become increasingly sensitive to what's going on inside you.

Shortly after my separation from my second wife, I dated a wonderful woman named Mina. Mina had an uncanny knack of stopping in the middle of a conversation when something was disturbing her and saying, "Wait. Let me feel about that." At first I was intrigued by this because it was so foreign to my way of doing things. Sometimes this trait would annoy me because Mina wouldn't let anything rest. If anything bothered her in some way, she'd let me know. I remember once after we had talked for a long time on the telephone late at night and had said our good-byes, I turned off the light and snuggled into bed, ready for sleep, feeling nice and warm about the conversation. It was well past midnight. Just as I was nodding off to sleep the phone rang. It was Mina. She was bothered by something I had just said, and she wanted to talk it over. This was one instance of several where she showed a remarkable capacity for attunement to her inner senses and could be totally empathic. I'll always appreciate this about her, because it was one of the first times I had met anyone who could be so intimately related to herself.

Truth # 2: There is no such thing as "instant intimacy."
Someone once observed that if an Adult Child goes to a party where there's only one other Adult Child, he'll immediately zero in on her, and they'll probably end up leaving the party together. Then they will fall in love within the next 24 to 48 hours, telling each other their life's stories within the first week. If you have ever had a similar experience, you have succumbed to acting out a belief that is common to Adult Children: There is a special someone out there, that one right person, a "soul mate," and if you can only find him, you will fall rapidly and madly in love and be together for all of eternity.

This myth needs to go the route of tooth fairies and eternal damnation. This is more descriptive of an addictive relationship than of an intimate one. Intimacy is not an all-or-nothing project, one in which you immediately give all of yourself over to that special person or to the relationship. It doesn't happen overnight but requires time to build trust, understanding, and a closer and closer bond.

While it is true that you can feel closer to some people more readily than others, much of what you experience as "instant intimacy" is idealized fantasy coupled with projection. Whether or not you're consciously aware of it, you carry around a fantasy of your ideal mate. When you meet someone you really like, someone who seems to come close to your ideal, you tend to project onto that person all of these fantasied expectations and to overlook any possible drawbacks. It's likely that you have been carrying around a parcel of unmet needs, and you imagine all sorts of ways this new person will be able to meet those needs. All the while, you are trying your best to be the person that you imagine this new acquaintance will want, watching closely to see if he approves.

Of course, your partner is playing the game, too. He's doing his best to try to convince you that he is, in fact, the man of your dreams, because he's needy as well. So he goes about denying those parts of himself that he thinks would cause you to reject him. He sees in you his own idealized projections.

After my second marriage ended, I intentionally avoided any heavy involvement with a woman. If I was really attracted to anyone, I immediately looked the other way. I was breaking some addictive patterns and starting to feel a sense of myself as a separate person, but this independence was still fragile. Then along came Jan Marie. I fell instantly in love, as did she, and we started hinting at a lifetime together after we had known each other just a couple of weeks. Lust was the overriding emotion that sustained us for several months. I became so obsessed that I put my work and friends to the side. I projected all my needs onto her, expecting her to be the perfect lover, one who would be there for me forever. It was a painful realization that she was a human being, with flaws and limitations. Our mutual addiction to sex numbed us to the realities of intimacy. I tried to stretch the myth of instant intimacy over several months, only to have it shatter with our breakup.

Your childhood training makes you susceptible to adopting this version of intimacy, and our addictive, co-dependent culture tends to idealize and glamorize it. The images and words to which we're exposed on television and radio and in newspapers and magazines suggest that if we only wear the right perfume, drink the right kind of beer, drive the right car, dress the right way, have the right kind of body, and get the right credit card, we will be okay and will be able to have the right kind of relationship. That's an incredible amount of idealization to sift through, especially for an Adult Child. It was not only the influences from your family that were significant in your learning about intimacy but also the influences from society.

Popular songs suggest that when you see your loved one, you will know because sparks will fly, the earth will move, and you will have eyes for no one else. Although love songs can speak to the beauty and joy in touching another person in an intimate way, these ballads are also inundated with romanticized, co-dependent idealization that tends to reinforce the myth of instant intimacy.

Frank has hopped on the bandwagon of instant intimacy on more than one occasion. "I remember reading *Bridge Across Forever*," he says with a chuckle. "I was determined that I just had to be more open to my 'soul mate' and that there was someone out there just for me. After this I met a woman I thought at first had all of those special properties that made her qualify as a soul mate. We spent the whole weekend together—I really thought she was the one—and we had practically moved in together by the third week. One of my best friends sat me down and had a talk with me and straight out told me not to do it, to slow down. Thank God for friends like him! I slowed down with her, and when I did, she got very desperate and clingy and, per my usual pattern, I pulled away. We broke up after four months because it just got to be too much, and I realize now how addicted I was to her. Now I'm sure that intimacy isn't something that's going to happen in an evening or even a week. It's going to take time."

Yes, it's going to take time. Although you can experience moments of closeness with people after first meeting them, true intimacy takes time. If you act too fast on these feelings of closeness, you are acting out of your own neediness, trying to find intimacy through another person. Remember the first truth about intimacy is that you must know intimacy with yourself first. What a relief to enjoy other people and perhaps even to feel intensely close with some without having your searchlights on, without having to mold or shape the friendship or to desperately try to delude yourself into thinking that there is only one special person with whom you can share intimacy.

Truth # 3: Intimacy is a process, not an event.
When you know yourself intimately, have an adequate sense of your own boundaries, and are willing to be fully present with another person, it's likely that you will experience intimacy with a number of people. As you develop your capacity for this type of intimacy, the main danger comes from misinterpreting the meaning of this closeness. What it means is that you are surrendering to your innate capacity and desire to make contact with other human beings in a significant way and that you are developing a stronger sense of your self and of your own boundaries. You are actively remembering your ability to love.

It's only been in the last three or four years that I have been able to develop greater closeness and intimacy with both men and women. I had assumed that any intimacy shared with a woman had to be sexual and that if I felt emotionally and spiritually close to any other man, that meant I was gay. I continue to challenge these old fears and beliefs and keep a bead on them. It's opened up new textures in my friendships, and I feel fortunate that I have some incredibly rich and full friendships.

One thing that's contributed to this richness and fullness is the fact that I've known these friends for a period of time, typically a few years. It's the *process* of getting to know someone that adds to the depth and character of the relationship. To experience a deeper, stronger intimacy with another person takes time. It won't happen overnight. It won't happen just because you're now living together, or because you're married, or because you've had a child together. It requires time, patience, attention, and lots of love.

Intimacy is a process, not an event. In the relationship with your mate, intimacy is deepened by sharing many different experiences. Two people must share their love, their sadness, their anger, and their joy in order to nurture the intimate bond between them. Ultimately this bond is felt as a deeply spiritual connection. You come to appreciate that the two of you together are greater than the sum of the parts. You must be able to look that other person in the eye and let him really know that you want to experience a deepening of your connection. You must forgive yourself for your transgressions and release your shame about being you. These things certainly don't happen the first few times you are with someone.

Some couples report that because they have shared so much over time, they can appreciate simple moments together as being profoundly intimate experiences. Peter and Marianne have been married about 12 years and have two children, Dana, 10, and Joshua, 8. Marianne describes one such moment: "We were walking along the beach while the children were playing in the surf. It was late in the afternoon but still warm. I remember how the sand felt beneath my feet—kind of cool and squishy—and how the surf slapped against the beach, reminding me of how steady and consistent life really is. Peter and I were talking about this and that. We talked about the fact that although we'd been together for many moons, it seemed like a really short time. We laughed about some of the funny times we'd had, like the time I crazy-glued my fingers together fixing one of Dana's toys. All this time we were holding hands. We got kind of quiet for a while and were just together walking on the beach, watching our children, feeling each other's presence in the presence of God, and tears started filling up my eyes. These were tears of quiet joy. Neither of us really had to say anything at that moment to understand what was going on. I felt my deep love and appreciation for life and for sharing it with Peter."

Captured in Marianne's description is the sense of how a greater depth of intimacy can be experienced with another person over time. I don't mean to idealize the experience of intimacy, but to point out that the intimate moments you experience with another person have a cumulative effect. It is the process of a series of moments that makes a walk on the beach with your partner so special and meaningful.

Remember these three simple truths, and you can begin to correct some of the common myths that you and most other Adult Children subscribe to. Let's look now at some practical skills you can work with to pave the way for greater intimacy in your relationships.

SOLUTIONS: HOW TO DO
THIS THING CALLED INTIMACY

We've seen that to develop intimacy in your relationships, you must first know yourself intimately. Your lifelong process of active recovery sets the stage for knowing yourself, so it's important to continue participating in your recovery in whatever way is appropriate for you at any given time, including reading, writing regularly in your journal, being involved in counseling, and participating in a 12-step program. You're used to doing most things in isolation, but recovery cannot be done in isolation. You must work your recovery with at least one other person involved, someone who is safe. You need validation and support from others. You grew up in a community called your family, one that was dysfunctional, where there was little or no validation for your real self. Now as an adult you can surround yourself with healthy people and let your Inner Child be validated in a healthy community.

By working your recovery, you are automatically working on your relationships. When you are specifically working with intimacy issues in your relationships, it helps to acquire some skills that you did not have a chance to develop while growing up. The exercises that follow are designed to help you develop trust, vulnerability, empathy, clear boundaries, and appreciation—all the essential ingredients for intimacy.

Most of the skills described in this section are designed to be worked with a partner, preferably your primary partner. However, since you can use most of them in any relationship where there is the potential for intimate exchange, it need not be your primary partner.

As you work with the various exercises designed to expand on your capacity for intimacy, certain childhood feelings may be aroused that create some anxiety. Do not be alarmed; this may simply indicate that some of these feelings are on the move, getting ready for release. You have had much training in intimacy avoidance, so give yourself time and attention in this particularly vulnerable area. Always be open to getting some professional help, either for yourself or for your relationship, if you get into a bind.

Softening Boundaries

When you're working on intimacy, it's vital to consistently practice the ways to identify and establish boundaries suggested in the previous chapter. In *Beyond Codependency*, Melody Beattie writes, "The goal of having and setting boundaries isn't to build thick walls around ourselves. The purpose is to gain enough security and sense of self to get close to others without the threat of losing ourselves, smothering them, trespassing, or being invaded. Boundaries are the key to loving relationships.

"When we have a sense of self, we'll be able to experience closeness and intimacy. We'll be able to play, be creative, and be spontaneous. We'll be able to love and be loved."

The more confident you become in your ability to set and maintain boundaries, the more you will be ready for the next step: learning to relax them, especially when you're with someone you can trust. As you gain greater confidence in your ability to define your self, to trust that you will not get lost in your relationship, you'll find it easier to soften your boundaries and let your partner in.

Following is an exercise adapted from one shown to me by Stephen Gilligan, Ph.D., designed to help you experience a "merging" of boundaries, which is a prerequisite for intimacy. This merging requires you to trust and be vulnerable and can help you develop an empathy for your partner. The exercise is unusual and may not seem very logical. It's designed to get you and your partner past your logical, rational minds into mutually intuitive, relational states of mind, and so you may experience a period of confusion when you start the exercise. Keep going even if it seems to make no rational sense.

If you're doing this with your mate, you may find it arouses powerful feelings and perhaps some familiar patterns of conflict. If conflict is generated, don't consider that you've somehow failed the exercise. This may happen, and the conflict itself may have to be resolved before you try the exercise again. Whatever the case, this process of exploration can help you be more acutely aware of your need to be clearer about your boundaries. It also opens the possibilities of merging with another person in a healthy way.

This exercise promotes awareness and attention—and you cannot have intimacy without awareness and attention. If you're in a relationship, mark a date to do this exercise with your partner once every four weeks. It will keep you both attentive and encourage you to relax your boundaries.

When you first try this you'll find that you will continue to feel the effects for some time afterward, and it may not be immediately apparent what this has to do with intimacy. Go ahead and try it anyway. I dare you! It will be fun and you'll no doubt learn something about intimacy.

> EXERCISE: Mutual awareness.
> Choose a quiet time when there will be no distractions for at least 30 minutes or so. Sit in comfortable chairs facing each other, no more than a few feet apart. (It's okay if your knees are touching.)

Take three or four slow, deep breaths together, remembering to exhale very slowly and deliberately, letting your body relax as you do. Make eye contact. If you and your partner find yourselves giggling and laughing at first, accept that this is your way of dealing with your nervousness and apprehension, and continue with the exercise.

Below are a number of unfinished statements that you and your partner are to say out loud simultaneously, finishing each statement in your own way. You will likely finish each sentence differently, and at first this may seem distracting. Don't let that stop you. Simply continue repeating each sentence the required number of times, each time finishing it with whatever words come into your awareness. Maintain eye contact and, if possible, your deep breathing pattern throughout. If you get off track in some way, pause for a moment, and begin again wherever you left off. Continue all the way through and I think you'll find the process completely absorbing.

Here is the sequence of unfinished statements:

"Right now, I'm aware that I'm seeing . . ." (repeat 5 times)
"Right now, I'm aware that I'm hearing . . ." (repeat 5 times)
"Right now, I'm aware that I'm feeling . . ." (repeat 5 times)
"Right now, I'm aware that I'm seeing . . ." (repeat 4 times)
"Right now, I'm aware that I'm hearing . . ." (repeat 4 times)
"Right now, I'm aware that I'm feeling . . ." (repeat 4 times)
"Right now, I'm aware that I'm seeing . . ." (repeat 3 times)
"Right now, I'm aware that I'm hearing . . ." (repeat 3 times)
"Right now, I'm aware that I'm feeling . . ." (repeat 3 times)
"Right now, I'm aware that I'm seeing . . ." (repeat 2 times)
"Right now, I'm aware that I'm hearing . . ." (repeat 2 times)
"Right now, I'm aware that I'm feeling . . ." (repeat 2 times)
"Right now, I'm aware that I'm seeing . . ."
"Right now, I'm aware that I'm hearing . . ."
"Right now, I'm aware that I'm feeling . . ."

When you have finished the entire sequence, sit quietly for a few moments without speaking. Then, spend a few minutes sharing with each other your observations and your experience. Especially note how you experienced any blending of boundaries or any fears or apprehensions about doing so.

After Ed and Marion tried this for the first time, Ed said, "I couldn't figure out what was supposed to happen, so after a while I stopped trying. When we finished, I felt completely relaxed, and very, very close with Marion. In fact, I'd say I felt as close to her as I have ever felt."

Marion too was enthusiastic. "I loved it! It was a little strange trying to finish the sentence and listen to what Ed was saying at the same time, but after a while it didn't matter. For the first few rounds I was busy trying to make sure Ed was okay with doing the exercise, but that passed, too. The couple of times we both said the same words at the end caught me by surprise. It's as if we were one mind. Closeness? Yes, I definitely feel closer to him now, but I'm not sure why."

Sharing Feelings: Appreciation

In moments of intimacy you connect through your heart, not your mind or body. Your body or mind may follow and join in, but the most precious connections are made when your heart is open to your partner's. The path to intimacy is through sharing feelings.

Sharing feelings is different from talking *about* feelings. When you are sharing feelings, you are expressing what is going on here and now with your emotions. For instance, if you are in a conversation with your partner and you notice a feeling of warmth and affection, by expressing this you are sharing what is current. Talking *about* feelings is conversing about emotions you have each experienced in the past, even if that past was 10 minutes ago. Sharing feelings requires you to be fully present and to notice what is going on inside yourself—in other words, to know yourself intimately.

Paul talks about how this shift took place in his communication with his wife, Lois: "I started paying attention to our conversations and noticed I had a distinct tendency to ramble all over the place when it came to feelings. Just last night I had a taste of what it was like to *share* feelings. Lois has this great ability to tell me how she's feeling at any given moment. Well, last night I tried it a couple of times, and I found out I could identify what was going on at that moment and share it with Lois. I told her I was scared when she started coming on to me sexually. I was so pleased. It's like a whole new world."

I can understand Paul's enthusiasm at this discovery. It's only been in the last few years that I can more easily share some of my feelings rather than just talk about them. Before then, being a therapist, I knew all the right words to say, the right expressions to use, but there was one thing missing: my self. I could use feeling words like "angry," "sad," "pleased," "happy," but since I wasn't completely present, I expressed them like I was giving a report rather than communicating an experience.

As described previously, the feeling of appreciation is one particular ingredient that can enhance intimacy. Here is a simple exercise that can not only help you and your partner focus on the more immediate expression of your feelings, but can also fine-tune your attention to what you appreciate about each other. You might also want to review some of the exercises in chapter 2 and do them with your partner.

> EXERCISE: Sharing appreciation.
>
> On a sheet of paper, write the incomplete sentence, "What I appreciate about [partner's name] is . . ." On the left side of the page put the numbers 1 through 20. Now take a few moments to consider what it is about your mate that you like. Be as specific as possible. Think of things your partner does for you as well as personality characteristics and attributes you enjoy. Finish the sentence in as many ways as possible. If you come up with more than 20 items, put down as many as come to mind.
>
> A few of the items Cyndi came up with about her husband John were as follows:
>
> What I appreciate about John is . . .
> 1. his sense of humor.
> 2. that he gives me room to be myself.
> 3. he fixes things.
> 4. his strength.
> 5. he fixes me coffee in the morning.
> 6. he wipes the sink out after he shaves.
> 7. he picks up after himself.
> 8. he's really easygoing.
>
> Now, for the next week, use the list of items to focus your attention on those things you appreciate. Whenever you notice your partner doing or being anything on your list, tell him so. Be sure to say it without sarcasm—be sincere. At least three times each day, let him know when you feel your appreciation for something he does or for some quality you like that you see him expressing. To comment on some quality of your partner's being or expression is more personal than noting actions, and would likely make more impact.

Cyndi reports, "This was harder than I thought. I tended to joke about it, or I'd say something and then follow it with, '. . . but, on the other hand, you didn't put your dishes in the dishwasher,' or something like that. I don't like doing that, because I found out there is a lot about John I do like and appreciate, and I want him to know it."

A complementary skill to sharing feelings is the ability to hear your partner's feelings, whether or not he is expressing those feelings directly. This takes us to our next intimacy-building skill, active listening.

Active Listening

Most people think listening means waiting patiently for the other person to finish talking so you can have your turn. Obviously, this idea of listening will not encourage intimacy but instead will tend to encourage self-righteousness, advice-giving, and argumentativeness. The two people "listening" will be engaging in parallel monologues, always missing the point of each other's communication.

Active listening, on the other hand, encourages more intimate communication. It encourages trust and empathy. This skill is one that, with practice, will provide you with a vehicle for touching your partner's feelings. It will encourage more open dialogue and create a more empathic relatedness between the two of you. It's similar to sharing feelings except that with active listening you now take a more receptive, responsive stance, paying close attention to what your partner is really communicating at a feeling level. It requires you as the active listener to put aside any personal agenda for the time being and pay careful and close attention to what your partner is saying.

Watch so that you don't give advice, defend yourself, correct, or criticize, but instead simply listen with your eyes and ears. In fact, active listening has been called "listening with the third ear," in that you are listening not so much for content as for the textures of the communication as shown by your partner's body language and voice characteristics. Your partner won't necessarily state her feelings, but your challenge is to see, hear, and feel them. The task of active listening is to articulate those unstated emotions for both of you by your verbal feedback.

Active listening requires three important steps:

1. *Observe.* When your partner looks like she is feeling something important or emotionally charged, observe her body language and listen for her voice tone. Pay less attention to the content of what she's saying. For instance, if her brow is furrowed, shoulders tense, jaws tight, voice sharp and choppy, and she's saying, "I can't take this job anymore!," she's obviously expressing

deep frustration. Don't intervene by giving advice or criticizing, but instead think of what she may be feeling.

2. *Paraphrase*. Next, while making eye contact and paying attention to your partner, paraphrase the feeling as follows: "You feel (or felt) [feeling word] ." In the example above, you might say to your partner, "You feel angry," or "You feel frustrated." (For a vocabulary of feeling words, refer to chapter 2 on emotions.)

3. *Listen*. Now pay attention to your partner's response. If you were close or right on, you'll likely get an acknowledgment plus some further words on the situation, such as, "Yes, I am frustrated! I can't stand that boss of mine. He's such a jerk!" The wonderful thing about active listening is that you don't have to be absolutely right for the skill to work; if you were not accurate in your paraphrasing of feelings, your partner will most likely do the clarifying. For instance, if you had said, "You feel sad about your job," your partner might come back with, "No, not sad. I'm angry." Right or wrong, you can accomplish the objectives of helping your partner feel heard and helping her identify and clarify her feelings. The result is a greater feeling of closeness.

A friend of mine recently confirmed how valuable active listening can be. "Norma and I were in an argument just the other day," he said, and at one point I stopped arguing and started to use active listening. The whole tone changed, and after a while she started to listen to *my* feelings. After a while we reached an understanding of what each other was feeling. It's so simple to do, but so easy to forget sometimes."

This skill invites intimacy by putting you in touch with what you are feeling, and especially with what your mate is feeling. As evidenced by my friend's comment, it can even change the direction of a conflict with your mate. It requires you to be open to what your partner is saying without being judgmental or defensive and to put your own issues aside for the time being. This doesn't imply that you should deny your own feelings or sacrifice your own needs, but you should delay addressing these and instead be there for your partner.

Here's a useful exercise for learning how to do active listening:

> EXERCISE: Listening for feelings.
>
> With your partner, agree to take 10 minutes apiece to practice active listening, using the guidelines listed above. Decide who will be the speaker and who will be the listener. Sit facing each other. The speaker then proceeds to tell a story about his day, or about some event that happened the past week, or about something that has to

do with the relationship. The listener's sole job is to practice active listening by paraphrasing the other person's feelings. As the listener, be careful to avoid judgment, blame, criticism, or sarcasm. Especially watch that these don't creep into your vocal inflections in a subtle fashion.

Do this for 10 minutes, then switch speaker/listener roles. Practice this faithfully once each day for the next 21 days, and I think you'll find that it will become a healthy habit in your relationship.

Craig and Allison agree that it was helpful. They both liked the idea of spending some focused time with each other sharing, not just swapping stories about their day but sharing in a way where each felt acknowledged and heard. Craig saw it as relaxing, while Allison felt it helped her feel more connected to Craig.

Next we'll move from the mind to the body as we look closely at two overlapping areas that cannot be left out of a discussion of intimacy: physical affection and sexual sharing.

Expressing Physical Affection

As an Adult Child, you probably have some confusion and mixed feelings about physical affection. If you were sexually abused you probably equate touch with betrayal and boundary violation. Physical affection may have become sexualized for you. Since you were exploited sexually by an adult before you were capable of comprehending adult sexuality, physical contact became confused with sexual contact. Now for you as an adult, these borders may be fuzzy or completely absent.

If you were physically abused, touch is associated with physical and emotional pain. You may find yourself now either rejecting any kind of touch or in a situation where touch continues to be painful—perhaps you are involved with someone who abuses you. Kathy, who was a battered wife for a number of years, came to realize that her willingness to put up with this abuse was directly connected to a childhood filled with beatings and emotional abuse from her father. Simply put, that's what she was used to. "I never really thought much about it," she says. "I guess Ken was a lot like my father—they both could get pretty mean. Ken would stay quiet for long spells of time. During times like that I'd get nervous wondering whether or not he really cared. It was usually after one of these quiet spells that we'd have a huge fight and he'd slap me around. I'd threaten to leave, and he would go out of his way to make up for it." Whether or not this is specifically the case for you, the abuse you suffered as a child has had a profound effect on the way you deal with physical affection.

In another scenario, there may have been little or no physical affection or contact in your childhood, so you have no criteria for knowing how to deal with touch. You find as an adult that you continue to avoid any risk of physical affection or physical intimacy because you simply do not have any direct experience upon which to build. You may continue to avoid all touch, or you may satisfy this basic human need through sex that is devoid of any emotional or spiritual connection.

Up until the last few years, I had always felt awkward about touching. My family was not a very touchy family. I had the type of training a lot of boys do, which says that if you're a real man, the main time you can be affectionate with a woman is during sex, and touching or hugging other men is completely verboten. These rules made it difficult to be relaxed with any kind of touching or hugging, other than with a woman for sexual gratification. Needless to say, my attitude about touching was rather one-dimensional and bereft of fulfillment. It left me hungry for sexual contact to fill in the gap.

There are many ways the boundaries between physical affection and sex can get blurred. The tricky part is to learn to differentiate loving touch from hurtful touch from sexual touch. While sexual contact obviously includes physical contact and sometimes affectionate contact, it's possible for touching to be nonsexual. Nonsexual touching means that sexual arousal is not the intent of the physical contact. If these borders are blurred for you, it will take some time and attention to more clearly differentiate the various expressions of affection that can occur between two people who love each other.

The following exercise will be helpful as you learn to give and receive physical affection. It gives both partners a chance to explore further your trust in each other and your willingness to be vulnerable. Agree ahead of time that you will take turns giving and receiving and that you will share your experience when it's complete.

> EXERCISE: Sensual foot massage.
> One partner is the giver, the other is the receiver. It's best for one of you to give the foot massage to your partner one evening, then receive one from your partner the next evening. That way your complete attention can be on your particular role with no anticipation of having to "even things up" by immediately reciprocating. The proper attitude for the giver is one in which you are completely focused on your partner, with no expectations for anything in

return. The proper attitude for the receiver is to be receptive to what your partner is giving to you and to provide feedback as to what feels especially good or what doesn't feel good. In either role, pay close attention to your experience in that role.

Assemble the following items:

A small basin of warm water
A washcloth
One standard-size bath towel
One large soft bath towel
Massage oil

I recommend safflower, canola, musk, or almond oil, because these are absorbed easily by the skin. Although not as readily absorbed, another choice would be coconut oil. You can keep the massage oil warm by putting the container in a bowl of warm water.

For the one giving the sensual foot massage, it is your responsibility to provide as comfortable a setting as possible. While not absolutely necessary, music and soft lights are pleasant additions to help provide a relaxing setting. The room should be warm enough to be comfortable. Have your partner sit facing you, with one of her feet in your lap. You should be sitting slightly lower than she so that she doesn't have any strain in the backs of her legs when you are massaging her foot.

The first step is to gently wash each of your partner's feet, one at a time. Take care in drying each one with the smaller towel, rubbing them dry with gentle yet brisk motions. Next, take one of her feet and lightly rub with your dry hands. Make sure you do not tickle her feet. Be responsive to any cues from your partner that your touch is too light, too rough, or just right. Groans of pleasure are fairly good cues that she's enjoying a particular touch.

Take some of the heated massage oil and work it into all areas of your partner's foot. Again, be attentive to how your touch is being received. It's permissible to ask how it feels at any point during the massage, and it would be helpful for your partner to tell you when a touch is particularly pleasurable. Start by massaging the whole foot with both your hands in broad, encompassing strokes. Then use your fingers to gently massage each toe, one at a time, moving your fingers into the crevasses between them.

If your partner enjoys it, spend some time rubbing the bottom of the foot. This is an area that usually receives little attention. Use your thumbs and fingers to work the contours of the bottom of the foot, slowly stroking each curve several times. More than any specific technique, however, it's useful for you to experience how it feels to be giving this massage. Note your own sensations in your fingers and hands as you do the massage, and enjoy. Cue in to how your partner is receiving your touch. Listen with your hands and with your heart, and be willing to experiment with different ways of massaging.

Do the other foot in like fashion. Spend about 10–15 minutes on each foot, or whatever time you or your partner can reasonably tolerate. After each foot is done, take the larger bath towel and rub gently yet briskly. Allow your partner a few minutes to quietly relax after the total massage is finished, then spend a few minutes talking about what each of you experienced. Repeat this process the following evening but switch roles. Plan to do this exercise every four to six weeks.

Joanna and Steve tried this exercise over a couple of evenings. "We flipped a coin," Joanna reports, "and I won the toss, so I elected to give Steve his foot rub first. Of course, he didn't object at all."

"I loved it!" Steve interjects.

"Yes, you sure did," Joanna continues, "and so did I. There was really something special about giving to Steve in this way. We were quiet sometimes, sometimes we giggled and laughed, and I found out where Steve is ticklish."

"Now you know some more of my secrets," Steve says.

"I hope I learn a lot more before this lifetime is done," she responds. "The next night was my turn to get the foot rub. I was surprised at how nervous I was. All my co-dependency stuff was there. I kept telling him that if he didn't feel like doing it, that it would be okay. He insisted, but it took me a while to relax. I kept wondering if he was okay doing it. I felt so loved and so appreciative of Steve during that whole time."

"I was fine giving her the foot rub," Steve says. "I had to keep reassuring her that I was enjoying myself. It was very sensual, at times bordering on erotic, but it never really got sexual. It was pure giving and pure pleasure. I'd like to see us make it a regular part of our lives."

As you explore the depth of meaning for you of physical affection through this exercise and other experiences, you may naturally want to explore the dimension of sexual intimacy. In the next section we'll begin to explore this domain of sexual intimacy, which can potentially redefine what sexual sharing can be.

Sexual Sharing

Perhaps the most profoundly intimate and vulnerable experience a man and a woman can have is to share sexual intimacy—not just when they are having sex but when they are truly sharing their sexuality with each other. There are a number of creative possibilities as to how you and your partner can share sexual intimacy, intercourse being only one. It's unfortunate but true that many couples get locked into sexual intercourse as the only vehicle for sexual expression. Although intercourse can certainly be pleasurable, when this is *always* the goal of sex a wide range of other possibilities are excluded.

Think of it: You are completely covered by the organ we refer to as skin, which is incredibly sensitive to a variety of sensations. There is an innocent sensuality that is a part of your being yet is contaminated by a lot of shame and guilt from having grown up with abuse. As you develop your capacity to be intimate, one of the prime areas to explore creatively is sexual sharing. To deeply share your sexuality is to be at your most vulnerable.

The word "sharing" with regard to sexuality doesn't mean exploiting, being self-sacrificing, manipulating, controlling, using, or treating each other as objects. It means a mutual exchange of giving and receiving, rather than demanding and taking. You are honoring each other spiritually and emotionally, rather than just rubbing two bodies together.

I think a good ground rule when you are in a sexual relationship is that you spend at least 30 minutes with each other talking and sharing, clothed or unclothed, before allowing the relating to become specifically sexual. In an intimate adult relationship, you can't take the sexual play and sharing out of context. If you do, you objectify the other person and you objectify yourself.

If, as a woman, you let your man be physically inside your body just to keep him happy, to calm him down, or to get a respite from his pestering you to have sex, you are selling out and face the danger of re-creating a familiar pattern of victimization. If, as a man, you are pressing to have sex against your partner's wishes, you are not only objectifying her, you are acting like you are a penis without a body, disconnected from any feelings or emotions. In either case you deny your real self. Any time you deny your real self, you are not capable at that moment of being truly intimate.

If you were sexually abused as a child, this whole area of sexual sharing is loaded for you. Either your body was used for sexual gratification by an adult or you were in some other way demeaned sexually. In either case, vulnerability through sex is risky business, to say the least. In addition, you may need to learn to love and care for your own body. If these exercises are too threatening, seek the help of a therapist to guide you through the restoration of your sexual self.

Given these qualifications, the following two exercises will allow you and your partner to enhance your sexual sharing. You may feel awkward and nervous at first doing them, but go ahead and explore them. Strong feelings may be triggered in the process, and I encourage you to talk these through with your partner, sponsor, a trusted friend, or your therapist. If you find these exercises useful, repeat them every few weeks. Most of all, know that by doing them you will learn something about yourself, about your partner, and about intimacy.

EXERCISE: Talking about sex.

The point of this exercise (adapted from *Healing Together* by Wayne Kritsberg) is to help you feel comfortable talking about your sexuality. An important aspect of sexual intimacy is to be able to reveal your thoughts, feelings, preferences, and needs to your partner.

Follow these guidelines in doing this exercise:

- Sit facing each other in a comfortable position.
- Take turns completing each sentence honestly in your own words.
- When your partner is sharing, you must simply listen. When you are sharing, your partner must simply listen. After completing the exercise you and your partner can discuss your experiences and observations.
- Either of you can refuse to complete any of the sentences.
- Either of you can end the exercise at any time.

1. My body is . . .
2. The part of my body I like most is . . .
3. My mother's attitude toward sex was . . .
4. I think masturbation is . . .
5. When I talk about sex, I . . .
6. The part of my body I wish I could change is . . .
7. The name I use for my genitals is . . .
8. My father's attitude about sex was . . .
9. Right now, what I notice in my body is . . .
10. The most erotic area of my body is . . .
11. I like it when you touch my . . .
12. When we make love, what I like best is . . .
13. If I don't have an orgasm during sex, I feel . . .
14. If you don't have an orgasm during sex, I feel . . .
15. The first time I had intercourse, I felt . . .

16. After we make love, what I like best is . . .
17. My favorite way of touching you is . . .
18. Something we haven't done that I would like to do sexually with you is . . .
19. I get nervous when . . .
20. I get really turned on when you . . .
21. I don't like it when you . . .
22. I feel closest to you when . . .
23. I feel most desired when . . .
24. The times I feel most sexual with you are . . .
25. Sexually, something I really enjoy is . . .
26. I feel most vulnerable during sex when . . .
27. What would make my sex life with you even better is . . .
28. My favorite sexual fantasy is . . .
29. Something I haven't asked for sexually is . . .
30. Right now I feel toward you . . .

Now that you have both taken some risks with self-disclosure, spend a few minutes discussing your experience. There may be surprises each time you do this exercise, since the responses may change over time.

Bob and Vicki tried this exercise. According to Vicki, "It was scary and exciting at the same time. I have a lot of messages in my head that say sex is dirty and you don't talk about it. For the longest time I referred to my sexual organs as 'down there.' Anyway, Bob and I got through about a dozen or so items, and we launched into this very frank discussion about our sex lives. It seems it has gotten really routine, so doing this sparked us into making some changes."

"I found it kind of embarrassing," Bob confesses. "I'm not sure I liked doing it, but I like the results. I found out just how repressed I am, and I thought I was pretty liberal when it came to sex. I also found out a lot about how Vicki likes to be touched. That night after our discussion, we just held each other and talked some more. She really seems like she's willing to try some things sexually. That night I felt really close to her. It was great."

Next we move to another exercise that is even riskier yet can be incredibly informative and even pleasurable: sensate focus.

EXERCISE. Sensate focus.

The purpose of this exercise is twofold. First, it encourages you and your partner to introduce nondemanding pleasuring into your sexual sharing and take the focus off performance. The objective of the experience is to be completely process oriented rather than goal oriented. In other words, there is no orgasm to get to. Second, it allows each of you to discover and perhaps release some of your inhibitions about giving and receiving sensual pleasure.

You must both agree that there is to be no intercourse following the sensate focus exercise. This is extremely important, as this agreement encourages an atmosphere of trust and relaxation between the two of you. The first couple of times you do this exercise do not include the genitals in your touching. That way you can rest assured about the nondemanding nature of this exercise. After this, you may include the genitals if you mutually agree to, but still retain the no-intercourse rule. As you are doing the exercise, both of you will find thoughts and feelings surfacing. Note these reactions so you can talk with your partner about them once the exercise is completed. If the exercise feels too threatening, I would advise you to work with a therapist.

To proceed, both of you get ready for bed. Take your clothes off, shower if desired, and relax. As the woman, lie on your stomach. As the man, sit or kneel comfortably near her and caress her back very gently and very slowly, being sensitive to her responses. Moving your hands very slowly, caress the back of her neck, her ears, upper and lower back, and move gradually down to her buttocks, legs, and feet. Concentrate on your sensations, on how it feels for you to touch her body, her skin, rather than worrying about how she is receiving your touch. Use your hands and/or your lips.

For you, the woman, focus your attention on the sensations you feel when he caresses you. Be aware of any emotions that arise, while doing your best to simply focus your attention on the sensations. Stay as focused as possible, trying not to let your mind wander. Don't worry whether your partner is enjoying it or not or getting tired or bored. Keep your attention on your own sensations, your own experience. Let yourself feel as much as you possibly can. Tell him what feels good—he can't really know unless you tell him. Tell him where you want to be touched, how you want to be touched, and when his touch feels especially good. Tell him if his touch is too light or too heavy, or if he is moving his hands too quickly. Don't just "put up" with it if it is unpleasant—talk to him. Notice also those areas of your body where you are particularly sensitive or responsive.

After a few minutes of this or until you have both had enough, you, the woman, turn over on your back. Now you, the man, can caress the front of her body. Once again, the first couple of times you do this exercise, skip her sexual organs—nipples, clitoris, vagina. Start by gently and slowly touching her face and neck and work your way gradually down to her toes. For you, the woman, concentrate on what it feels like to be caressed. For the man, concentrate on what it's like to caress. Stop before either of you gets too tired or the exercise becomes tedious.

After you have had a brief rest, it's the man's turn to be the receiver. Follow the same procedure, only this time the woman is the giver. Once you have completed both ways, you may want to discuss your experience of this exercise. Repeat once every three to four weeks.

Since this is probably a new way to approach sexual intimacy for you, be patient with yourselves. Couples have all sorts of reactions to this exercise, but a typical response is that it is ultimately relaxing to be together when there are no expectations for sexual performance, but instead a sharing of touch and sensual pleasuring.

George and Sally went off to do this exercise after a counseling session. In the next two follow-up meetings, they had excuses as to why they hadn't done it. As we talked, it became clear that they had some real fears. George was concerned that he would get an erection and wouldn't be able to stop himself from wanting to have intercourse. Sally realized that she had a hard time imagining herself receiving pleasure, since receiving in general was difficult for her. When they finally tried the exercise, George was relieved that although he did get an erection a couple of times, he was able to turn his attention back to the process and found both giving and receiving quite enjoyable. Sally enjoyed the giving but had a bit of a problem with the receiving. "I was nervous most of the time. I kept thinking about all the things around the house I had to do, which I know was just my resistance. At one point I felt George's penis brush against my foot as he moved to the other side. I got really tense then. It brought back memories of just how vulnerable I felt when I was abused. I got really tearful toward the last of it. I was feeling sad that I was so uptight, and pleased that something was beginning to change with that."

Don't be alarmed if you have similar reactions. It's a sign that something is moving, that some feelings are being freed up. And have fun, too!

Now that you've had some forays into intimacy, I'm sure you realize that not every moment of a relationship will be close and fluid. Even some of these exercises may have aroused disagreement and dissension. Just as with intimacy, as an Adult Child you have not had the kind of training that prepares you to deal with conflict constructively. So on to another critical area: dealing with conflict in your relationship.

CHAPTER 6

CONFLICT

*P*at was flushed as she approached Sean. "Sean, sit down," she demanded. He sat down. "You're going to find out anyway, so I want you to know. I signed up to go back to school."

"You *what*!?"

"I signed up to go back to school," Pat repeated. "You remember I was telling you how I always wanted to be a counselor and help people? Well, now I'm going to do it."

"Oh, great!" Sean groaned. "I suppose that means you're going to be gone at night and I'll have to be here by myself. And what about your job? You can't just quit. We need the money. This sounds like another of those half-baked schemes you're always coming up with."

"That's not fair, Sean." Pat's voice started to rise. "This is important to me. You're always so quick to make me wrong. You never think of anyone else but yourself and you never support what *I* want to do."

"I would, but it's always so half-baked," Sean said. "Knowing you, you'll go for a year and then drop out. You never finish what you start. You put all that money into photography, and now the stuff just sits. You bought a membership in that gym, and you *never* go. And this is going to be just the same. I have half a notion to . . ."

"I do use the camera and I do go to the gym sometimes." Pat's voice began to shake. "And don't threaten me! At least I don't come home every night and sit in front of the TV for hours!"

"Look, damn it! Don't talk to me that way!" Sean stood up, shaking his finger at Pat. "I've had enough of your whining and complaining. How could you ever be a counselor when you can't even make your marriage work?"

"It takes two, you know," Pat yelled as tears came to her eyes. "Maybe the marriage would work if I was married to the right man. Somebody who cared about me and wouldn't put me down all the time."

"Well then, why don't you just go ahead and find Mr. Right?" Sean replied with heavy sarcasm in his voice.

"I could do better," she said. "Right now I'm married to Mr. Rude, to Mr. Lazy, to Mr. Going Nowhere."

"You can leave any time you like! But if you do leave, just don't plan on ever coming back! I can get along fine without you!"

"All right, then, I will!" Pat stomped off into the bedroom, grabbed her purse and keys, and slammed the front door while Sean sat back down and started angrily flipping through a magazine.

And so a variation of a scene that had been repeated several times before is once again played out, with both Pat and Sean feeling hurt and angry and not knowing where to go with these feelings or how to resolve the conflict.

Corinne was upset. She had just come home from a week in Memphis and anticipated making up for lost time with her husband Larry. Instead he was mowing the lawn and talking on the telephone and watching basketball on TV. She felt angry inside and wanted to lash out. Instead, she said, "Larry, I have a problem I'd like to discuss. Is this a good time?"

"The game's over in ten minutes. How 'bout then?"

After extracting a solemn oath from him, Corinne agreed and, 10 minutes later, began. "Larry, I'd like some attention. After all, I've been gone a week."

"You think I'm avoiding you."

"Yeah, I'm feeling neglected. I'd like some cuddling. I'd like us to lie in bed and talk about what we've been doing and do some kissing, like we did when we were new. Is that okay with you?" Corinne asked.

"Heck yeah," Larry said with a shrug. "I'm game if you are." With that, he took her in his arms and kissed her passionately. "Okay," he said with a smile. "You start."

Any time two unique individuals come together as spouses or lovers, they bring with them their own needs, drives, and wants. Sometimes these are compatible and in alignment, and other times they are not. When they are not, conflict occurs. Simply defined, conflict is contention resulting from these opposing needs, drives, or wants. Conflict can be mild, such as when your spouse wants to eat Chinese and you prefer Italian; or major, such as when you want to move to New York because of an exciting new job prospect and your mate wants to stay near her family in Indiana.

Conflict is a part of life even in the best of relationships. One partner wants to buy a big house, the other wants a small one. He wants to take an exotic vacation, she wants to save money. A wife wants to return to school, her husband wants her to keep on working. Conflict can be constructive and creative or destructive and damaging, depending on whether it's handled in a healthy or unhealthy way.

Sean and Pat demonstrated an unhealthy way to manage conflict. They are both very defensive and accusatory. They don't focus on the issue or aim to do any problem-solving, but instead personally attack each other. They show no empathy for each other's feelings, and neither really hears what the other has to say. Issues totally irrelevant to the problem at hand are brought in and used to bludgeon each other. The conflict escalates, threats are made, and they end up "ending" their relationship—for the umpteenth time.

On the other hand, when conflict in a relationship is dealt with in a healthy way, the process itself can lead to increased closeness, appreciation, and understanding. Corinne and Larry are also in a situation where their wants and expectations differ. Yet both are able to express themselves and work things out amiably. Corinne feels angry, but she doesn't let her emotions get the better of her. Instead she focuses on the desired outcome.

In healthy ways of dealing with conflict, the people involved express what they think and feel about the conflict and take constructive steps to resolve their differences. They may not feel comfortable during the conflict—there is usually some tension— but they work through those difficult times and arrive at resolutions that help them both feel good.

This is not what you witnessed in your training ground for conflict—your family.

BACK TO THE FAMILY

Your relationship with your parents and the relationship between your parents were the first models you had of how to handle conflict in close relationships. Your parents handled conflict as children would handle it, only with far more damaging consequences to all concerned. In your family, conflict was played out in extremes. Your family may have responded to conflict with long, agonizing silences. You could feel the tension, but you had to pretend it wasn't there. These tense periods of silence may have been the norm for your family or may have loomed suddenly after some sharp words or after a bout of violence.

Amy describes how this happened in her family: "After my mom and dad would have these knock-down, drag-out fights, my mom would ignore my dad—treat him like he wasn't there. She'd walk in and not say hello, and the rest of the night they wouldn't say a thing. In one sense, it felt good because if they weren't talking, at least they weren't fighting."

Conflict in your family may have meant verbal and/or physical abuse. In that case, you learned to equate anger with violence, with someone getting hurt. The abuse may have been predictable or may have come at unexpected moments. Margaret's family was like this: "Sometimes I'd get excited about something, and I'd forget to turn the light off in my room. My dad would walk up to me and—just like that—slap me across the face. He'd start yelling that I was intentionally trying to waste his money, to spite him, and then he'd hit me some more as he shouted, 'I'm gonna kill you!' "

In another extreme, there may have been a total absence of conflict. You never heard words of anger or hate, but you never heard words of love or compassion either. Your parents seemed to be in a world of their own, and they left you in a world of your own. It wasn't that you had poor modeling for dealing with conflict; you had *no* modeling. You had no way to learn how to deal constructively with conflict. You learned to handle conflict by avoiding it. Your parents denied and repressed their feelings so much that they simply weren't there for you spiritually or emotionally.

Hazel comments: "I thought I came from this perfect family, because no one ever fought. I used to brag about it. From talking with my mother, I realize now just how unhappy she was. She recently told me that she had seriously considered leaving my father when I was ten years old, but at the time I wouldn't have guessed. I always saw her as such a saint—maybe that was part of the problem."

From your family, then, you drew certain conclusions about conflict, some of them accurate, many erroneous. Not only did you carry some of this dysfunctional patterning over into your adult relationships, but since you were never exposed to any constructive ways to resolve differences, you don't see any other options.

ADULT CHILD STRATEGIES
FOR DEALING WITH CONFLICT

As an adult, you still don't know how to handle conflict with your spouse or lover. Anger in you and your mate terrifies your Inner Child, who has had to deal with this her whole life. She's afraid you or your mate will lose control and lash out violently. She panics at the thought that conflict and disagreement may well lead to abandonment, and so you continue to deal with your anger and hurt in the style you perfected in childhood.

The Silent Treatment

One way you and your partner may deal with each other is the silent treatment. Both of you may be boiling with anger, but you pretend to ignore each other. The intent of your silence is to punish your partner; you choose this method because any more direct and overt expressions of anger are too threatening. You passively expect your partner to get the message and feel bad enough to change her behavior.

"Day after day," says Lucy, "my husband would just make his breakfast, dress, and leave. If I tried to talk to him about what I said to his boss, he'd just say 'Yep' or 'Nope.' I thought the whole thing would blow over in a day or two, but it would go for weeks!"

Going Along

You may decide to take another passive route, which is to "get along by going along." Again, anger and confrontation are just too terrifying, so you say nothing. But you go beyond the silent treatment. You do your best to keep things peaceful, doing whatever you can to placate your mate. This may work in the short term, because there is a semblance of peacefulness on the outside, even though there is turmoil on the inside. You present an image to your partner and your friends of a loving, workable relationship and of a thoroughly happy and agreeable mate, but this strategy is fraught with destructive consequences.

The most common of these consequences is that you lose touch with your feelings after a while. You risk getting so involved in denying your anger and other so-called negative emotions that you get totally out of touch with *all* your feelings. When you repress your anger, sorrow, and hurt, you end up repressing your joy, happiness, and love as well. Soon you shut down your feelings for your partner. Living without emotions, as you discovered in childhood, isn't really living at all.

On the other hand, you may express your negative emotions, but indirectly. This is also called passive-aggressive behavior. The objective is to somehow "get" your mate, to somehow make him feel guilty or angry while you profess complete innocence. For instance, you find yourself burning your partner's toast or picking him up late or letting sarcastic remarks slip out. One of my favorite examples was related by a student in one of my seminars. She had done a good job for a long while of acting out the role of the "perfect wife." One day she just "happened" to spill hors d'oeuvres on her husband's boss. She claimed no conscious intent, and her husband railed at her later.

Another consequence of going along with things is that your anger and frustration may build up to the point where you can't contain them anymore and they burst forth loudly. You'll get angry at one situation, such as when your husband picks you up late, but you deny you're upset at all; you hold it in and hold it in. When you get home, you yell at him for not putting some of the dishes in the dishwasher, or you take it out on the children or your pet. This is known as displacing your feelings, or "kicking the dog."

Another problem with going along submissively is that you don't get to live your own life. You put all the responsibility squarely in your partner's lap, and so end up feeling powerless and victimized. It may seem attractive at first to let the other person be the decision-maker, since he gets to be accountable for how things turn out. But you soon find that this dead-end strategy only perpetuates the feelings of victimization you had in your childhood.

Still another common consequence of being submissive is that, although you give up everything in order to be loved, your love doesn't last. Your partner doesn't have a whole person to relate to and loses respect for you. Worse still, you begin losing respect for yourself and the way you have been living your life.

Fighting It Out

The third way you may deal with conflict is by simply fighting it out, with one or both of you yelling, swearing, and bringing up lots of grievances at once. This is the "Virginia Woolf" school of conflict resolution (so called after Edward Albee's play *Who's Afraid of Virginia Woolf?*), in which conflict is never really resolved. It has also been called "kitchen sink" fighting, because everything is thrown in but the kitchen sink (sometimes that is thrown in, too).

"I didn't want to," says Robert, "but when we'd fight, I'd look for the worst things I could think of to get back at her with. I wanted to hurt her bad. I'd drag up all the time and money she once wasted starting a multilevel business. Or I'd tell her she was just as crazy as Samantha, her nutty sister—anything to drag her down, to hurt her."

Unfortunately, this type of approach to dealing with conflicts can lead to physical violence. In relationships where there is spousal abuse, it's common that both partners come from backgrounds where they were abused in some way. As much as you may detest the abuse you endured, until you begin to practice constructive methods of resolving conflict you risk re-creating similar circumstances in your present relationship.

WHY DOES IT HAVE TO BE THIS WAY?
THE CAUSES OF CONFLICT

Whatever style of conflict resolution you find yourself using as an adult—the silent treatment, going along with things, or fighting it out—there are five major underlying causes that perpetuate destructive ways of dealing with conflict.

"I Must Have My Way!"

The number one cause of conflict is a couple's attempts to control each other. At the core of the conflict is the idea that your mate is not doing, acting, or being how you think he "should." Your anger and frustration with him are rooted in this unrealistic, demanding belief. Thus your behavior is aimed at controlling your partner, at getting him to do what you want. At the root of these attempts is your fear of abandonment.

By giving your partner the silent treatment, you're manipulating him into feeling guilty. If he does feel guilty, then you will seem to have control. Going along with things, being passive and submissive, is an attempt to control by avoiding all conflict, hopefully keeping your partner from abandoning you. Fighting it out is a more direct and aggressive attempt at maintaining control by intimidating your partner into giving you your way. All these attempts at control are destined to fail, since you cannot ultimately control another person anyway.

"I was talking to a friend about Frank playing tennis all the time," Marge relates, "and she stunned me by saying, 'Why not let him play all he wants?' I didn't have a comeback for that one. She went on to say very bluntly that she thought I was trying to control him with the way I was always complaining to him about it. At first I didn't like hearing that, but she's right."

"I'm Afraid to Get Angry"

You feel afraid of your anger, and the more you try to repress it the more it escalates. You may use alcohol, drugs, or any other addiction to try control it or to cover up the intensity of your anger, to stop the emotional dam from bursting, but these eventually fall short. There is no such thing as unexpressed anger. It will get expressed somehow.

There's nothing more terrifying to your Inner Child than rage—yours or another person's—so you put a lot of energy into suppressing anger. You're like a steam kettle: when the pressure builds to a certain point, you have to have some way to release it. You may internalize it, in which case it can contribute to physical illness, or you may externalize it. Your anger may be expressed outwardly in some of the ways described, such as displacing it, passive-aggressive behavior, or verbal and/or physical fighting.

Sandra gives an example of how her attempts to suppress her own anger failed: "I'd be so nice when my husband would leave his socks and underwear out. And then when he'd keep me waiting half an hour, I'd be so nice, so calm. And then one day he went to the grocery store and came home without the spices I needed to fix a meal—and wham!—I blew up! Screaming and yelling—I totally lost it. Poor guy, he didn't have a chance."

Like Sandra, you may repress your anger until you can't hold it back anymore and then lash out. Often the fights that result have little to do with the real issues; they are ostensibly about the little things that drove you over the edge. As a result, loved ones may be surprised at the intensity of your reactions and feel hurt and angry. You, in turn, find yourself feeling remorseful, only to return to your more passive, "nice" persona until further tension builds and you have another explosion.

"How Else Can I Act?"

That's a good question, given that you had poor models for how to resolve conflicts. You saw your parents handle their differences by having intense conflicts or by never talking at all about these differences. Until you got to adulthood, you had little or no opportunity to see healthy ways of handling conflict.

"The other day," says Cindy, "my husband asked me about a real estate investment I was working on, and I lashed out at him. I yelled and screamed that he knew nothing about real estate, that I had been in it seven years, and that if it was up to him, our money would be in a bag buried in the backyard. Then it occurred to me—this is exactly how my mom would always treat my dad. If he'd ever question her, she'd yell and scream at him and try to make him look small. At the time I remember thinking, 'Dad's right to ask.' And here I was, twenty years later, acting the same exact way toward my husband!"

"Don't Get Too Close to Me!"

Another thing that may drive you to have frequent and intense conflicts is fear of intimacy. As discussed in chapter 5 on intimacy, we Adult Children have erected all sorts of defenses in the name of avoiding something we don't know much about and are therefore afraid of: closeness and intimacy with another human being. You very much want this closeness with your mate, but getting close makes you feel uncomfortable. It's a reminder of the pain you suffered at the hands of those you used to be closest to, your parents. To get close means you risk being vulnerable to being hurt, to being abandoned.

So you have an approach/avoidance way of relating with your mate. You want to love and be intimate with her, but when you get close your defense mechanisms kick in and you start a fight to restore your distance.

This has been a familiar routine for me. I recall one time in my marriage to Susan when we had spent an evening together and I felt particularly close to her. It was wonderful. The next day I "built a case" against her. My style of fighting was more passive-aggressive, so I didn't come out and tell her directly what was going on. Instead I started thinking of all the negative things I could—she didn't treat our baby daughter in the way I thought she should, she wasn't affectionate enough toward me, she didn't take very good care of the house—so I could generate enough conflict to justify keeping my distance. When she reacted to my distance by getting upset, I could make it *her* problem. It was just too scary for me being so close.

"Things Are Just Too Calm"

Because conflict and tension are so familiar to you, you may be addicted to crisis. Your body has become accustomed to the periodic surge of adrenaline, so in its absence you unconsciously set about looking for ways to create that surge. While you don't exactly "enjoy" the tension and pain of conflict, the feelings you experience when things are tense are familiar, and vaguely comforting in their familiarity. The adrenaline that flows is like a drug to which you become habituated. When everything is calm and peaceful, you automatically assume that something will go wrong, that some crisis is immi-. nent. How many times have you said to yourself, "Things are just too peaceful around here. Something's bound to go wrong soon." This is the declaration of crisis addiction! When things are going relatively easy, you set about to stir the pot and look for something to become upset about. If nothing is wrong, you may go ahead and create a crisis.

As an Adult Child, this may be the only time you experience emotional intensity, as your feelings are flattened out and not easily aroused much of the time. It's as if it takes a shock to your system for you to feel something, and conflict will certainly arouse more intense feelings. Also, pain may equal love for you, as you saw fighting and loving linked in your family.

As Carol puts it, "I don't know why it is, but my husband and I are probably the closest after one of our huge fights. We get into our routines and don't have much to say to each other for a long time, and then something gives and we have a fight. I don't like the fighting part, but I sure do like the making up afterward!"

Now that you have some ideas about your style of dealing with conflict and some of the causes for this style, let's move to skills that your parents never taught you—skills that can help you and your partner use conflict as a creative tool for improving your relationship.

SOLUTIONS: WE CAN WORK IT OUT

Because you've had poor modeling and little or no exposure to using conflict to constructively problem-solve, the following section will give you and your mate some ideas and skills to use when you're in conflict. The tools here must be practiced to work, and ideally they should be practiced with your mate. It takes two to create conflict, so it will take two to resolve it. If conflict is a major part of your relationship, I strongly encourage you to seek professional counseling as well.

These skills and ideas will give you different ways to view conflict, as well as practical steps to take to encourage more creative problem-solving.

For the first step, we'll explore certain attitudes that can fuel the fire of conflict, and some alternate ways of thinking that can potentially lessen the tension.

Changing Your Self-Talk

We all talk to ourselves. Sometimes we say things aloud, but much of what we say is in the form of thoughts. When conflict arises with your partner, listen to what you are saying to yourself. You're probably saying things like, "Gosh, I hope he doesn't blow up," or "Oh no, and things were going so well!" or "Now I'm really gonna let him have it!" This self-talk shapes how you approach the problems in your life and how you feel about those problems. Much of your present self-talk is the result of what was generated in your childhood, at a time when you made conclusions and decisions about yourself and about life that were in black-and-white, absolute terms.

If you are willing to pay close attention to what you say to yourself and to specifically rethink some of these outmoded attitudes about conflict, you can develop a much more positive and functional attitude toward it.

The following are some myths about conflict you may be telling yourself. When you change your self-talk and actively start telling yourself the truth, you won't make yourself nearly as upset. Conflict will be far easier to deal with and less likely to escalate to the point where it causes a lot of pain and damage.

Myth: Conflict and anger mean violence.
Truth: While conflict and anger mean tension and
discomfort, they are temporary and need not lead to violence.
In your childhood this myth may unfortunately have been true. Mom and Dad's fights may have led to violence, or you yourself may have been the victim of violence. This has led you to be supersensitive to anger and conflict and eager to avoid any trace of them.

But anger and conflict with your partner need not mean violence. As an adult you are not under your parents' control, and you can learn healthy ways to work out any conflict in the relationship. There is inevitably some tension associated with conflict, and you will no doubt feel uncomfortable. But this, too, shall pass, and you can remind yourself that this discomfort is only temporary. Further, you can learn to protect yourself by learning how to establish and defend boundaries (see chapter 4).

Myth: Conflict isn't part of healthy relationships.
Truth: Conflict is a part of every
relationship; the key is how you work with it.
Conflict is inevitable in all relationships. There never has been and never will be a relationship without conflict. Where two people are involved, there will be differences of desires: one wants to spend money freely, the other wants to

save for the future; one loves the country, the other prefers the city; one wants to watch "Roseanne," the other prefers an old movie.

This myth comes from comparing your family with idealized versions. The Ward and June Cleavers of the world exist only in fantasyland, but witnessing these models inevitably sets you up to fall short of meeting these standards in your adult relationships. To try to prevent or circumvent conflict only creates more tension or distance.

Conflict is not only inevitable, it can be healthy. Sharing your feelings with your mate and working constructively with the inevitable differences in needs, drives, and wants are good for the relationship and can lead to real understanding and better solutions.

Myth: When there is conflict, one of us has to be right, the other wrong.
Truth: There is no right or wrong, only differing points of view.

This polarized, dualistic thinking of right and wrong simply is not true. There is a common belief that someone has to be right. For to be right, the other person must be wrong. This type of righteousness is at the core of arguments and fights. It's not only what feeds arguments in a relationship—this myth is what starts wars.

Instead, consider that most of what you believe is simply a point of view. If you thought the movie was good and your mate thought it wasn't, it doesn't mean either of you was right or wrong, but instead that you had differing points of view. Why try to ram your point of view down your partner's throat in the name of righteousness?

Try this exercise and see if it doesn't illustrate how you handle your own righteousness with your partner.

> EXERCISE: Stand facing your partner and take each other's right hand, holding your right arms clasped as if you were about to arm wrestle. Then, push down on your partner's hand while saying out loud, "I'm right!" while your partner resists your push. Next, your partner pushes against your hand and says "I'm right!" while you resist. Alternate several times, being sure neither of you pushes so hard you hurt your partner. Pause and share your experience. Then, do the same process, this time saying, "My point of view." Note your experience and share it with your partner afterward.

Doug tried this with his wife and observes, "I felt a lot more committed to the fight when I was saying 'I'm right!' Saying 'My point of view' made it obvious that mine was just one of many, and maybe not even the best."

Another version of this myth is, "It's got to be someone's fault." The truth is that it takes two to have a conflict, and the more you take responsibility for your contribution rather than believing you're being right and blaming your partner, the more smoothly you will discover ways to work out the conflict.

*Myth: There must be an immediate
and perfect solution to every problem.
Truth: Conflict resolution takes time and
often there is no "right" solution—only workable ones.*
When you operate as though this myth is true, you are setting yourself up for a lot of frustration and anguish. As an Adult Child you find yourself approaching conflict in an all-or-nothing fashion. Your search for the perfect solution inevitably ends in defeat as there is no perfect anything in the world. At the same time, the time and energy you spend in your search deprive you of the chance to find other potentially workable solutions. Conflict resolution takes time. Often, to try to come up with an immediate solution only breeds bitterness and resentment.

Unless it's a rare emergency where an immediate solution is called for, you can take your time and think about possible solutions with your partner. When you allow yourself the time to work through the conflict and keep yourself open to other potentially workable solutions rather than looking for the "right" one, you won't get frustrated as easily.

Problem-Solving

The greatest educator of his time, John Dewey, formulated a process that you and your partner can use to resolve problems. As adapted by Dr. Thomas Gordon, the founder of Parent Effectiveness Training, these steps are:

1. Define your problem in terms of needs.
2. Brainstorm possible solutions.
3. Select the best solution or solutions.
4. Decide how to carry out the plan.
5. Carry out the plan.
6. Evaluate your progress periodically.

1. Define your problem in terms of needs.
Needs are your general requirements in a given situation. Solutions are the specific ways you and others hope to satisfy those needs. Suppose, for example,

that you and your mate see a movie every Friday evening. You want to see *Black Rain*, while your partner wants to see *Teenage Mutant Ninja Turtles*. Each of you dislikes the other's choice, and at first it seems as though only one of you will have your way; win/lose outcomes are typical when you define your problems in terms of solutions. When you examine the problem in terms of needs instead, it becomes obvious that what you and your partner really want is entertainment, not merely those particular movies. You clearly agree on this, though you haven't agreed on specifics.

When you look at the problem this way, a world of other options opens up—other movies, plays, TV shows, and videos that both of you would find entertaining. Additionally, you both might find entertainment by going for a drive, visiting friends or relatives, or taking in a lecture. Literally hundreds of options for meeting your need for entertainment come to mind when you define your problem in terms of *needs* instead of solutions.

Peg reports this experience: "Glenn and I had endless fights—it seemed like we were *always* fighting. There just didn't seem to be any solution in sight. We discovered that almost all our fights were about solutions and that they almost always followed the same pattern: One of us would take a stand ('We're getting rid of our old car and buying a new one.'). Then the other one would take an opposing stand ('No, we can't afford one.'). And then, from those opposing stands, we would fight it out. It was almost like we were two knights fighting over territory. When, instead of stating our solutions, we shared our needs ('I need a car I know will start when I turn the key'), we were able to have fabulous discussions about how to satisfy those needs instead of vicious fights over who would get their way."

Peg and Glenn's case is not unique. Many couples find that most of their fights result from their thinking in terms of solutions rather than needs.

> EXERCISE: Define your problems in terms of needs. Take a problem that is currently troubling you. Begin by writing down the solution or solutions you have been thinking of implementing. Then, ask yourself, "What need or needs would this solution fill?" The answers you write down are the answers you require in defining your problem in terms of needs.

Randi tried this exercise in the following way: "Elliot and I were house hunting, and each of us fell in love with a different house. His was twice as big and reminded him of the big old house he grew up in. We fought and fought over which house to bid on. Then, when we thought in terms of needs, the answer became clear. Yes, we needed housing, but we also had other needs, like food and an occasional vacation, which were not going to be met if all our money was going for the mortgage on the house he wanted."

Judy's experience was particularly interesting: "My case was kind of weird. I had decided to divorce my husband. That was my solution. But when I asked myself the needs I wanted to fulfill, it came down to that I wanted to go out more and have more fun, and he's always busy working. We went to a marriage counselor and she helped us schedule dates just like my husband schedules business appointments. And now that my needs are being pretty well met, I've found that those bad thoughts about him and my desire to get away and try again with someone else have evaporated. I'm really pretty happy."

> EXERCISE: Practice defining other people's problems in terms of needs. The next time someone tells you she plans to take action in some area of her life that affects you, ask her, "Why are you going to do that? What needs of yours will that action fulfill?" This will give you practice in identifying needs, practice that will help you in working out solutions that meet both her needs and yours. Next, use active listening to draw her out still further, as in the following example.
>
> *Greg*: You say you want us to move to the country. Why do you want to do that?
> *Patty*: I think it's easier for us to make friends in the country. We don't have any real friends here.
> *Greg*: You'd like us to have more friends, that's a need you feel.
> *Patty*: Yes, when I grew up in the country, we had all sorts of friends, and I'd like us to have that.
> *Greg*: You want us to have the same sociable atmosphere you had when you were little.
>
> Through his questioning, Greg defines Patty's problem as a need for more friends, not for a move to the country. This opens up a wide variety of possibilities that would not have been available had they simply stuck with discussing the solution of moving to the country.

If Pat and Sean, whose story began this chapter, had defined their problems in terms of needs rather than solutions, they would have been better able to work out an amicable solution. Pat might have found that her need was not for enrolling in school, or even for becoming a counselor, but rather for working with and helping people. Sean might have found that his need was not for having Pat keep her job, but rather to be able to afford to maintain his lifestyle and make the mortgage payments. Going through this step would have opened up new possibilities for them to accommodate each other's needs and wants. We will explore these possibilities as we go through the remaining five steps.

2. Brainstorm possible solutions.

Once you have defined your problem in terms of needs, it's time to brainstorm possible solutions. Brainstorming means coming up with as many solutions as you can think of. The key to making it work is to voice your suggestions as they pop into your mind, without pausing to censor them, and to write them all down without anyone criticizing them. By all means, come up with crazy solutions, the crazier the better, and build on each other's suggestions.

Greg and Patty, who were featured in the example above, were new to the city, having transferred from Abilene, Texas. After six months they still didn't have any close friends to have fun with. "We're surrounded by people," Patty said, "but we're isolated almost as if we lived alone on an island." Their need, then, was for more friends. In my office, the three of us brainstormed and came up with the following suggestions:

- Have a huge barbecue and pass out flyers inviting all the neighbors.
- Have several barbecues and invite the neighbors over in small groups.
- Invite the Ransons over for lunch.
- Join the church couples group.
- Take out a personals ad in the newspaper seeking the friendship of another couple.
- Start a couples club.
- Go to a PTA meeting and see what couples look interesting.
- Go to Chamber of Commerce mixers.
- Take a walk every day around the neighborhood and talk to people.
- Take the time to get to know their children's friends' parents.
- Join a film club.
- Instead of heading for the parking lot after church, stick around and meet people on the patio.
- Wear smile buttons.
- Smile more and take more time in daily life to make contacts.
- Spend more time with the next-door neighbors.
- Drive around town asking people, "Will you be my friend?"

- Accept loneliness as inevitable in modern society.
- Pay someone to be a friend.
- Join the Sierra Club or a bicycle club.

When Greg and Patty got rolling with their brainstorming, they discovered they had dozens of alternatives. Many were frivolous, but almost all were preferable to doing nothing and enduring the present situation.

EXERCISE: Think of a recent situation in which you and your mate were having a conflict. Perhaps it was over what color to paint the kitchen, which preschool to send your three-year-old to, where to go for an evening's entertainment, or where to move to. Next, write out as clearly and simply as possible a statement of the conflict.

For instance, Alex wrote: "Madeline and I disagree about where to take our vacation. She wants to visit her parents in Minneapolis, and I want to go to Maui." Madeline wrote out her version: "I want to go home and spend some time with my parents, while Alex wants us to relax on Maui. I kind of want that as well."

Compare what you have written to see where you and your partner agree about the needs of the situation. In Alex and Madeline's case, they agreed that they needed to get away from the pressure of their everyday life and needed to relax.

Next, brainstorm 5 to 10 possible solutions that would fill both of your needs. Alex and Madeline wrote the following:

- Go to Maui.
- Go to Minneapolis.
- Spend three days in Maui and four in Minneapolis.
- Go to Minneapolis this vacation, then go to Maui the next.
- Go to Maui this vacation, then go to Minneapolis the next.
- Invite Madeline's parents for a visit for Christmas.
- Go someplace closer to save money.
- Take a cruise.
- Stay home and take one- or two-day excursions.
- Rent a room at the beach for a week.

Open up your mind to ordinary solutions—and to crazy, off-the-wall solutions. The more possible solutions you have, the greater the likelihood that one of them will work for both of you.

3. Select the best solution or solutions.

The next step is for each of you individually to look at the list and pick out the solution or solutions that best meet the needs of both of you. Be sure to give due consideration to any "wild and crazy" suggestions. Then share your selections, paying especially close attention to those that are on both of your lists. Decide together on one or more of the proposals.

Once you have made your choices, decide to put your energy into making them succeed. Don't bother worrying if you made the right choices—if they don't work, you can always drop them and work on new ones.

Patty and Greg were delighted to see that most of the ideas they came up with looked like they would do the job. So as not to be overwhelmed, they decided to focus on the following solutions: Inviting the Ransons over for lunch; joining the church couples group; taking a walk every day around the neighborhood and talking to people; and joining the Sierra Club and making friends there.

> EXERCISE: Look over your list of possible solutions from the previous exercise. Agree on one or two with your partner.

Alex and Madeline agreed that they would go to Maui and invite her parents to visit them sometime during the winter. Madeline discovered that much of her longing to go to Minnesota was out of a sense of duty and obligation, and that above all else she wanted to be with Alex in a relaxing setting.

4. Decide how to carry out the plan.

Deciding on your solution is a major step, one that most people never reach. But, like so many New Year's resolutions, merely deciding on a solution is not enough to ensure its completion. You and your partner need to lay out plans for how you will realize your solution. You need to decide who will do what and by what date. Do this and you will find yourself solidly oriented toward the achievement of your solution. You will be able to tell when you are getting closer to meeting your solution, when you need more time, and when you need to put out more effort.

You can set plans in several ways for realizing your solution. One is to set a goal and pick a date and time by which it will be achieved. Patty and Greg decided that by 9 o'clock that evening they would invite the Ransons over for lunch Saturday. Having been so specific, if 9 o'clock rolled around without their having made the call, they would know that they had in fact failed to meet their goal. They could then immediately make the call or could set a new time for making it. Either way, by getting specific they were orienting themselves toward making progress and enabling themselves to monitor their progress. Compare this with what would likely happen if their goal was merely to get together with the Ransons "soon."

Another way to set goals, useful for achieving complex or long-term goals, is to set step-by-step objectives. If, for example, your goal were to be able to retire in 20 years and live off your savings, you might set various goals for getting educated about investments and saving and investing money.

A third way to set goals is to establish ongoing goals for doing certain things periodically. Patty and Greg decided to establish a goal of attending the church couples group each week. Every other day, they decided, they would take a walk around the neighborhood and talk to the people they saw. And every time there was a Sierra Club social event, they would attend.

No matter which way you choose to implement your plans, decide on one or more dates when you will evaluate your progress and decide what more needs to be done.

> EXERCISE: The next step is to decide how you will implement the plan. Write out as specifically as possible the times and dates when you will accomplish your goals.

Alex and Madeline decided that by 9 P.M. the next night they would call Madeline's parents and invite them to visit. Alex agreed to call the travel agent on Friday to find out about some package deals to Maui. Madeline agreed that by Friday she would talk to a friend of hers who was born and raised in Maui to see if he could offer any suggestions. They further agreed to discuss their options over dinner Saturday night. They not only decided on a plan, they both got a dinner date out of it!

5. Carry out the plan.

If you take all the other steps in this program and don't do this one, your efforts won't mean a thing. This step is really the one that counts. It is only by taking real action in the real world that you can ever make progress. Despite this, lots of people define the problem, brainstorm possible solutions, select the best solution, decide how to carry out the plan—and then do nothing. Do not be one of them. If you are serious about making progress, you must take this step. If the action does not achieve the desired result, so be it. You can try some other action. But it is vital that you make efforts on your own behalf if things are to improve in your life and your relationship.

6. Evaluate your progress periodically.

On the date chosen in step 4 and periodically thereafter, pause to evaluate your progress toward meeting your goals. If your goals are being met, pause to congratulate each other and decide what more you might do. If they are not being met, take time to think about why and what you might do differently.

A month after their initial meeting, Patty and Greg paused to talk about their progress. They had met three couples they liked at the church couples group and one couple at a Sierra Club meeting. On one of their walks they had gotten to know a couple they had briefly met earlier. They had invited each of these couples over once, and one of the couples had visited twice. In turn, two of the couples had invited them over, and they had enjoyed both visits. Both were delighted by the progress they had made in one short month, but Greg voiced the opinion that socializing was taking up far more of his time than he could comfortably give. "Honestly," said Greg, "I enjoy the friends, but we're doing it so much, this is beginning to feel like a job." They decided for the next month to issue or accept invitations for weekends only. A month from that date, they decided to have another follow-up meeting.

Talking It Out

If the world were perfect, each time you and your partner had a problem you would calmly sit down and go through Dewey's six-step process for problem-solving. In the real world, however, you and your partner will sometimes want to talk out your problems in a less formal way. To keep the process from breaking down into old dysfunctional behaviors, you still need some structure. Here are some steps for talking out your problems.

1. Ask for time.
2. Relate your problem.
3. Make sure your mate understands.
4. Give feedback.
5. Listen.
6. Repeat steps 2 through 5 as long as the process appears to be worthwhile.

1. Ask for time.

Tell your partner, "I have a problem I'd like to discuss," and ask if this is a good time. Doing this is important, as the other person may be too tired to talk or may be preoccupied with other matters.

Gene describes his experience: "I had just turned on 'America's Funniest Home Videos,' and Alison walked in and blurted out, 'We have to talk.' 'Later, later,' I said, shooing her away as I watched this baby spit out her birthday candles. Alison stalked over to the TV and shut it off! 'I need to talk to you!' she said. I started yelling."

According to Beverly Hershfield, a noted San Diego therapist specializing in the problems of couples, Gene's situation is common. "I frequently hear from men and women who come home from work wanting nothing more than to kick off their shoes, look at the mail, and read the paper—while their mates insist on bringing up some problem right then and there. If they would just wait ten minutes or half an hour, they'd probably save themselves half the fights they have. And further, they'd often find their partner quite willing to talk."

So ask if it's a good time to talk. If it is, begin. If it's not, ask, "When would be a good time?" and make a specific appointment to talk about the situation.

2. Relate your problem.
Be sure to tell why it is a problem for you and how you feel about it. Use "I" statements rather than "you" statements. For example, instead of saying, "You never take me out to dinner," say, "I'd like to go to dinner." Statements that begin with "you" tend to sound accusatory.

3. Make sure your mate understands.
Ask your mate to use active listening (see Intimacy, chapter 5) so you'll know your message got through. If the other person doesn't know the skill, say, "Will you please tell me what you think I said?"

4. Give feedback.
Let the other person know if the message was accurately received. If it wasn't, clarify it and repeat steps 3 and 4 until you are confident that the other person got it right.

5. Listen.
The other person gets a turn to speak, expressing her views and feelings, while you use active listening until she is satisfied that you got her message.

6. Repeat steps 2 through 5 as long as the process appears to be worthwhile.
The following is a fairly typical example of two people using the steps outlined above.

Al came home. Maggie wanted to talk with him right away, but she waited until half an hour after dinner. "I have a problem I'd like to discuss with you," she said.

"Okay, let's hear it," Al replied.

"And just so we can be sure we understand each other, let's use active listening."

"Fine by me."

"Al, you and I talked about our going to Bali this summer, and you said you'd make the arrangements. And here it is mid-April, and I'm upset because I haven't heard a word about tickets or hotels or anything."

"So you think I'm hoping you'll forget the whole thing."

"No, that's not it," said Maggie. "I'm worried that you're so busy, you'll put off making vacation plans until the last minute. I'm really excited about our going to Bali and I'd be upset if I didn't get to go. Now can you tell me what you think I said?"

"You're looking forward to Bali, but you're worried that I'm going to mess up and wait so long that we won't be able to go or won't get good rooms."

"Right. Now tell me what's going on with you, while I tell you what I hear you say."

"I've been so snowed under at work," Al said, "that I haven't had time to even *think* about Bali. But I wrote into my schedule to make reservations this week."

"You've just been so overloaded at work you haven't had time," Maggie responded. "But you're going to make time this week."

"That's right," Al said. "What's more, I asked my boss today if we could have ten days instead of a week for our trip—and he said yes!"

"We're getting three extra days for our holiday!" Maggie exclaimed.

"Right," Al replied. "Won't that be wonderful?!"

Sandy used this skill with her husband. "It feels weird at first—but *it really works*! My husband was going to lend someone ten thousand dollars and I was going crazy. But when we sat down and used this skill, we didn't fight or yell, we just worked on achieving an understanding. It turned out my husband had checked out the guy and had good security backing the loan. Talking about it made me feel a whole lot better about the loan—and my husband."

When You Do Fight: Ten Rules for Fair Fighting

Every now and then, you and your mate will get into a fight. You won't feel like problem-solving, you won't feel like using the talk-it-out format—you'll just want to let the other person have it! Such fights, with charges and swear words and grievances flying every which way, can inflict deep damage on your relationship. Arnie, one of my clients, recalls: "During a fight with my now-ex, she told me she thought I looked ridiculous, that my thin little body was a turn-off and my little bald spot was a joke. Even after we made up, that made me really withdraw from her and finally led to my totally withdrawing from her."

Another client, Andrea, described how deeply hurt she had been by her husband's tirade one night after he had been drinking: "He called me fat and stupid. He said I'd been going downhill for years, letting myself go. And he said he'd never thought I was very bright and ran down a whole list of mistakes I'd made. I never quite forgave him for that."

Words can and do hurt. Remarks made during the heat of fights often inflict serious and lasting damage on relationships. Therefore it is important that the two of you agree on some ground rules for fighting, boundaries that will protect you both during conflict. *Do so before they are needed, and put them in writing*. Use the 10 rules below or make up your own, but do it now and write them down. That way, when you need them the rules will be in place to serve as guidelines. The following, then, are suggested rules. Feel free to modify them and add to them to suit your needs.

Rule # 1: STOP the fight before it gets out of hand.
Rule # 2: No hitting, yelling, or swearing.
Rule # 3: Don't make interpretations.
Rule # 4: Don't threaten to leave.
Rule # 5: No gunnysacking (see explanation below).
Rule # 6: Be specific about your problem.
Rule # 7: Express your feelings.
Rule # 8: Listen, listen, listen!
Rule # 9: Compromise when possible.
Rule # 10: Speak up if any of the rules above aren't followed.

Rule # 1: STOP the fight before it gets out of hand.

Call a time-out if tension is mounting and the conflict is getting out of hand. A time-out is when, at an agreed-upon signal, you *stop* for at least 20 to 30 minutes, and you both go to your "corners"—whether you go to separate rooms or one of you takes a walk. The idea is to physically separate for a while. Either of you can declare the time-out. Then, it's up to the one who called the time-out to initiate a discussion by following the talk-it-out format. Be willing to continue the time-out overnight if necessary, but be sure to initiate your discussion within 24 to 48 hours of the time-out at the latest.

Another option is to halt the fight in its tracks by stopping and going through the talk-it-out format. Andrea, for example, surprised herself by halting a fight in its tracks: "Josh and I were beginning a 'discussion' which I knew was going to turn into a huge fight about whether to send our child to private school. Tensions were mounting, and I was getting ready to explode. I wanted to call him cheap and to throw in lots of other ways he's cheap. And he would have no doubt countered by saying I waste money and am driving him to the poorhouse—his favorite expression. Well, I decided instead to do something different. I took a deep breath. 'Josh,' I said, 'instead of one of our usual fights, why don't we try the talk-it-out format we heard about.' Well, we did it! It was terrific, because instead of getting angry and screaming and fighting, we both calmed down and got a good understanding of each other, and we came up with a solution we're both pretty happy with."

Rule # 2: No hitting, yelling, or swearing.

This is sometimes a difficult rule to follow, given your upbringing and the modeling your parents gave you. Gail reports, "I got married to get away from all the abuse. And the way we were carrying on, it was just as tense at home as it had been in my childhood. When our marriage counselor got us to agree to no more hitting, scratching, and yelling, at first it was hard for us to say anything at all. An eerie silence would descend on us. But then we began to talk about our feelings and our disappointments, and that's when we began to work our marriage out."

Rule # 3: Don't make interpretations.

People often become angry when you not only tell them what they did that you don't like ("You didn't talk to my brother all evening") but go on to say *why* they did it ("You deliberately snubbed my brother!"). Allan was late picking his wife up at the spa. "As soon as she got into the car, she let me have it. 'You're deliberately late,' she said. 'You hate my working out because it takes time from you.' The truth is, I was late because I got tied up at the office. But that began a stupid, unnecessary fight."

Rule # 4: Don't threaten to leave.

Threatening divorce or separation is easy in the heat of a fight, but it is a controlling tactic that is highly destructive to the relationship. It taps into you and your partner's basic fears about abandonment. Don remembers being "floored the first time my wife said that if I was going to be this way, she was going to leave. We were having a fight about I don't even know what, and all of a sudden, boom! It's like you're having a water fight and someone brings out a real live hand grenade. I had never even thought of leaving before. I promised to marry her and love her forever, and that was my intention. But when she brought it up, that's the first time I ever thought about what life would be like without her. And then she'd threaten it again and again and, I think that's one reason we finally did call it quits."

Rule # 5: No gunnysacking.

Gunnysacking is bringing up 2 or 5 or 10 complaints at the same time. Your mate stays out late but you say nothing; you just deposit the gripe in a little sack. He insults your mother, and you put that in the sack. He forgets to bring home milk, and you put that in the sack. Then he forgets to fill up the car with gas, and you take out the whole sack and dump it over his head! This is gunnysacking, and it is highly destructive to a relationship. Your mate, besieged by what appears to be indictment after indictment, will not likely respond to your many objections. He will probably either take off or counterattack.

Instead of gunnysacking, bring up your problems as they occur, one at a time. Ralph relates the following experience with his live-in lover: "When we used to fight, Jean would bring up every darn thing she could think of. The subject might be my forgetting to pick her up on time, but she'd be getting on me for buying a car that always breaks down, for getting fired, for being late to work, for looking at girls who pass by. With so many charges, how could I possibly respond? 'Execute me!' I shouted so everyone could hear. 'Kill me! I deserve to die!' Nowadays we laugh at that. We've decided to just handle our problems one at a time. It works a lot better, though it's sure quieter around here."

Rule # 6: Be specific about your problem.

General complaints like "You don't love me anymore" or "You're not being nice to me" won't help you get what you want. Rather, be specific about just what did or didn't happen: "You haven't brought me flowers in five months." "You haven't told me you love me since my birthday." One time Matt's wife, Myra, said to him, "That was rude of you." Says Matt, "I didn't have a clue as to what I had done, and she wouldn't tell me! Only after all sorts of questions did she let me know that I kept her waiting longer than she would have liked while I was talking on the phone."

Rule # 7: Express your feelings.

It's important for you to let your partner know not only what you *think* but also how you *feel*. Charlotte reports her experience: "I was upset that Dan had failed to plan for our weekend. He hadn't made reservations or anything. I found that before getting to the solution part, the 'What do we do now?' part, I needed the release that comes from at least telling him how mad I felt."

One caution: Be careful that you don't use your feelings to manipulate. As we discussed in chapter 3 on control, Adult Children have learned to use their helplessness or anger in order to manipulate others. Although this may work in the short term, ultimately it leads others to feel resentful and angry toward you. Better to express honest feelings and to ask others for what you want but to give up trying to control them with your feelings.

Rule # 8: Listen, listen, listen!

Give your partner every opportunity to speak fully. Use active listening as much as possible to encourage him to speak. Says Marsha, "When Sam would interrupt me, he'd probably be thinking he was winning our fights. But all it ever did was make me madder and more determined to have my say and get my way. Now that we hear each other out, I feel better, and I'd say I'm less interested in winning than in working things out."

Rule # 9: Compromise when possible.

A good way to do this, once again, is by focusing on *needs* rather than solutions. Says Donna, "One time one of our cars broke down and we fought over who would get the other one. When we thought about it, all we wanted was *transportation*, not the car. So we worked out schedules, who would drive who where and all that, and it worked out pretty well."

Rule # 10: Speak up if any of the rules above aren't followed.

If you don't speak up about violations, these rules will soon be forgotten. Each of you should have your own copy, and keep a copy posted in plain view. Sandy and Kevin, for example, found it useful to keep the rules on the bedroom door: "We took the rules and some of the problem-solving skills, changed them a bit to suit ourselves, and posted them. That way, when we have a problem, we can easily look them up and see what we agreed to do. And when somebody breaks a rule, we can point that out easily. It's worked well for us."

> EXERCISE: Think of the most recent argument or disagreement you have had with your partner. Look over the list of the 10 fair-fighting rules and see which ones you and your partner violated. If it's appropriate and safe to do so, discuss the conflict with your partner and talk about how you would handle it now. Do so only if there is no longer a great deal of tension around that particular issue.

Tim and Mindy tried this. Tim reports, "Five out of ten isn't too bad, I suppose! We went over Mindy's complaint that I spend too much money. We decided that she did some gunnysacking, she wasn't specific, and was yelling. I didn't take a time-out before I got really mad, and I made a lot of interpretations, telling her why she was really upset and all. Oh, yeah, I guess there was a sixth one—neither of us stopped to listen. Playing by the rules isn't a piece of cake, but it's sure nice to have some rules to play by. Never did before. I think we can make it work!"

You now have some ground rules for fighting and some tested ideas for working through your conflicts. My best advice at this point is to be extremely patient with yourself and your partner. Like Tim, you never had any rules to play by before. It will take considerable attention, willingness, and a whole lot of love to work with these guidelines and make them an integral part of your relationship. But it is possible to do so, and by doing so you can discover how conflict can be both creative and constructive for you and your partner and for the relationship.

In the next chapter we will explore commitment, an idea that strikes fear and trembling—or at least caution and consideration—in the hearts of men and women everywhere. Everything else we've covered—emotions, control, boundaries, intimacy, and conflict—will be valuable as we consider how commitment can secure and empower your relationship.

CHAPTER 7

COMMITMENT

*P*atrick met Karen through a dating service. You couldn't have designed a better match. They both liked long walks at sunset, folk and soft rock music, quiet evenings at home, and travel. They were both nonsmokers, detested violence of any kind, and thought of themselves as spiritual but not religious. Both enjoyed their work and considered a career to be high on their list of priorities. Either one would be considered a "good catch."

They dated six months before Karen started noticing the change. "At first, Patrick was very attentive. He called at least three times every week, always listened closely to me, brought me flowers, and was always a gentleman. After a while we started spending most of our weekends together. Then he started to change. He got more distant, withdrawn. I thought at first it was just a mood—you know, another side to him or something. But it kept going on. When I asked him if anything was wrong, he totally denied there was a problem. He stopped holding my hand in public, stopped saying he loved me, and when we'd talk he seemed like he was in a different world most of the time. By the time he called me and told me he had to stop seeing me, it was no surprise. I was really upset, because this relationship had had so much promise. I keep wondering if it was something I had done or said—maybe I pressed him too soon for a commitment, I don't know—but he had acted as if he wanted a steady girlfriend."

From Patrick's point of view: "She wasn't perfect or anything, but I liked her a lot. I don't know what it is, or what it was. The more involved we got, the more nervous I got. I started noticing things about her that I didn't like. Her hips were too big, she smiled too much, she wasn't aggressive enough in bed. It all sounds too familiar. My therapist told me that I just couldn't handle someone who was good to me. I think he was right. I think I set about sabotaging the relationship, but I didn't know how to stop myself. Now I wish I had her back, but I'm afraid I really blew it—again!"

Jan was packing a lunch, Nick and Michelle were getting their bikes out, while Tony helped their son Robin pump up a tire on his bike in preparation for their bike ride. "Looks like you're getting big enough for a new bicycle soon, Robin," Tony said with a smile as he steadied Robin's bike. Tony watched as his eight-year-old showed considerable finesse in hooking the tire pump up to the tire valve and then set about using the hand pump. Tony reflected back on the day Robin had been born. He and Jan had gone through a rough pregnancy together. For the last two months Jan had had to stay in bed most of the time. Then they almost didn't make it to the hospital. But the labor went well, and even though he had also participated in the births of his first two children, Tony remembered how awesome it felt when he saw his third child coming into the world.

Tony reflected further on the 15 years he and Jan had been together, married 13 of them. "She's a tough woman," he thought. "How hard I had to fight to keep her." For example, there was the time just before they got married when she wanted to call the wedding off. In his opinion she had been listening too much to one of her friends. He knew at the time she was just scared. That's why he showed up at her door, guitar in hand, and sang his rendition of "Let Me Call You Sweetheart" and Jackson Browne's "I Thought I Was a Child." He smiled inwardly as he recalled how she had first cried, then laughed, then invited him in for tea. The wedding took place as planned.

His thoughts turned to the time he had decided he'd had enough with his computer business and had impulsively called it quits. Boy, was she angry! It almost split them apart. He didn't work for almost a year, and they thoroughly gouged their savings. Jan went back to work, and Tony stayed home with the children. They came close to losing their house but were able to pull through somehow. Even though that was one of the roughest times, it was also a time when they shared some incredibly happy moments.

"Dad! Dad!" Tony came out of his reverie. "I got the tire pumped up! All by myself!"

"So you did. Good job, Robin!" Tony gave him a hand hug on the back of his shoulder.

About that time Jan came out with the daypack full of their lunches. "Where are Nick and Michelle? Are they ready yet?"

"They're getting their bikes. They'll be here any minute."

"Well, good, because we should've left a half hour ago." Jan handed Tony the daypack. "Is my bike in the garage?"

"Yeah. I'll get it for you," Tony said. "But first . . ." He set down the daypack and took Jan by the hand. "Come here. I want to give you a hug." Tony embraced Jan very slowly. Jan gradually relaxed and put her arms around him. "I just want you to know I really appreciate you and I really love you."

"Oh, Tony," Jan whispered, "I love you, too."

In many ways this was the hardest chapter for me to write (it was hard to get committed to writing about commitment!). When I talked to my editor, I would jokingly refer to this as "the 'C' word chapter." After all, I'd been through two marriages and a couple of long-term relationships that I'd broken off largely out of unconscious fears of intimacy and commitment. My last intense relationship ended painfully about three years ago, and in retrospect I can see how starkly addicted I was in my unacknowledged co-dependency. I was engulfing and she was abandoning, which was a switch, since I was usually the abandoning partner. For the last three years I've been extremely careful about getting involved in any type of committed relationship. So who am I to be writing about commitment?

Frankly, I don't think there are any experts on commitment, and I don't think anyone has the "right" answer to this question, including myself. But I do think, having "been through the wars" and having counseled hundreds of couples as a marriage counselor, that I've clarified considerably what commitment in a relationship is all about. I've learned how, like many other Adult Children, I tend to run when things get sticky. I see how unconscious I have been in the past about my commitments, and how isolation, although unsatisfying and lonely, has been my first choice when togetherness became uncomfortable.

Most important, I'm beginning to understand that the key is *balance*, rather than approaching commitments or anything in life in an all-or-nothing fashion. Specifically with regard to commitment, there is a balance between blindly running from making or keeping a commitment and just as blindly making a commitment impulsively or keeping one that is destructive for both parties involved. The more consciously I make and keep my commitments, the more I'm able to keep my commitment to balance in my life.

A commitment is when you make a promise to give yourself—your time, energy, and attention—to something you value. Your commitment is what you stand for. It's inextricably interwoven with how you think, how you act, and how you feel. Your commitments are at the top of your list of priorities. They can be to your work, your health, your recovery, your spirituality—or to your relationship. While you may have apprehensions and fears about making and keeping a commitment, particularly to a relationship, doing so provides a structure that can potentially embrace those apprehensions and fears.

In Patrick and Karen's situation described above, it's clear that Patrick had some fear and apprehension about his commitment in his budding relationship with Karen. In the earliest stages of the relationship, he acted like a man interested in commitment. Then something changed, and by his own admission, Patrick "set about sabotaging the relationship." Perhaps he has a deep fear of intimacy and closeness, perhaps a fear of being smothered or trapped. Robert Bly, a poet and author of *Men and the Wound*, has suggested that men who go from one woman to the next, never staying long enough to make any kind of commitment, be dubbed "flying boys." Perhaps it's a modified version of the saying, "When the going gets tough, Adult Children leave." Whatever the nature of Patrick's underlying fears, it's clear that he is having trouble with commitment.

Tony and Jan, on the other hand, have obviously endured a great deal in their relationship. What has made them stay together through their hardships and their victories? It certainly isn't just their love for each other. It is their commitment to the relationship and their family. As described, it hasn't always been easy—they've weathered some distinct rough spots. Over the 15 years they've been together, each of them has seriously questioned their commitment on a few occasions, yet they made a choice each time to stay with it in spite of the hardships. Their willingness to sustain their commitment has given a structure to their relationship in which their love and respect for each other have deepened tremendously over the years.

Besides their commitment, other important elements have provided sustenance for their relationship: love and respect for each other, honoring each other's boundaries, the willingness to risk being intimate, and their love for their children, to name a few. But when these factors wax and wane, as they inevitably do in any relationship, their commitment sustains their togetherness. In short, their commitment is constructive rather than destructive. Their commitment is alive and conscious rather than lifeless and reflexive.

'TIL DEATH DO US PART: FAMILY TIES

The kind of commitment you witnessed as a child has made you think of commitment as something constrictive and damaging, something to be feared and avoided, or something that is downright confusing. Your parents' marriage may have been an example of a commitment that was lifeless and reflexive—

lifeless because there was little vitality; reflexive because they stayed together out of habit or routine more than out of conscious choice. Because of their own co-dependency, your parents looked to each other to make themselves feel whole and complete. One or both may have been actively addicted to drugs, alcohol, or some other substance or process. Yes, they did make a commitment to marriage, and yes, they did keep their commitment. But did the path they committed to have heart? Perhaps not. More than likely, they stayed together because that's what married couples were supposed to do.

"I knew they weren't at all happy," Frank says. "They didn't ever talk much, and I never once saw them hug or kiss. I think my dad had affairs throughout the marriage, though I'm not sure. My mom seemed to find some comfort in eating, because she was really overweight. I don't ever remember her even smiling—she always looked glum. They acted like zombies most of the time. Yes, they stayed together, but there sure wasn't much happiness at home."

In your parents' day, divorce was considered sinful and to be avoided at all costs. An unquestioned moral or societal authority stated that marriage was for life. The marriage may have been empty or chaotic and abusive, yet because of social and religious pressures, husbands and wives stayed together. They did so not out of a conscious commitment, not out of a promise generated from within themselves, but out of an obligation, a blind obedience to an external authority—the church or the community.

Strictly following the marriage vows "'til death do us part" seemed to sanction the notion that anything that happened, short of murder, was part of the deal. For most people it was. The patriarchy that had been dominant for hundreds of years still considered a wife and children to be part of the man's property, and he could pretty much do whatever he wanted with them. A wife often stayed with an abusive husband for economic reasons or for the sake of the children.

Rachel watched her mother get beaten one time after her father went on a drunk: "I took my little brother Jonny and started to go into our room, but my dad yelled at me to 'sit there and watch what happens to your bitch of a mother' as he then proceeded to hit her with his fists. We sat shivering in the corner, terrified he was going to kill her and that he would do the same to us, but instead afterward he just took off—probably to go drink some more. After he left, I practically screamed at my mom, 'Why don't you just leave him?' You know what she said? She said she was staying with him for our sake. For our sake! Believe me, it couldn't have been any worse if she had left him."

Other experiences as you were growing up gave you poor models for commitment. Perhaps, like Frank in the example above, your parents were in a rather empty, affectionless commitment, or one or both were having affairs.

Perhaps you were caught up in a divorce that itself was fraught with concerns and fears. Or maybe you grew up witnessing a relationship characterized by tension, fighting, and insecurity.

My parents have been together all of my life. My mother had been married once before and brought three children into the marriage with my dad, then they had me. Even though I remember some times that were pleasant, I recall a lot of chaos and uncertainty. With the drinking, the fights, the threats, and confusion, the conclusion I came up with was that marriage was a miserable proposition. I vacillated between thinking that I'd never get married, or that if I did it would be much better than their relationship. Two marriages later, I realized that I had carried my confusion about commitment in a relationship into my adult life.

GROWING UP UNCERTAIN: COMMITMENT AS AN ADULT

For much of my adult life, I never really understood what making and keeping a commitment meant. Even though there was a part of me that was afraid of getting married, I did so—twice. My need to be attached was greater than any fears or considerations about being in a committed relationship. It wasn't a big problem to make a commitment (or pledge) to be married, but what I didn't anticipate was how being married would bring up all my fears. Because of those fears, I found ways to run from my commitment, from staying with my vows.

My first wife, Beth, who was also uncomfortable with closeness and intimacy, agreed to an "open" marriage when I suggested it as a way to manage our discomfort. With the kind of stifling commitment we had both witnessed in our families, it's no surprise that each of us looked for a way out. The open marriage was an interesting experiment, but it didn't bring us any closer. It certainly didn't help us deal with the more fundamental issues each of us had brought into the marriage. For both of us, it was a way of running from intimacy and commitment. I've already related how quickly and easily we agreed to a divorce. We didn't give much thought to the possibility that we could repair what was broken—we just ran.

In my second marriage, to Susan, I still had little knowledge or awareness of what commitment meant. Yes, I agreed to "love, honor, and cherish," but I didn't understand what those words really meant. Operating within the commitment of marriage meant I had to be real and honest, but my big fear was that if I was real and honest, then she'd see the me I didn't like and would leave. My way of dealing with this was to present to her my ideal self, the self I thought she would love and accept, and hide all the blemishes. Because she too was an Adult Child, I think she looked for me to be ideal as well. I also think her sweet smile masked a lot of unresolved and unacknowledged anger.

The more we hid from each other, the more distant we became. I looked to other women to provide the kind of comfort that was missing for me in the relationship, but the guilt over doing so only thickened the barriers. One summer what had been boiling inside each of us for four years erupted in a series of heated arguments. Things got very tense. We made a halfhearted attempt at some marriage counseling but didn't get to the core of the problem. As the tension crescendoed, one night the word "divorce" came into the conversation, and we agreed to do so—just like that. We lived together for another two months, then moved out of our house and proceeded with the divorce. It was one of the most painful, gut-wrenching experiences I've ever been through, partly because in addition to the pain of the divorce, the feelings that had been lying dormant since childhood were erupting to the surface. Again, I took the only route I knew as an Adult Child—when the commitment wasn't working, I ran.

Coming out of the environment you did, you also no doubt felt uncertain about a lot of things—yourself, other people, how life worked, what "normal" really was—and most especially about what commitment in a relationship was all about. For most Adult Children, this is a confusing issue.

Many Adult Children get involved in relationships in which commitment is based on addiction and co-dependency. If you were raised in an alcoholic family or in a family where any other addiction was dominant, your training prepared you for a co-dependent attachment in your adult relationship. The flowering of co-dependency often shows itself up as a relationship addiction. Rather than making a conscious choice to be in the relationship, your co-dependency shows as a pattern of addictive attachment and self-denial, an unhealthy commitment to an unhealthy relationship.

Sharon typifies this pattern. "I've been married to Merv for twenty-two years, and I'm beginning to see how much he is just like my father. At my first Al-Anon meeting, one woman was talking about her marriage to an alcoholic. She talked about how she sacrificed her own needs most of her life, how the drinking controlled the both of them. That could have been me talking! I'm looking at my husband in a whole new light now. I'm not sure what I'm going to do, but one thing's for sure: things will never be the same after that meeting."

Commitment as an All-or-Nothing Deal

Whatever the particular configuration in your family, as an Adult Child you tend to approach commitments in an all-or-nothing fashion. You find yourself either taking a very rigid approach to commitment, sticking with it come hell or high water, or fearing it so much that you avoid commitments altogether or sabotage them when you do make them. Either way can be a trap.

The potential trap in rigidly sticking to a commitment to a relationship is the risk that you will stick with it beyond the point of common sense. For instance, if your partner consistently breaks promises or agreements, or if you are continually being abused and all the intervention you've tried hasn't changed that fact, it makes sense to seriously reevaluate whether to stay in the relationship. Tammy Wynette's song, "Stand By Your Man," comes to mind as an example of our culture's influence on the mentality that assumes you should stick it out no matter what. How ludicrous! I think there are times in a relationship where you *must* re-evaluate your commitment and consider the alternative of ending it.

Georgia was two years into the relationship with Desmond when she decided to call it quits. "I thought long and hard about doing this. He kept telling me he wasn't interested in a commitment beyond our dating and sleeping together, and I went along with it because I really cared for the guy. Plus I've found out you just can't push men into commitments. He wasn't mean to me or anything, he just wasn't ready for what I wanted. I can't blame him or make him wrong for that, but I want someone who wants just me. I finally told him that it just wasn't going to work and I had to stop seeing him. He called a lot, and we tried being lovers one other time, but it didn't work. I have to stay with this decision."

The fear of making a commitment can also be a trap. In this instance you are trapped by your own fear. As long as you are run by your fear of making a commitment, you don't really have a choice either. You are still reacting to what you witnessed as a child. Even your body may give away the overwhelming threat you feel when you are confronted with the opportunity of getting into a committed relationship.

"After I had been dating Trina for a few months, things started getting more serious," Walt says. "Once when we were out for dinner, the conversation turned to marriage and children. Trina made the comment that she thought she and I would make a great husband and wife. I didn't know what to say. I actually broke into a sweat! It makes me think of that Steve Martin movie, *All of Me*, when his girlfriend told him she didn't think he could even say the 'M' word. Rising to the challenge, he gave it a noble try but all he could get out was

'M-M-M-M-M.' Anyway, Trina and I are still dating, but I'm just not sure where I want to go with it."

And there Walt remains—uncertain and ambivalent, aware of his fear yet still trapped by it. It will be useful now to identify some of the fears that lie behind this wariness of commitment.

What's So Scary About Commitment?

Behind the sweaty palms and labored breathing are more specific fears that haunt you as an Adult Child. The most common fears include the following.

Fear of intimacy.
We've already seen how frightening it is for most Adult Children to be close to another human being. To be intimate implies that you are vulnerable, real, and honest, and risk rejection or abandonment. For a commitment to have some life, this kind of risk is required, yet this goes against the grain of your experience in childhood that taught you to protect yourself at all costs. It rarely occurs to you that you can work with most of these fears *and* be in a committed relationship.

Walt continues with his description: "I've been realizing that being close to Trina—or anyone, for that matter—scares the hell out of me. I do like her a lot. She's real good to me, so I know it's not her. Last night we went out to dinner and she pointed out that I don't look directly at her as much. When we were in bed the other night, I got real nervous about spending the night. I kept thinking of all these things I had to do the next morning, but I didn't say anything and instead just had a lousy night's sleep. It just seems that the more we are together the less comfortable I feel. I'd almost prefer one-night stands to this—but those don't work anymore, either."

Fear of being trapped.
Perhaps for you the prospect of commitment means a tremendous burden and obligation that you will be stuck with forever and ever, from which there will be no way out. Without a clear sense of your own boundaries, you may picture yourself as being totally consumed by the relationship. In fact you may have had this sort of experience, so you are gun-shy about risking another one. If this is your biggest fear, you may set up all sorts of defenses against commitment: you avoid relationships altogether, you bail out just when you start feeling close, or you get involved with people who are passive and meek, who will not represent a threat to your leaving the relationship.

Joan, an attractive woman in her 30s who has never been married, describes how this fear has operated in her life: "I've gone through men like water. With the exception of one relationship that lasted three years, most haven't lasted more than three or four months. I seem to either get involved with these guys who want to put me in a box or else guys who want me to take care of them. Either way it's a losing deal. I'd rather stay single all my life than be trapped in a dead-end relationship."

Fear of losing control.

Living with another person over a period of time means that inevitably you will have to make some compromises. You won't always have your way or be able to do whatever you want. In a committed relationship you will usually have to take into account another person's needs and wants before deciding on a course of action. As an Adult Child, being in control is high on your list of priorities, so the thought of making any compromises can be intimidating. Perhaps in a past relationship you did give up control to another person, so now you hold onto control like a prized chalice. Naturally you will pause before jumping into a commitment.

"I spent seventeen years in a marriage that was like a prison," relates Dorothy. "He was my master and ruler, and I was his servant. I had an okay job, but no say in where his—and my—money went. I looked to his approval on everything. He decided what I wore, where we went—everything. I stayed for the sake of the kids, and it reminded me of my mother and father. He ran her life just like my husband ran mine. I've been divorced for seven years now, and I've met a wonderful man who wants to marry me, but I'm just plain scared that this will repeat itself all over again."

Fear of being hurt.

You can imagine being hurt in many ways by making a commitment, but they all relate to the fundamental fear of being abused or abandoned. It bears repeating that for you, closeness and commitment at one time meant abuse and/or abandonment. You don't really expect that a mate could be good to you. Your Inner Child expects to be mistreated in some way, so all your defenses are geared toward avoiding that mistreatment. An unspoken fear that goes along with this fear of being physically or emotionally hurt is the fear that if you got into a committed relationship, your mate would leave you, just as you were abandoned in childhood.

"Seems like whenever I really like someone," Charles confided, "I start picking them apart in my mind. I met this woman recently, and I really like her and she seems to like me. I see a lot of potential for a relationship with her, though I know it's too soon to tell. But I have these nagging thoughts about what's wrong with her—she's too young, she's probably a really angry person, she's never been married. *Something* must be wrong with her—especially if she likes me. I think I'm just afraid that if I got really involved then she might leave me. The kid inside is really scared about being abandoned again."

You may identify with some or all of these fears that stand in the way of making commitments. In addition to issues about *making* a commitment, there are issues about keeping that commitment. One issue in particular is related to our society's emphasis on immediate gratification. This societal emphasis tends to reinforce your tendency as an Adult Child to run whenever you're frustrated or disillusioned.

Throw-Away Commitments

It's easy to indict "society" and blame it for a lot of our ills. Rather than an indictment, however, this is an observation of the way things are in our society in general and how this relates to the difficulties many people, specifically Adult Children, have in keeping a commitment in a relationship.

Our immediate-gratification, make-me-happy society supports "throwaway commitments." Everything is designed for disposal. Use it, then throw it away. Many of our products come in "convenience size" packages, and every year new products are introduced, such as shavers and even cameras, which are designed to be used once, then tossed into the growing garbage heap of consumer refuse. There is undeniable evidence that this garbage heap has reached critical mass, and we are drowning in it. Mother Nature is crying out for us to treat her with greater dignity, love, and respect.

Our society is geared for immediate gratification. "I want what I want, and I want it now" is the cry that is heeded by corporate America in catering to the consumer's low frustration tolerance. Thus we have fast-food restaurants, "3's a crowd" signs in supermarkets, and instant credit. If you have ever mounted up bills on your credit cards or, like a friend of mine, borrowed from your VISA to pay your MasterCard, you have a taste of how addicted you can become to the immediate gratification of every whim or want.

This emphasis on rampant consumerism and immediate gratification further supports the illusion that it's possible to be happy all the time and that the responsibility for individual happiness rests outside the individual. We tend to look outside ourselves for something to make us happy, and on occasion we do find temporary things, achievements, or people that seem to fit the bill. But typically these are short lived, and we then go about our search for the next item that will seem to fill the deep void that will *never* be filled from the outside. As someone once said, happiness is an inside job.

For you as an Adult Child, these societal influences support your already entrenched tendency to run from a commitment when things get difficult. You tend to figure that if this relationship doesn't work, well, maybe the next one will be better. This attitude, coupled with all-or-nothing thinking, leads you to see no alternatives other than either sticking with it "'til death do us part" or bailing out when things are rough.

SOLUTIONS: MAKING COMMITMENTS THAT WORK

In spite of habitual attitudes you may carry about commitment, you can make commitments that are workable and can get better and better at conscientiously keeping your commitments without being blindly rigid about doing so. This section will differ somewhat from the format of the solutions sections of the other chapters; specific exercises for you and your partner to do will be at a minimum. The relationship itself *is* your exercise on commitment. All the areas that you've worked on so far culminate here. I've outlined some ideas to spark dialogue between you and your partner. I encourage you to discuss all of the issues that are triggered by the material in this section.

The more consciously you make your commitment and the more conscientiously you maintain it, as long as it's alive for you, the more successful you will be at your relationship. Your steady willingness to work within that relationship and to keep the promises you make will demonstrate this commitment.

Commitment = Freedom

Making and keeping commitments can actually be a freeing rather than constricting experience. Without a willingness to make commitments, you risk bouncing around in life without a clear direction. Sometimes a lack of direction is mistaken for personal freedom.

Being committed helps you bind and focus your energies, thus freeing you up to generate accomplishments in your work and closeness and intimacy in your personal life. I have a good friend, Kenneth, who was more or less drifting in his love life and to some extent in his career. He had a lot of talents but was somewhat unfocused in applying them. He had many of the common Adult Child fears of intimacy and commitment and tended to drift from relationship to relationship without ever seriously committing. At age 35, having grown tired of the dating scene, he met a wonderful, loving woman who also had a very practical business finesse. He liked her a lot but struggled for a while over whether to commit. Finally he decided to pursue a committed relationship with her. He told me, "I might do different, but I won't do better." In the three years they've been together, two of them married, he has been much more focused with his work and has experienced considerable financial success. He seems to be genuinely more loving and affectionate, not only with his wife and new son, but with his friends. His harsher side has softened considerably. Once in a while he complains to me about their conflicts or their differences, but he always qualifies this with his commitment to love her in spite of these rough times. His commitment has freed him up to experience greater love and affection and has contributed substantially to his sharper focus in his career.

What Do You Value?

Since commitment is a promise to give yourself to something you value, it's useful to consider what it is you value and to which values you're willing to give your promise. This is especially true when promising something to another person in a relationship. Committing to these values is the first step; taking action on that promise is the ongoing challenge in the relationship.

Some examples of values that many couples believe in when it comes to relationships:

Love	Cooperation
Honesty	Spirituality
Trust	Communication
Keeping your word	Sexual intimacy
Monogamy	Personal recovery
Affection	Separate time
Play	Raising children

This is certainly not an exhaustive list, but one that will serve as a trigger for the following exercise.

> EXERCISE: Looking over the above list with your partner, brainstorm any additional values that you feel you incorporate in your relationship or you would like to incorporate. When you've come up with a complete list, make a copy for each of you, and each of you rank the values in order of most important to least important. This is not intended as a way to see who's "right" about any particular values, but to see what's important to each of you with regard to the

values you are willing to commit to in your relationship. Share your lists with each other and use them as a basis for discussing your commitment.

Take each item and talk about how you can more specifically express this value in your relationship. For instance, if you both agree that communication is important, how can you enhance this in your relationship? Perhaps you could set aside 20 minutes every day to talk with each other. If spirituality is important, you might agree to go to church weekly or to read to each other out of some spiritual works three times a week.

After Dean and Stephanie did this exercise, Dean reported these discoveries: "This really brought out a lot to talk about—we're still talking although we did this two weeks ago. I was surprised that we both had put 'play' near the top of our lists, because we haven't been doing much of that lately—we've been so busy, wrapped up in our projects and all. So we agreed to do something in the way of play at least two times each week, one of those times being the weekend. Last weekend we rented some roller skates—we had a ball!"

Commitment Is the Container

The commitment is the container for the relationship. It describes the agreed-upon boundaries of the relationship and provides a structure for all the other changes and processes that take place in a relationship. As a house contains the furnishings within, a commitment contains the values that you agree to, the promises that you make based on those values.

Within the structure of that commitment, you have room to deal with your wants, needs, and feelings. The commitment both includes and transcends the two individuals' needs, wants, and feelings. It doesn't have to enmesh them, nor do they always have to coincide—the commitment makes room for the two people involved *and* for the relationship.

Unlike your parents, you have the opportunity to make a conscious choice about your commitment. While your parents may have made the conscious decision to get married, they probably lived out their commitment in a lifeless and reflexive way. As an Adult Child you may be tempted to go into a commitment impulsively, to leave it just as impulsively, or to avoid commitment altogether, but you need not be run by any of these patterned behaviors.

As you work with your commitments more consciously, you'll realize that there are only three ways to deal with any commitment: keep it, renegotiate it, or break it. If you never make commitments, you can skip this section. One certain advantage of never making commitments is that you never have to worry about keeping them or breaking them. When you do make a commitment, no matter what form the commitment takes, consider these three ways to follow up.

Keep a commitment.

Rather than approach any commitment in a haphazard way, it's better to treat each one carefully and considerately, to approach making it—and especially, keeping it—with your eyes wide open and your conscious mind in gear. If I could suggest a general guideline, it would be: *Never make a commitment you don't intend to keep*. This includes a pledge as seemingly innocuous as "I'll call you tomorrow." When you keep your promises, you generate trust and a sense of safety. Others know where you stand and what you stand for. Following this guideline will help you become increasingly conscientious about making and keeping commitments and will prompt you to value your own word more highly.

When it comes to a relationship commitment, this is even more true. When you make a commitment, it becomes the container for everything else in the relationship. As that commitment endures over time, the partners share an increased sense of security and durability. If the commitment is clear and is not constantly tested or threatened, greater trust and safety are generated over time. Trusting that your partner won't run away helps you through all the ups and downs. Being assured that the relationship is strong enough to withstand the rough spots makes it easier to be vulnerable with each other and creates the opportunity to explore intimacy in greater depth.

Some friends of mine, Ed and Maggie, have been married more than six years and seem to have a workable, committed relationship. Maggie comments: "It's hard to describe. It's a different way of feeling love—not always passionate and exciting, but there are times when the intensity goes beyond anything I've ever imagined. I totally trust Ed—to be exactly the person he says he is. I suppose during sex is when it's most obvious. We're willing to explore all sorts of nooks and crannies—not just physically, but emotionally and, I would say, spiritually as well. I can honestly say it's never been better."

Renegotiating a commitment.

When you enter into long-range commitments in a relationship, you can count on the fact there will be changes in you and your partner and, in turn, the relationship. Some of these changes may be quite welcome, others may be fraught with conflict. There may be long periods when you and your partner are confronted with serious challenges that shake the foundation of your commitment. A good general guideline is to stay with your commitment if at all possible and if doing so is not harmful.

You may find that certain changes in your partner or the relationship are difficult to adjust to. Your mate or lover may develop new behaviors that are unacceptable to you, or you may no longer be able to accept habits that seemed acceptable when you entered into the commitment. Your husband's drinking may have become intolerable, or you may not have noticed how emotionally abusive and hurtful your wife could be. It's not a question of getting your partner to change; that enters into the realm of manipulation and control. Nor does this mean running away the first time your partner acts in an unacceptable way. You need to work within the parameters of the relationship (the container) and renegotiate the specifics of your commitment. You did *not* commit to being emotionally or physically abused, or to having a partner who isn't totally in the relationship. To renegotiate requires you to ask for what you want, clarify your boundaries, and outline your contingencies (see chapter 4 on boundaries) so that you can communicate where you stand. It will require your patience and persistence; constructive changes will take time. It's been my observation that for deeper, significant change to take place in an individual or in a relationship, an absolute minimum of two years is needed.

After eight years of marriage, Wendy decided she had had enough of her husband's silence and distance. "I talked with a friend from my ACoA [Adult Children of Alcoholics] group, and she gave me the name of a good marriage counselor. I told Mike that I wasn't willing to live like this anymore and that I wanted to see a marriage counselor. I had already made an appointment, and I told him that if he wouldn't go, I would keep the appointment for myself because I had to do something about it. He didn't go for the first two appointments, but after that second appointment he asked me what I had talked about with the counselor. I was very blunt and told him we talked about whether I should stay in the marriage. After some bickering he agreed to go. We've been twice now, and so far it seems to be helping."

Another creative way to renegotiate your commitment is along the lines of what my friends Rob and Chris did. When they neared their tenth wedding anniversary, they decided to get married again. They wrote the ceremony, invited all their friends and family, and included their two children in the rite. Everyone there was deeply touched by this ritual act of Rob and Chris recommitting to their marriage. The wedding vows reflected an even greater depth of meaning as to what they were committing themselves to, and all at the wedding were moved as the pair tenderly spoke these vows to each other.

Breaking a commitment.

You've done your very best to honor your commitment, have made several attempts to renegotiate it, and these have failed. The next option you have is to break your commitment.

Commitments are usually broken either as an act of fear or as an act of courage. If the commitment is broken out of fear, it's usually because of one or more of the fears described earlier in this chapter and it's usually broken impulsively, without much planning or forethought. On the other hand, if a commitment to a relationship is broken out of courage, it's because one of two situations exists.

In the first instance, you decide to break your commitment because you are being physically, sexually, or emotionally abused or, as in Wendy's situation, your mate is there physically but not in any other way. You've attempted some intervention and renegotiation, you've set boundaries and contingencies, but the abuse continues. Or you've tried to reach your mate in a number of different ways but there is continually—habitually—no response.

Emotional abuse in a relationship may not seem to be grounds for renegotiating or breaking a commitment. Many people do not accept that it *is* abuse. On the surface it doesn't seem as destructive or dramatic as physical or sexual abuse, and it leaves no scars. I think it can be just as destructive, only the wounds are invisible. Words can and do hurt; if you were emotionally abused in your childhood you know how much they hurt. To stay in an environment that is emotionally abusive wreaks havoc with your self-esteem. I'm not talking about an occasional fight or a few angry, harsh words—nearly everyone will have that happen even in a committed relationship. I'm talking about steady and systematic emotional abuse. This is where your partner continually demeans you, puts you down, calls you names, and generally uses you for a verbal punching bag. If renegotiating your commitment doesn't eventually halt the emotional abuse, it may be time to consider breaking the commitment.

"Norma was a sewer mouth," Barry says, "and she could say the most mean and spiteful things. For the first year or two I'd just sort of put up with it—I guess I thought I deserved it or something—but finally I got fed up with it. One time I up and slapped her face, and that scared me a lot. I didn't want to hurt her and I told her so. I started telling her that I didn't want her to talk to me that way, and she'd cool it for a while, then it would start in again. She refused to go to counseling. I finally left her after about another year."

A second instance in which a commitment can be broken out of courage rather than fear is when you and your partner's needs and directions in life have diverged to the point where the structure of the relationship can no longer accommodate them. This case requires a lot of soul-searching; if you identify with this type of situation, I recommend that you and your partner get into some counseling. If your partner won't go, then go yourself. Again, a commitment to a relationship should not be taken lightly—there was a reason you got into your relationship in the first place. If and when these avenues exhaust any hope of compromise or reconciliation, it's time to accept the reality of the situation: you and your partner have grown apart in ways that cannot be reconciled. There's no need to blame your partner or yourself. The best you can do is to forgive yourself and move on.

Dan and Cory had lived together for three years, and both claimed that other than their one major predicament, they were basically happy with the relationship. The problem was that Cory wanted to be married and have children, and at age 36, her biological clock kept ticking. Dan was adamant on both counts. He didn't want to be married, and he definitely didn't want children. They had talked it over time and again, with no clear resolution or compromise. Cory was faced with the dilemma of giving up her lifelong dream to have children, or leaving Dan. "This was the hardest decision in my life," she says. "I really loved Dan—I still do, but I really want to have a shot at having a child, and Dan was really clear about it—he doesn't want any part of it. I told him of my decision to leave, and we talked and cried together, then I moved out. I still see him, but it's not the same. I know I'll always love him, and maybe someday he'll change his mind. But I just can't wait around until he does. It's just a really sad situation."

It's a reality that some committed relationships are temporary. In one sense, none are permanent—they will all be over someday, whether through death or by choice, through separation, divorce, annulment, or an amicable parting. The end of the relationship may come after two years or after fifty.

It's also true that not every relationship you enter into is somehow destined to be a commitment. You're not obliged to make a commitment if the relationship is not substantial or if you're simply not ready. To date someone doesn't mean you have to marry him, nor do you have to feel obligated to commit just because the other person wants a commitment. There can be wonderful friendships that are mutually beneficial without requiring a specific commitment. To enter into a commitment is an individual decision that requires some consideration of its "fitness" for you and for your prospective partner.

If you do decide to commit, it's useful to explore some of the qualities present in a relationship that makes the commitment work.

What Makes a Commitment Work?

Through my own personal experience, my 15 years doing marriage and relationship counseling, and some serious conversations with close friends who are in committed relationships, I have discovered that the following characteristics, or core values, help to a make a commitment work.

Trust
A healthy sense of self
Personal responsibility
Commitment to love

One note of caution: This is not a recipe for an ideal relationship—there's no such thing. It's better to think of a workable relationship or a "good enough" relationship. Nor do you have to "have it all together" before you can enter into a relationship. You can consistently work on developing these qualities even while you are in a relationship. If you're not in a committed relationship, you can practice most of these values to some extent in other friendships.

Trust.

The most essential ingredient in commitment is trust. As an Adult Child, you may have problems developing trust because of the inconsistency and unpredictability in your family. Trust in a committed relationship centers around two components: *emotional safety* and *keeping your agreements*.

Caryl S. Avery addresses this well in "How Do You Build Intimacy in an Age of Divorce?" (*Psychology Today*, May 1989): "Although trust in a partner means different things to different people—dependability, loyalty, honesty, fidelity—its essence is emotional safety. Trust enables you to put your deepest feelings and fears in the palm of your partner's hand, knowing they will be handled with care. While feelings of love or sexual excitement may wax and wane over time, ideally, trust is a constant." So, trust comes from a sense of emotional safety, and emotional safety comes from your partner being there for you with *reasonable* consistency.

The other building block for trust is so simple yet so profound in its implications: keeping your agreements. I referred to this earlier, but it bears reiterating. The automatic consequence of keeping your agreements, of doing what you say you're going to do, is trust. The automatic consequence of breaking your agreements is lack of trust. The more consistently you keep your agreements, the more your partner will trust you. When you consistently break your agreements, your partner learns not to trust you. When you promise to be there for your partner, and you live up to this and provide emotional safety by not putting down, abusing, criticizing, or avoiding, then over time a deep sense of trust in the relationship will develop quite naturally.

A healthy sense of self.

Before you can have a healthy relationship, it helps for both parties to have a sense of their own individuality, their own personhood. As an Adult Child you carry the illusion that somehow a relationship is going to make you feel whole. That fantasy will make you continue to look outside yourself, to your partner and to the relationship, to make you feel like a real person. This is a sign of unhealthy co-dependency. We tend to look at a relationship as an entity unto itself, neglecting to note that two people compose the relationship. The traditional notion is that $1 + 1 = 1$; a more realistic formula would be $1 + 1 = 3$— you, your partner, and the relationship.

The greatest gift you can bring to the relationship is the unique person you are—your joys, sorrows, creativity, personal growth, and love. These will always be primarily generated by you—not your partner, not the relationship, but you. If you're not in a relationship now, it's a great opportunity to focus on developing a sense of self. This is a matter of personal exploration and discovery, with the emphasis on getting to know yourself intimately. It also allows you to clarify what commitment means to you.

These past three years for me have been a chance to break my relationship and sexual addictions. I see how I have used these as ways to numb myself from relating intimately and from finding out who I am. It feels as if a lot of these addictive habits have gradually peeled away like so many layers of old skin, to where I feel an intact sense of who I am.

Through this process I've clarified my priorities with regard to commitment. First and foremost I am committed to my Higher Power. A sign above my desk continually reminds me of this primary commitment: "My sole purpose every moment I live and breath is to worship God in innocence and with humility." Next my commitment is to love—to love my friends and neighbors, love myself, and love life. Perhaps these are truly one and the same commitment.

If you are in a relationship and you're struggling with "finding yourself," don't blame your partner for keeping you from doing so. You must take some risks and initiative and give yourself two or three years, and possibly more, of exploration. Get involved in a recovery program, such as Co-dependents Anonymous. Talk with your partner, keep her posted about what's going on with you. If you've been selfless for most of your relationship, you may need to go through a period of selfishness to balance the scales. It is possible to do this in the context of your commitment.

Jackie has been married for 38 years. She and her husband, Mervyn, have raised four children. She came to counseling three years ago with complaints about her husband's lethargy and inactivity, his unwillingness to take risks and try new things. Frequently when one partner complains about something in the other, it may say more about the complaining partner than the one being accused. Jackie soon discovered that while, yes, Mervyn was rather inactive, her complaints were more about her own inactivity. "As I started to realize that, I started thinking more about what I can do with my life. I started going to Al-Anon meetings, and that got me started. After three years, I'm still going to meetings, volunteer my time at the local hospital, take tennis lessons, and have been taking classes in real estate at the local community college. I'm feeling better and better about myself. I'm still not sure what to do about my marriage, but I've decided to stop trying to fix it, or to fix Mervyn, and learn to take care of myself."

Personal responsibility.

Correlated with a healthy sense of self is the willingness to assume personal responsibility for your commitment and for your role in the relationship. This means recognizing that it's not up to your partner to make you happy, and it's not your responsibility to make your partner happy. While your partner certainly influences you and vice versa, he is not the cause of your misery or your happiness. You are in the driver's seat, even when you are in a relationship. This does not imply that you shouldn't care, and certainly doesn't rule out sensitivity, empathy, and compassion. It does mean that you are not your partner's caretaker, nor is he yours. The more you are able to assume full responsibility for yourself in your relationship, the less likely you will be to blame your partner. This becomes a bedrock for your commitment.

A traditional way to think about responsibility in a relationship is that each partner assumes 50 percent. However, I would suggest that each partner can assume 100 percent responsibility for himself or herself in the relationship. Not only does $1 + 1 = 3$, but 100 percent $+$ 100 percent $=$ 200 percent. Putting this notion of total personal responsibility into practice in your relationship takes you farther from any remaining feelings of victimization that were so familiar in childhood.

Following is an exercise borrowed with permission from an excellent book for couples, *Lifemates: The Love Fitness Program for a Lasting Relationship*, by Harold Bloomfield, M.D., and Sirah Vetesse, Ph.D. The exercise can help you and your partner assess to what degree you accept personal responsibility for your own happiness and well-being in your relationship.

EXERCISE:
Read each of the 33 statements as if you were speaking to your partner. If you are not presently in a relationship, read them as they apply to your most recent committed relationship.

Next to each statement, write the number that most accurately applies.

3 = rarely
2 = sometimes
1 = often
0 = always

1. I struggle to be more of an individual person in our relationship. _____
2. I try to guess what you need and feel frustrated when I am wrong. _____
3. I expect you to know what I want and to give it to me without asking. _____
4. I feel guilty saying no to your requests for fear of making you unhappy. _____
5. When I want something from you, I feel hurt when you say no. _____
6. I don't feel happy unless you are happy also. _____
7. I feel I cannot live without you. _____
8. I feel guilty if you are not sexually satisfied. _____
9. I feel used rather than loved and appreciated. _____
10. I feel pressured to change my thoughts, feelings, or behaviors. _____
11. I feel as if you complain or nag about my failure to make you happy. _____
12. I tend to blame you when I'm not feeling good about myself. _____
13. I tend to blame you when things go wrong. _____
14. I regret giving up professional career goals for our relationship. _____
15. I place responsibility for my life's happiness on you. _____
16. I hold myself back from expressing my full abilities, competence, and intelligence. _____
17. I find myself playing the role of Prince Charming or Cinderella, trying to rescue you and make you feel happy. _____
18. I feel our love for each other can solve all problems. _____
19. I don't need friends; I need you. _____

20. I don't need family; I need you.   _____
21. I feel I have to be strong and responsible so you won't
    feel scared or disappointed.   _____
22. If you are not happy, I feel guilty.   _____
23. I feel if you don't need me, you won't want to be
    with me.   _____
24. If I make myself happy, I'm afraid of being
    considered selfish.   _____
25. I fear you will outgrow our relationship and
    leave me.   _____
26. I have to give up my desires in order to make
    you happy.   _____
27. I feel that I need to protect, defend, and save you.   _____
28. I feel that our love is a prison; I've lost my freedom
    and happiness.   _____
29. If I am happy and successful, I won't need anyone,
    including you.   _____
30. I count on you to make major decisions when I am
    unsure of how I feel.   _____
31. If you love me, you will do what I say to make
    me happy.   _____
32. I wish I could take more financial responsibility
    and were less economically dependent upon you.   _____
33. I feel responsible when you are hurt or upset.   _____

Now add up your score. For each of the above, "rarely" signifies that you feel free to be yourself and enjoy taking responsibility for your own happiness. An "often" response suggests that you relinquish responsibility for your personal happiness and are prone to excessive dependence on your love partner. The following analysis of your overall score will help you calculate the level of freedom and autonomy in your relationship.

80–99 You experience an abundance of freedom in your relationship. You are a whole individual who enjoys interdependence and understands that the source of personal happiness lies within.

60–79 You enjoy above-average autonomy in your love relationship. You know how to meet your needs and don't make your love partner responsible for your personal satisfaction.

40–59 Although you have enough independence to hold your own in a relationship, you may often feel "If you really love me, you would . . . ," causing you a good deal of unnecessary frustration. There is a heavy price to pay for these expectations. You need to develop your independence and self-sufficiency.

20–39 You tend to be excessively dependent and look to a relationship as a prime source of happiness. If you have difficulty sustaining a love relationship, your expectations may be excessive or demanding.

0–19 If you are in a relationship, you are probably locked in a pattern of co-dependency where you and your partner looked to each other for personal happiness. Freedom to take responsibility for your own emotional well-being is probably limited. You and your lover blame each other for your frustration and lack of happiness. There may be problems in your relationship that could benefit from professional consultation.

Pay particular attention to statements on which you scored 0 or 1 and ask yourself how those attitudes and beliefs have an impact on you and your relationship. If possible, have your lover complete this quiz as well. When reviewing the results together, beware: Don't use the quiz to blame, but rather to learn. Be sure to acknowledge yourself and your lover for the courage and commitment it takes to look honestly at the hidden assumptions in your love contract.

Commitment to love.
Although most of us rightfully think of love as a feeling, it's possible to experience love as something that includes those warm, tender, affectionate feelings yet is more than a feeling. As Gerald Jampolsky sums it up in his book of the same title, love is letting go of fear. Love is the bond, the connection, and the commitment to your partner that can be continuously acknowledged *no matter how you feel*. Love is expressed when you are willing to be fully present with your partner.

I suggest that making and keeping a commitment to love, a promise to always treat your partner lovingly and with respect, becomes the light that gets you through the inevitable passages into darkness your relationship will take. Your commitment will be clear, and emotional maelstroms will not damage the overall commitment. Making this commitment will also allow you to see your partner's love for you even when it's hidden behind walls of anger, fear, or hurt.

Love expressed as a commitment typically involves loving action. It isn't enough to say "I love you" and then take actions that are less than loving. Many men have beaten and neglected their wives while at the same time contending that they "love" them. When you have in the background a *commitment* to be loving, any unloving actions in the foreground stand out in marked contrast.

Further, when you and your partner rely on your mutual commitment to love each other, you can feel far more secure in your love than when you just hope that loving feelings are still there. One of the reasons we Adult Children often don't share our feelings is that we are not used to somebody being steadily there for us. When the first sign of conflict appears, we panic and run as those old, familiar fears of abandonment creep up. When you feel secure that the other person will continue to honor his commitment regardless of his feelings, it gives you room to be more open and honest.

Making a commitment to love takes some getting used to. Len and Kathleen agreed to be committed to love since they got married two years ago. Says Kathleen, "This was hard for me to do. Here I would feel so angry, I would just hate Len's guts—*and I'd still have to love him!* I'd even say to him, 'I love you—as a commitment.' There were times I'd be so mad, I'd say, 'I love you as a commitment, but *only* as a commitment!' It was hard, but you know, it also gave me a sense of security, saying that, hearing him say it back. I could tell the marriage would go on and we would ride out the storm because we still had that commitment to rely on. Our feelings may have gone all over the map, but our commitment stayed the same."

> EXERCISE: Use the simple affirmation, "I am committed to loving [partner's name], no matter how I feel." Once a day for the next 21 days, repeat this affirmation out loud at least 10 times, pausing after each time you state it to notice any feelings or thoughts that are sparked by using the affirmation. Do not dwell on these thoughts or feelings, but instead return to stating the affirmation. If your partner is also doing this, I'd suggest you perform the exercise individually but share whatever you notice in doing so. It can generate some meaningful discussion as to what committing to love really means.

Kathleen tried the affirmation and reported, "It helped to work with this. I think I softened a lot and felt much more convinced that it was very possible to still love Len, even if I didn't *feel* my love for him."

Commitment can generate real depth of intimacy and love in a relationship. You have that opportunity in your present relationship or in a future relationship. You will probably have to make some changes to have a healthy, committed relationship; this will mean giving up some attitudes and behaviors left over from childhood that get in the way. This will take patience, persistence, and—you guessed it—commitment.

If you want to change, you have to do what it takes. If you make a commitment to your relationship, then I suggest you do it 100 percent. In fact, I suggest that whatever you do in your life, you do 100 percent. This includes reading this book and doing the exercises contained within. Change does not come as a result of reading books alone—it comes in great part by your willingness to commit to action as well as words. It comes with your commitment to love and care for yourself enough to make *you* important enough to be good to, and to make you important enough to have exciting, fulfilling relationships and perhaps that one special relationship with your husband, wife, or lover.

SUGGESTED READINGS

*W*hile certainly not exhaustive, these are some of the better books that I'm sure you will find helpful in your recovery as an Adult Child and in your relationship as a husband, wife, or lover.

Adult Children of Abusive Parents: A Healing Program for Those Who Have Been Physically, Sexually, or Emotionally Abused, by Steven Farmer. Los Angeles, California: Lowell House, 1989.

Beyond Codependency, by Melody Beattie. New York, New York: Harper & Row, 1989.

Earth Honoring: The New Male Sexuality, by Robert Lawlor. Rochester, Vermont: Park Street Press, 1989.

Escape from Intimacy, by Anne Wilson Schaef. New York, New York: Harper & Row, 1989.

Healing the Child Within, by Charles L. Whitfield, M.D. Deerfield Beach, Florida: Health Communications, Inc., 1987.

Healing the Shame That Binds You, by John Bradshaw. Deerfield Beach, Florida: Health Communications, Inc., 1988.

Healing Together: A Guide to Intimacy and Recovery for Co-dependent Couples, by Wayne Kritsberg. Deerfield Beach, Florida: Health Communications, Inc., 1990.

How to Make Love All the Time, by Barbara De Angelis. New York, New York: Dell Publishing, 1987.

I Don't Want to Be Alone, by John Lee. Deerfield Beach, Florida: Health Communications, Inc., 1990.

Lifemates: The Love Fitness Program for a Lasting Relationship, by Harold Bloomfield, M.D., and Sirah Vetesse, Ph.D., with Robert Kory. New York, New York: New American Library, 1989.

Lifeskills for Adult Children, by Janet G. Woititz and Alan Garner. Deerfield Beach, Florida: Health Communications, Inc., 1990.

Stage II Relationships, by Earnie Larsen. New York, New York: Harper & Row, 1987.

When Society Becomes an Addict, by Anne Wilson Schaef. New York, New York: Harper & Row, 1987.

Abandonment, fear of, 36–37, 44,
    72–76, 82–84, 135
  catastrophizing about, 53
  and control of mate, 38–39
  reevaluating, 82–84
Abuse. *See* Emotional abuse;
    Physical abuse; Sexual abuse
Acceptance, of mate, 56–58
Addiction
  as barrier to intimacy, 106–107
  to crises, 137–138
  to relationship, 108
*Adult Children: The Secrets of
    Dysfunctional Families* (Friehl
    and Friehl), 22–23
Adult Children of Abusive Parents
    (Farmer), 2, 21, 83
Adult Children of Alcoholics
    (Woititz), 45
Affection, physical, expressing,
    119–122

Affirmation(s)
  of right to personal boundaries,
    80–82
  of unconditional love, 57–58
Alcoholics Anonymous (AA), 49
Anger, 21, 24
  as control mechanism, 46–47
  denial of, 46
  determining source of, 47
  expression of, 47
  fear of, 136
  and identification with the
    aggressor, 47
  internalization of, 44
  as manipulative behavior,
    46–47, 50
  reactions to, 133–134
Appreciation
  and intimacy, 97–98
  and risk-taking, 97–98
  sharing, 115–117

Asking for what you want, 58–60
Attentiveness, 113–115
Awareness, mutual, 113–115

Beattie, Melody, 70, 105, 112
Beyond Codependency (Beattie), 70,
    105, 112
Blame, 30
    as barrier to intimacy, 103–104
Bloomfield, Harold, 177
Bly, Robert, 20, 160
Boundaries, of relationship, and
    commitment, 170
Boundaries, personal, 2, 63–90
    and abandoning behavior
        patterns, 74–76
    and ability to say no, 71
    definable, need for, 64
    in dysfunctional families,
        66–69, 95
    and engulfing behavior patterns,
        75–76
    enmeshment of, 66, 73, 76
    flexibility of, 77
    in healthy relationships, 63–65
    identifying need to set, 78–80
    inconsistency of, 68–69
    and intimacy, 70–71, 92–93
    maintaining, 86–89
    merging of, 95, 113
    mutual respect for, 64–65
    negotiating, 85–86
    permeable, 69–70
    physical, 65
    preparing self for setting, 78–84
    psychological, 65
    reality testing of, 79
    in relationships, 69–90
    relaxing of, 71, 95, 112–115
    retraining exercises, 79, 81,
        83–84, 88, 89

    right to, 80–82
    rigid, 67–69, 73–74
    and role confusion, 67
    setting, 62, 65–66, 74, 84–86
    and sexual contact, 70–71
    support for, 86
    unclear, 66–67
    in unhealthy relationships, 63, 64
    violations of, 88–89
Bradshaw, John, 104
Brainstorming, 144–145
Broken Record technique, 87–88

Caretaker role, 36, 41–42, 105
    as barrier to intimacy, 105
Catastrophizing, 49, 52–56
    about abandonment, 82–84
    changing, 54–56, 82
Cermak, Timmon, 11, 13
Change, in individual or relationship
    commitment to, 182
    time necessary for, 172
Childhood trauma, and Post-
    Traumatic Stress Disorder, 11
Co-dependent behavior, 13, 19,
    42, 48
Co-dependents Anonymous, 176
Commitment(s), 2, 157–182
    versus addiction to immediate
        gratification, 167–168
    breaking, 172–174
    to change, 182
    as container for relationship,
        170–174
    defined, 159
    in dysfunctional families,
        160–163
    fear of, 165–167
    as freedom, 168–169
    healthy, 158–160, 170
    and healthy sense of self, 175–177

love as, 180–182
making and keeping, 168–182
and personal responsibility, 177
reasons for breaking, 173
reasons for renegotiating,
171–172
renegotiating, 171–172
retraining exercises, 169–170,
177–181
rigid approach to, 164–165, 168
in "throw-away" society,
167–168
trouble with, 157–158, 160
and trust, 171, 175
unhealthy, 160–161, 163, 170
to values in relationships,
169–170
willingness to make, 168
Communication
by asking for what you want,
59–60
of consequences, 58, 60–61
in dysfunctional families, 99
of feelings, 26–28, 115–117
honesty in, 71
lack of, 7–10
nonmanipulative, 58–61
of wants, 59–60
Compromise, 35, 62
in committed relationships, 166
Conflict, 2, 129–155. See also
Conflict management
Adult Child reactions to,
132–135
causes of, 135–138
changing ways of thinking about,
139–141
passive or submissive reactions to,
133–135
Conflict management
in dysfunctional families, 131–132

through fighting it out, 134–135
healthy styles of, 130–131
poor models for, 131–132,
136–137
through problem-solving method,
141–148
rules for fair fighting, 150–155
through talking it out, 148–150
unhealthy styles of, 129–130
Consequences of behavior,
communication of, 60–61
Contact, emotional or physical,
lack of, 67–68
Contingencies, versus threats, 89
Control, 2
"all or nothing" view of, 48
alternates to, 49–62
attempts at, 62
as barrier to intimacy, 102
as cause of conflict, 135
common strategies of, 40–48
in dysfunctional families, 35–38
eliminating all efforts at, 56–58
of expression of real self, 36
and fear of abandonment, 36–39
in healthy relationships, 34–35
illusion of, 37–40, 61–82
and irrational thinking, 50
letting go of need for, 48–62
through lying, 45–46
need to maintain, 35–38, 48,
53, 166
retraining exercises, 51–52, 57,
59, 61
in unhealthy relationships, 33–35
Crises, addiction to, 137–138

Daddy's Little Princess role, 36, 67
Defenses, development of, 2
Demanding thinking, 49–52, 56
retraining exercise, 51–52

Denial, 45
    of anger, 2, 7, 36, 46 (*see also*
        Psychic numbing)
    of emotions, 99
    and lying, 45
Depression, versus vitality, 20
Dishonesty. *See* Honesty
Dysfunctional families. *See* Families,
    dysfunctional

*Earth Honoring: The New Male
    Sexuality* (Lawlor), 28
Emotional abuse, 47
Emotional distance, increasing,
    73–75
Emotions. *See* Feelings
Empathy, and intimacy, 96–97
Engulfing of mate, 73–76
Enmeshment of personal
    boundaries, 66, 73, 76
Escape from Intimacy (Schaef), 56–57
Expectations, 50
    examining, with partner, 51–52

Families, dysfunctional
    boundaries in, 66–69, 95
    commitment in, 160–163
    communication in, 7–10, 99
    conflict management in, 131–132
    control in, 35–38
    denial in, 7–10, 45
    and fear of abandonment,
        72–73
    and intimacy, 98–99
    isolation in, 98–99
    lying in, 45
    roles in, 36
    traits developed in, 10
    unhealthy commitment in,
        160–162

Fear, 24
    of abandonment, 36–37, 44,
        72–74, 135
    of anger, 136
    of being hurt, 166–167
    of being trapped in relationship,
        165–166
    of commitment, 165–167
    of intimacy, 137
Feelings, 2, 5–31
    awareness of, 21–22
    basic, identifying, 23–26
    communicating, 6–7, 26–28
    denial of, 2, 7–9
    expressing, 20–31
    in healthy relationship, 6
    listening for, 118–119
    and loose boundaries, 69–70
    naming, 22–26
    retraining exercises, 21–22,
        24–27, 29–30
    sharing, 115–117
    taking responsibility for, 30–31
    in unhealthy relationship, 5–6
    unlocking, 15–18
    validation of, 9
    variations and intensities of,
        24–26
Fight or flight responses, 9–10
Foot massage, sensual, 120–122
For Your Own Good (Miller), 16
Friehl, John and Linda, 22–23

Garner, Alan, 85
Gilligan, Stephen, 113
Gordon, Thomas, 141
Grieving, 15–18
    to awaken Inner Child, 15–18
    to undo psychic numbing, 15

Grown-up Abused Children (Leehan and Wilson), 43

Healing the Shame That Binds You (Bradshaw), 104
Healing Together (Kritsberg), 124
Healing Yourself (Kritsberg), 73
Helplessness, sense of, 43–44, 50, 53, 72
Hero/Heroine role, 36
Honesty, 102–103
    and risk-taking, 102–103
Hypervigilance, 11, 12–13

Identification with the aggressor, 47
If . . . then . . . contingencies, 88–89
Illness, psychosomatic, 44
    catastrophizing as cause of, 54
    and need to set boundaries, 78, 79
"Impression management," 45–46
"Incomplete Sentence" exercise, 26–28
Influence, nonmanipulative, 58–61
Inner Child
    awakening, 14–20
    fear of anger, 136
    protection of, 82, 105
    recapturing, 14–20
    repression of, 35–36
    validation of, 112
Intimacy, 2, 91–128
    and appreciation, 97–98
    barriers to, 102–107
    and boundaries, 68–69, 93, 95–96
    and boundary-setting, 70–71, 74
    versus co-dependency, 93
    in committed relationship, 182
    defined, 92

development of, over time, 110–111
    in dysfunctional families, 98–99
    and empathy, 96–97
    expanding capacity for, 112–128
    fear of, 68, 73–74, 137, 165
    fundamental truths about, 107–111
    in healthy relationships, 92–93
    and honesty, 102
    requirements for, 93–98
    retraining exercises, 113–114, 116, 118–121, 124–125
    and risk-taking, 94
    and self-knowledge, 110, 112
    and sense of self, 70, 74
    sexual, sharing, 123–127
    skills for developing, 112–128
    and trust, 93–94
    in unhealthy relationships, 91–93
    and vulnerability, 94–95
Invisible Child role, 36, 98–99
Irrational thinking
    changing, 49–56
    about intimacy, 107–111
Isolation
    in dysfunctional families, 98–99
    and rigid boundaries, 67–68

Jampolsky, Gerald, 180

Kritsberg, Wayne, 71, 124

Lawlor, Robert, 28–29
Leehan, James, 43
Lennon, John, 39
Lifemates: The Love Fitness Program for a Lasting Relationship (Bloomfield and Vetesse), 177

Lifeskills for Adult Children
(Woititz and Garner), 85
Listening, active, 117–119
Loneliness, and inflexible
boundaries, 67–68
Love
and acceptance, 57–58
and control, 56–57
mature, 57–58
as mutual commitment, 180–182
unconditional, 57–58
Lying, 50
as control mechanism, 44–46
justifying, 44–45

Manipulative behavior. *See also*
Control
anger as, 46–47
Martyrdom, as controlling strategy,
42–43
Massage, sensual, of foot, 120–122
Miller, Alice, 16, 20
Mommy's Little Hero role, 67
Mom's Little Man role, 36
Moyers, Bill, 20

Needs, defining problems in terms
of, 143–144
Negotiation, 35, 62
of boundaries, 85–86
renegotiation of commitment,
171–172

O'Neill, George and Nina, 75
Open Marriage (O'Neill and
O'Neill), 75

Passive behavior, 43–44, 53, 135
Passive-aggressive behavior, 46–47,
133–134, 137
Perfectionism, 68

Perfectionist role, 36
Physical abuse, 35–36, 47
Physical affection, expressing,
119–122. *See also* Touching
Play(ing)
to awaken Inner Child, 18–20
in relationships, 28–30
and willingness to risk, 19
Post-Traumatic Stress Disorder
(PTSD), 10–14
overcoming symptoms of, 14
symptoms of, 11–14, 19
Powerlessness, sense of, 37–38,
43–44
and illusion of control, 37–38
Preferential thinking, 52
Problem-solving, 141–148
Promises. *See* Commitment(s)
Psychic numbing, 13–14, 19
undoing, 15–16

Relaxation, 21–22
Respect, 77
Rigidity
of personal boundaries, 67–68
in thinking, 51–52
Risk-taking
and honesty, 102–103
and intimacy, 94
and play, 19
in safety, 3
in showing appreciation, 97–98
and spontaneity, 19
Roles, in dysfunctional family
Caretaker, 36, 41–42
Daddy's Little Princess, 36
Hero/Heroine, 36
Invisible Child, 36, 98–99
Mom's Little Man, 36
Mommy's Little Hero, 67
Perfectionist, 36

Sadness, 24
Schaef, Anne wilson, 23, 39, 45,
      56–57, 106
Self
   knowledge of, 107–108, 110
   and personal boundaries, 65,
      70, 73
   protection of, 36
   real, validation for, 112
   respect for, 77
   sense of, in committed
      relationships, 175–177
   trusting, 101
Sensate focus, 125–127
Senses, opening up, 16–18
Sensual pleasure, exploring,
      120–127
Sevareid, Eric, 20
Sexual abuse, 11–12, 47, 72, 123
   and role confusion, 67
   and violation of boundaries, 66
Sexual intimacy
   and personal boundaries, 70–71
   through self-disclosure, 124–125
   through sensate focus, 125–127
   sharing, 123–127
Shame, 16
   as barrier to intimacy, 104–105
Silent treatment, 133
Socrates, 107
Spontaneity, 14–15, 18–20
   recapturing, 18–20
Spousal abuse, 135
"Stinkin' thinkin'," changing, 49–56
Support, emotional, 17–18, 112
   for boundary-setting, 86–87
Survival mode, 9–10

Talking. *See* Communication
Therapy groups, support from,
      17–18
Time for self, as boundary issue, 71
Touching
   intimate, 119–127
   in sensate focus exercise, 125–127
   in sensual foot massage, 129–131
Trauma, reexperiencing, 11–12. *See
      also* Post-Traumatic Stress
      Disorder
Trust
   and commitment, 171, 175
   and intimacy, 93–94, 101–102

Validation, 101, 112
Vetesse, Sirah, 177
Victim role, 43–44
Vigilance, 54
Vitality, as opposite of
      depression, 20
Vulnerability
   and intimacy, 94–95
   through sex, 121
   taking risks with, 94–95

When Society Becomes an Addict
      (Schaef), 23, 39, 106
Wilson, Laura, 43
Withholding, 50
   as control mechanism, 40–41
Woititz, Janet, 45, 85

Steven Farmer, author of *Adult Children of Abusive Parents*, is a psychotherapist and marriage and family counselor with a private practice specializing in Adult Child issues, co-dependency, and men's issues. He teaches courses in Dysfunctional Families and Adult Children of Alcoholics at Saddleback College, and is the Director of the Center for Adult Children of Abusive Parents in Irvine, California. Steven gives lectures and workshops on Adult Child issues and co-dependency, including healing your Inner Child, self-esteem, assertive communication, intimacy, sexuality, and spiritual integration. For information about his workshops and audiotapes, call (714) 756-1415.